Books by Susan Day:

Who Your Friends Are
The Roads They Travelled
Hollin Clough
Back

Back

Susan Day

Leaping Boy Publications

Published by Leaping Boy Publications
partners@neallscott.co.uk
www.leapingboy.com

A CIP catalogue record for this title is available
from the British Library.

ISBN 978-1-9998401-4-3

Joan Jones' family

Father Arthur

Step-mother Vicky

Step-sister Viv

Step-brother Roland

Husband Martin

Daughter Rachel

Brother-in-law Colin

Bill Badger's family

Wife Lydia

Daughters Emily, Laura

Sister Carenza

SEPTEMBER

Monday

September again. Expectation in the air, warm days and cool dusky evenings. Seeing people again who have been out of your life for weeks, as if you were going back to school after the summer holidays. The first choir session of the new term.

Viv is among the first to arrive at the hall, short of breath from hurrying and loud of voice from excitement.

'Hello Richard,' she says boldly. 'Did you have a good summer?' He does not reply, but she never expected him to. He is hovering near the door, avoiding eye contact and trying to find something to do with his hands. Other men have aged more gracefully than this one. Thin hair and a drinker's complexion. Unshaven – maybe going for a beard?

The small hall is beginning to fill up. The chairs are set out, two rows in a three-quarter-circle, but today people are still on their feet, talking in small groups, telling their news. Husbands and wives are standing together, describing to another couple a daughter's wedding, or a new grandchild. Pamela is telling Sandra how she and her sister missed their Eurostar connection; behind her Viv can hear someone explaining that they didn't manage to get away because of the death of his father.

'What about you?' says Sandra, turning away from Pamela. 'Did you go away?'

'Only to see my brother,' says Viv. 'And my mother – she lives with him. But it's nice, you know, to have a change of scene. They live in Barnstaple, beast of a journey from here, but it were lovely – lots of cream teas, wine in the garden. You know.'

'My son brought his family to stay for a week,' says Sandra. 'Lovely to see them of course, but the food they get through! You forget, don't you, how much boys eat. And exhausting – I thought I would sleep for a week after they'd gone.'

The evening is rapidly cooling. Many of those now arriving are equipped with cardigans and jackets, but Viv has been too optimistic and her plump upper arms are exposed and goose-pimply.

'You'll be sorry,' says Pamela. 'You'll be cold.'

'Me?' says Viv. 'Never cold. You must have thin blood, you.' Pamela always makes her think of a small cross animal, gnawing at its cage. Viv likes to poke a stick through the bars to aggravate her.

Almost everybody seems to be here, there must be nearly forty people in the hall. Richard is still by the door as the last few people come in, chatting pleasantly, refreshed by their many and various summer breaks, suntanned and well fed and ready to get back to business.

'He likes to keep us waiting,' says Pamela. 'It adds to his feeling of power.'

'He's just giving us time to chat,' says Sandra. 'How's your toothache, by the way? Last time I saw you –'

'What do you think we'll be doing then?' says Viv.

'I'd like a nice musical,' says Pamela. 'I said that to him before we broke up for the summer. I said there's only so much Everly Brothers I can stand. Don't you think?'

'I don't care,' says Viv. 'I'll sing anything, anything'll do me.'

A stranger appears at the door next to Richard, a newcomer, with straggling white hair and a body that could have been constructed from wire coat hangers. He and Richard look at each other and laugh, loudly and a little incredulously it seems, and make a move towards a hug, which turns into a mutual shoulder touch. The whole hall looks on.

'Great to see you,' says Richard to him. 'Come and find a seat. What do we call you by the way? These days.' Which seems an odd thing to say to someone you've just almost hugged, however briefly.

'Bill,' he says. His eyes are dark and his expression impassive as he looks round at the group as if assessing them for some task.

'Let's start,' says Richard, 'just to warm up, with "Wake up Little Susie".' He is a different person, thinks Viv, as soon as he is in charge of them, and doing his job.

Beside Viv, Pamela groans audibly.

'Just to get us going,' says Richard. 'Then I'll tell you what I have in mind.'

The man beside him is looking at the floor and when he raises his head again Viv is sure that the smirk lingering on his face is an indicator of some advance knowledge.

Tuesday

Viv sits with Joan outside the coffee shop in the Botanical Gardens. The light is golden and the trees still fully green.

Joan has a fruit tea, not much stronger than plain hot water, and Viv has her usual croissant, and hot chocolate topped with cream. There have been times Joan has tutted, and Viv has said that she is half Spanish and a quarter French and that surely entitles her to a continental breakfast once a week, and Joan has said that she is certain Viv has already had her breakfast and Viv would say that she had but it were only Special K which surely doesn't count as food.

But on this day, Joan does not so much as glance at the amount of butter being spread.

'I love September,' says Viv.

Joan only says, 'Mm' and looks into the distance. Viv, people find, seems to love a lot of things.

There's a silence – not an uncomfortable one – and then Joan says that her daughter Rachel has moved house, she might go and help her do some decorating before the weather gets cold, she doesn't fancy going to Scotland in the winter, it is so wet there on the west side.

'What's her new address?' says Viv.

'I haven't got it on me,' says Joan. 'I'll email it to you.'

Viv dabs her finger on the croissant crumbs on her plate and licks them off. She sips her chocolate. Joan has already finished her tea.

'Throat made of asbestos,' says Viv between sips. She has said it on a number of previous occasions, and Joan takes no notice.

'What's up?' says Viv. 'You don't seem very with it today.'

'What? Oh. Nothing.'

'How about a day out?' says Viv. 'We could go to Chatsworth. I haven't been in your new car yet.'

'Well, as I said, I might be going away. I'll let you know.'

They sit in silence. Joan scratches the end of her nose; Viv rummages in her bag. At last, 'I think I'll get my hair cut,' says Joan.

'Again? You had it done not a fortnight since. It looks fine anyway.'

'I suppose.'

'You're only seeing Rachel.'

'Mm,' says Joan. 'Rachel won't notice my hair.'

'Oh! I knew I had something to tell you. Listen. Our next concert. You'll never guess what it's going to be.'

'No I won't,' says Joan.

'Go on, have a guess.'

Joan appears to make an effort. 'Last time you did songs from – was it *My Fair Lady*?'

'That were ages ago.'

'And then?'

'Then we did Liverpool Sound. And then early sixties stuff, countryish. You remember?'

'If you say so. So this time –?

'You'll never guess. I'll tell you.' Pause for effect. '*Hair*.'

Joan does not speak. When Viv phoned her friend Maggie to tell her this, there were jokes about being grey, or bald, which in all honesty most of the choir are, but Joan sits for a few minutes in silence while Viv waits, and then she says, wistfully maybe, 'I went to see that when it first came out. In London. 1969 it would be.'

'You should join the choir,' says Viv. 'It would be lovely for you.'

Joan shakes her head impatiently and does not answer.

'There were a bit of consternation,' says Viv. 'When he told us I mean. There were people saying some of the songs were too rude, and Pamela says they are all about taking drugs, but he says we don't have to do all of them, and it will make a change, he

5

says. Anyway, it's Richard's choir and we have to let him think he's in charge. Bring it on, I say, the ruder the better.' Viv cackles quietly.

'I don't remember that much about it really,' says Joan, and opens her bag for her purse to pay her share of the bill.

'And a new man has joined,' says Viv as they walk past the hothouses. 'Always good, to get extra men. Quite fit. Can't remember his name. You really should join the choir. You'd know people. And Fairlie's in it of course. You always got on well with him.' She looks sideways at Joan, as if hoping for a response, or a clue.

'No,' says Joan. 'I don't like singing.'

Viv opens her mouth, then shuts it again. Then opens it again. 'Your hair doesn't need cutting. You only just had it done.'

'I'm wondering about a fringe,' says Joan.

Viv looks at her. Joan's hair is, as always, a smooth auburn sweep on either side of her face. 'You haven't had a fringe in years. Not since those feather cuts went out of fashion. About 1976?'

'You remember the strangest things,' says Joan, and almost smiles.

'Well,' says Viv, 'If I don't see you before, same time next week?'

'I'll let you know,' says Joan. 'As I said, I might go and stay with Rachel for a few days.'

Viv watches Joan's back diminishing in the direction of the park, towards her flat. Her new flat that Viv has been in precisely once in three months. And that time had been uninvited. She had to ring the buzzer at the downstairs door, and wait for ages until Joan answered, and the invitation to go any further was what Viv would call grudging. But then, thinks Viv, turning uphill towards her own home, how many times has she visited me? Hardly any, even though I invite her all the time. I'm always saying, Come round, just drop in, no need to phone, just come.

She's just a very private person. The older she gets the more and more private.

At Broomhill, Viv catches a 52 bus to save her legs, her mind still on Joan. It is difficult, she decides, to believe that the Joan she knows now is the same person as the Joan she met at the age of twenty. That is, Joan was just twenty; Viv was almost nineteen. That Joan, that clever, casual, shining, fascinating person, seems to have very little to do with the Joan of now, however well dressed. Joan, cool and confident at her father's wedding to Viv's mother; Viv, short and plump, her eye-liner too harsh, her skirt too short, her laugh too loud.

Viv gets off the bus, takes a quick look in the nearest charity shop in case they have any good handbags, buys a couple of tomatoes and a bunch of grapes in the greengrocer's, and goes home.

My little house, she always thinks as she catches her first sight of it. My garden, she says to herself as she emerges from the jennel between her house and the one next door and sees her patch of flowers, her espaliered apple tree, her bird feeder and her wind chimes, her pots of herbs and her own back door.

She likes a terraced house; she has lived in one all her life and likes the feeling that her house is being held up on either side, both in a bricks and mortar sense, and in an intangible, almost spiritual sense. On one side of her are three young male students. She can hear them calling to each other through the house, and smell their cooking through their open back door – open because they often seem to need to let out the smoke caused by their cooking.

The house the other side stood empty for a year, ever since Marjorie first went into hospital after a fall, and Viv was always conscious of the lack of an occupant. Even when Marjorie died it stood empty waiting for the family to organise themselves; at last it was cleared and put on the market, after a cursory – if Viv was any judge – amount of refurbishment. Then two weeks ago a couple moved in, a couple of about the same age as Viv, a tired looking man and a plain but energetic-looking woman. So far they have made no contact. The man seems to go to work, though not every day; the woman – Viv has heard the noises – has been making herself busy painting and renovating. There have been boxes and bags of rubbish – bits of carpet, sacks of stripped-off wallpaper – in the back garden. Tradesmen have appeared from time to time – a plasterer, a man with a floor sander, two lads carrying a new cooker; they all came down the jennel and across Viv's garden to the back door of her new neighbours, the way people have to do in these old terraced streets.

Viv likes the look of these new neighbours, though it is unusual for people their age to be buying such a small house. Downsizing, she conjectures. But she will do no more at the moment than nod and smile in a friendly way – plenty of time to become proper neighbours, or even friends. You can never have too many of either, is Viv's opinion.

Sunday

The following Sunday, having finally come to a decision, Joan leaves her home.

She eats a larger breakfast than usual in order to use up the last of the loaf. She pours away the last of the bottle of milk. She cleans her flat – not that much cleaning is necessary – and tidies everything into its proper cupboards, empties the bins, does a little ironing and puts away the clothes.

She packs carefully, thinking through everything she might need. Clothes, summer and winter because in September who knows what weather she might encounter. Shoes, for various as yet unknown occasions. Cosmetics (few), toiletries (expensive), medication (statins). She has bought a new tube of toothpaste in case hers should run out before she returns. Spare glasses. She considers her choice of jewellery with care and takes only plain and minimal earrings. No rings for her fingers – she still looks at her hands with something like shock, since she took off her wedding ring when she moved house, back in the summer, hardly any time ago.

She puts in her rubber gloves, in case there is a need for house cleaning. She checks that all her addresses are put into her phone; she remembers to pack the charger. She chooses a good handbag and places in it all her usual necessities – tissues, lipstick, hairbrush, purse – credit cards? check – phone, pen, glasses and a supply of contact lenses. She puts in the postcard. She does not, unlike Viv, carry a bulging tote bag big enough for an extensive life-support kit, so there is no room for her supply of fruit for the journey; it will go on the passenger seat in a separate bag. She has loaded her Kindle with a few more books; she puts some CDs in the car to listen to on the way.

It is past midday before she is ready to go, and she loads her car, comes back and makes sure all the windows are closed. Takes out the plugs to the TV, the computer and the microwave. Takes a last look round. Closes her front door behind her and checks that it is securely locked.

Down the stairs, into the lobby, out of the street door. Into her car. She sits for several seconds, breathing. Starts the car, moves towards the road. Before she pulls into the traffic she pauses, puts the handbrake on and selects a CD. Other people, Viv being one, have adopted the iPod thing, but Joan is attached to her CDs. This one is an old one: Fairport Convention, *What We Did on Our Holidays*. She smiles. She sets off.

She has not mentioned the idea of going away to anyone but Viv, she has not in fact spoken to anyone except shop assistants since last Tuesday. Viv will think she has gone to visit Rachel. In fact, Joan sets off not for the M1 North, or even the A57 west across the Pennines, but south out of Sheffield to Chesterfield, and on by country roads through Nottinghamshire. There is no way on earth she would get to Paisley going in this direction.

It is rather a nice day.

The roads are less busy than on a weekday – no school run, fewer lorries – but there are still plenty of cars about. Where can they all be going? she wonders. Joan does not care to feel apologetic about the cars that line up behind her and finally, impatiently, pull out to overtake. I am a little old lady, she thinks. They will be looking at me and thinking, just a little old lady pootling along, off to buy knitting wool, or to see another old lady and talk about grandchildren. They will think this car belongs to my husband and that I shouldn't be let out to drive such a fast car, and that I probably don't know how to get it out of second gear. They don't know who or what I really am.

She is in no hurry. It does not really matter whether she gets there today or tomorrow, or even the next day. It will be good to take it slowly, and consider, on the way, how she feels about what she is doing. She feels – compared to how she usually feels

– excited. She feels daring, nostalgic, hopeful. She feels it might be seen as a romantic journey she is making. She feels young – or at least, younger than usual.

Although it is not an impulse. She has thought hard about it, ever since Tuesday morning when she found the postcard in her box in the lobby, with her old address crossed out and her new one squashed into the corner. Thinking for five whole days cannot be said to be an impulse, can it, but thinking some more can do no harm, and if she decides to, well, she can turn round and go home and no one will be any the wiser.

The stubble fields are dotted with crows, or maybe rooks. Wood pigeons fly across the road. As she looks towards Bolsover Castle, high up to her right, she sees a kestrel hanging in the air. A few of the trees now are touched with gold, barely touched, that is all.

Fairport Convention. Strange to think that they used to dance to this, there in the Hexagon, before the big dance hall was built. Not really danceable music. In her first year, was it? or second? Before she met him anyway. Had she been wearing that swirly-patterned dress, that barely covered her bum? But she had good legs, in those days, and even now they're not too bad.

She finds she has forgotten how much she enjoys the prospect of a long drive, with no need to hurry. She has a list of Premier Inns with her, she can stop for the night at any point she wants to. He will not be expecting her today.

He will not be expecting her at all.

She did try to phone him, several times, before she made the decision to set off, but there was no answer. Why had he never given her a mobile number? Surely he has one? If not, as a person who relies on a landline he has no right to leave his house. But she has his address safely in her phone. At least as long as he hasn't moved house and omitted to tell her.

She didn't expect him to get over Lydia's death so soon. Well, he won't be over it, she knows that, though he maybe thinks he is, but she hadn't expected him even to consider a meeting before next spring at the earliest. She would have sent the normal Christmas card. She would have given him her new address.

Do I really want to see him again?

It's all right. There is no commitment in meeting as friends. Only as friends.

Before she turns on to the A616 she pulls into to a lay-by, changes the CD to Neil Young's *Harvest*. These are not the songs he liked. His taste was for rock not folk, for Steppenwolf and John Mayall, Frank Zappa, Velvet Underground. Self-consciously alternative, Joan always thought. Obscure. He thought folk was soft and wishy-washy. They considered that having different musical tastes didn't matter. It would never come between them, they believed. Nothing would.

She is still in the lay-by, looking at a hedge full of sparrows and listening to "Heart of Gold". Even he grudgingly accepted this one, she remembers, it was the whiney ones he hated. I left all my records behind when I cleared out, I wonder what he did with them.

He was the love of my life.

Sorry Martin. She sits for a little longer thinking of Martin, then puts the car into gear and pulls out into a gap in the traffic.

Four years since Martin died. More than forty since her father died. How all those years have galloped away, leaving barely a hoof print of memory on the baked soil. Martin was not a fan of any music with words. Words get in the way, he said. He liked to make up his own mind maybe, about what a tune was telling him. Jazz, he liked, not difficult jazz but big band, swing, cheerful robust noise. When driving he liked Mozart, because, he said, it kept him calm.

Was Martin then not the love of her life? Ah, but there was time enough to become accustomed to him, for him to become no more or less than the element she spent her days in, that she thought no more deeply about than air. Essential and invisible. And when he was gone it was as if she couldn't breathe. He died without knowing – she is sure of this – that there was someone she once loved more than she ever loved him, her husband.

Not that it was a secret. Not that he didn't know about the existence of her previous love, of course he did. There were one or two photographs, there were anecdotes. In more recent years there was the yearly Christmas newsletter from Carenza, which he would pick up every year and say, puzzled, 'Who on earth is Carenza?' 'Oh someone from way back. I used to go out with her brother. She's one of those people who likes to keep in touch.'

'Oh yes, I remember.' Martin didn't care and forgot straight away. He was confident enough, solid enough, big enough, to tolerate such a thing. Even if he knew that Joan kept all Carenza's letters it would not have made him even slightly uneasy.

Martin. How she misses him still. Just because she's driving towards the Essex coast, all nervous and fluttery at times, just because she's going to meet someone else, doesn't mean – or does it?

The last time I saw him was in Corfu, standing there in the hot night as the taxi took me away. So dark, that unlit street, that it's not really true to say I saw him. He was there, still not believing this was happening. Neither of us, at that moment, I think, knew it was the last time. There were, of course there were, conversations afterwards. When he returned to London and found me gone, when I told him I had resigned from my job and was staying in Sheffield, when he called after midnight, drunk, and cried down the phone, when, finally, I told him I was married to Martin, yes already married, it was too late.

'It was an impulse,' I said.

'You're not impulsive,' he said.

'I am now,' I said, thinking, I must be, mustn't I?

I, she, her, me. We seem to be different people.

Joan continues on her road, looking out for a teashop, until – no teashops having presented themselves – she arrives at Newark-on-Trent.

Rather imposing, this – has she been here before? Anyway, there is parking, there are teashops, and Joan knows enough to know that they may close by four-thirty, and if she wants a cup of tea it had better be now. And, having had a large – for her – breakfast, and therefore no lunch, she decides she will have a scone or teacake.

The shop she chooses is composed, inside, entirely of dark wood. Floor, ceiling, counter, tables, chairs – all polished wood, brown and shiny as gravy. The pictures on the wall are marquetry – still wood, but of more varied shades of brown. The staff, however depressing the decor, are cheery and chatty.

'Going far?'

Joan is known for being secretive, but somehow it is not the same, telling total strangers your business. She could say anything, it wouldn't matter. But she tells them something approaching the truth.

'I'm on my way to Colchester. Visiting an old friend.'

'It will be dark before you get there,' says the younger of the two women. 'Cream or butter with that scone?'

'Cream please.' Joan has a sense of being rash. 'I'll probably stop over somewhere tonight.'

'Your friend not expecting you then?'

'I can send a text,' says Joan, thinking, If only I could. But maybe it's better this way.

She navigates to the A1 and follows it as far as Grantham. Birthplace of Margaret Thatcher, she remembers. Famous for nothing else, as far as she knows. She bypasses the town and allows her car to amble eastwards, past darkening fields, flat as ironing boards, and sinister. Ghosts, she thinks. Drowned witches and water sprites. She would not like to break down here. Miles and miles, fens and dykes, and lone trees and even lonelier houses. Sprinklings of lights in the distance. At last she turns south, and stops at her Premier Inn for the night. Wisbech.

Joan lies on her bed in her room. The television is on, with the sound off. She has eaten an apple and a banana from her bag and a packet of crisps from the vending machine in the hotel lobby. She has drunk a cup of tea, made with a decaffeinated teabag from the packet she brought with her.

She hasn't come far in an afternoon's driving, she knows that. Martin would have been scornful. What's the point of having a fast car if you drive like a doddering fool? That's the sort of thing he used to mutter at people going too slow on a motorway. But Joan is satisfied with her day. She is happy to approach slowly towards her goal, she has been happy all afternoon to look around her, to pull into lay-bys and change the CD, to look to either side and take in the greenness or the bleached blondness of the fields, the treeness of the trees. She has seen rabbits hopping near a hedge, seagulls following a plough, and she has not had second thoughts. Her course is set, still, she is going to visit her old friend, her old boyfriend, the one she thinks of still with affection.

The one who let her down. Yes, but that was just the way he was. She should not have expected anything different. But she wasn't thinking straight, and why should she have been? My dad died, she says that even now, in mitigation, it would have felt so wrong, to stay in Corfu, on holiday, it would not have been real. She left Corfu, she left him standing outside the scrappy little block of 'studios,' with its smell of drains, its suffocating heat and unopenable windows, where they had been happy. Hadn't we? Why would I have left like that if we were so happy? But I still believed he would get on the next plane. I waited all week for him to turn up on the doorstep, and there was nothing, not even a phone call until he had seen out his holiday and come home on his charter flight. What was the excuse for that?

And being at home, with her stepmother, that was awful too. Of course Vicky was upset, Joan would have been horrified if she wasn't upset. They had been married hardly three years and seemed to truly care for each other. What Joan found difficult, and shocking, was that Vicky appeared to blame him, as if he had done it on purpose to make her unhappy. Why didn't he go to the doctor before this happened? Why didn't he look after himself? Why did he go and play golf? Surely he must have had some warning that this was coming on. Why didn't he think of his responsibilities?

Joan arrived back at Heathrow, worn out with crying. She went by train to Sheffield, somehow falling asleep and ending up in Leeds. She woke up, thought, I'll call my dad to come and get me, realised again that he was dead, and sat crying on the station till all the trains had finished for the night.

It was Viv who drove up to collect her. Beyond their parents' wedding and a brief Christmas encounter Joan had had little to do with her. She was a vivid little person, big cloud of black hair, chubby thighs and a short red dress. Joan considered her tarty. But when she saw her slow to a stop outside Leeds station, she was a rescuer, almost an angel. They approached each other carefully, in case they had the wrong people, though Joan was sure it was her. She wasn't the sort of person to change much – she still hasn't. Older, of course, a bit chubbier, still battling with that massive bosom, still dressing in pinks and purples, still accompanied on all occasions by a massive handbag in red or gold.

'I brought you a sandwich,' she said, and handed over a thick home-made ham and tomato on white, wrapped in greaseproof paper. Joan dried her eyes and got into the car and ate the sandwich, while Viv talked all the way home. Maybe she was being insensitive – she can be – but actually, it helped. There was no need for Joan to reply, no need to think or react, Viv just rambled on, telling about who she was going out with, where she worked, what the weather had been like, what she had for her tea. Maybe she was scared Joan would talk to her, and tell her how miserable she was, but, knowing her now, Joan thinks it was only practical. She knew that she had to get them both home, she had to keep herself awake and Joan was in no fit state to do it, so she did it herself. She even made her laugh, a little, though it also made her cry, so she was careful after that not to do it again.

'Mum's in bed,' she said when they got to the house. 'Doctor's gave her a sedative. Bed's made up in your old room. I'm in the guest room. I won't see you in the morning, got to go to work.'

Viv. How strange that for forty years or more she and Joan have been so entangled. How odd that two people so different should have married two brothers so similar. How incestuous it all was.

Viv. That preposterous name, that raucous laugh, at the end of some daft story. Huge holes in her education – well actually, if her education was an article of clothing it would be a string vest. Viv who never reads a book, only magazines about celebrities. Viv who has folksy sentimental plaques hanging up in her kitchen, and sends birthday cards with pictures of kittens. Viv who never reads a newspaper, or watches the news but has always – and always will – vote Labour because that's what 'people like her' do. It has been embarrassing at times over the years, having to acknowledge her as a relative. Stepsister or sister-in-law – either description would cause a faintly startled look to cross the face of the person Joan was introducing her to, and Joan would have to fight the wish to explain that they were not really related, and not really anything like each other.

But then, everyone warmed to Viv. At work everyone knew her and liked her. She was helpful, she was funny, she was sympathetic when people told her their sad stories – which they did. Joan was relieved that she herself was never in a position

17

where she had to manage Viv, because she suspected that there was often more talking than working, more laughing than was necessary.

And she has stuck by Joan, in spite of the flimsy, semi-detached basis of their relationship, all these years. Whatever else Viv is, she is loyal, she doesn't let go of her friends, or allow her friends to let go of her. Joan thinks of the weeds that used to climb up her hedge, with their fuzzy sticky leaves and the annoying little seeds that had to be picked off her clothes one by one. It is similarly hard work keeping Viv in her place, not estranged but not too close. I would miss her, thinks Joan, if I never saw her at all. And let's face it, there are not many people I can think of as friends.

Joan has a sudden vision of what it might have been like if she had brought Viv along with her on this expedition. But it does not bear thinking about. What would he say? What would he think of her? I will never know, she thinks, and then, What does that mean? – that this is a one time only meeting? that I will never allow him into my life enough for him to ever meet my step-sister / sister-in-law / ex-colleague?

Joan gets ready for bed, turns off the television, swallows her statins, sets the alarm on her phone, gets into bed and turns off the light. She wonders what Martin would say if he could see her. She does not believe it is possible that he can. It has been, she thinks as she slides into sleep, a more interesting day than some.

Monday

Joan is on the road early next morning before her alarm has gone off, but even so there is noticeably more traffic than the day before.

She takes a wrong turn leaving the town and finds herself driving on strange, straight roads, with unexpectedly angular bends. She has no idea of her direction, travels alongside straight, canal-like rivers and comes, finally, to a signpost pointing to Ely. She stops and looks at her map. She is old-fashioned enough to prefer a map to a sat-nav – and besides, she dislikes that smug, know-all voice.

She tries, without success, to trace the way she has come and is entranced by the names. Euximoor Fen – how would you pronounce that? Wardy Hill, Wimblington, Apes Hall. Coldham – I bet it is. Sixteen Foot Drain – that must be how deep it is. Forty Foot Drain – even deeper? Or wider?

Get on with it, Martin would say if he were here. Stop fussing about the names and tell me which way am I turning. It has taken her an hour and a half to drive a very short distance, she does not even want to calculate how many miles she has wasted. She will go into the town, have some breakfast and plan her route properly.

She turns right and sees the tower of the cathedral in front of her, dimly through the mist of a fine September morning. Her CD is playing "Feeling Groovy". She smiles.

So on, out of Ely, towards Cambridge. Haverhill, Halstead, and before midday she reaches the outskirts of Colchester. It has changed.

Well, for sure, everything in the world has changed, but this A12, the one they used to drive up on from London for weekends, has grown, spawned new carriageways, new slip roads, more signs and instructions than she can take in and process. She is afraid she might not be able to get off this frenetic, frantic road, and will end up in Ipswich. (Nothing worse, she thinks.) But there is a sign for Clacton.

Clacton will do. Even if she has to go all the way there, she will find her way back to where she wants to be. And most likely there will be a sign. And there is, and she follows it, and the succeeding ones, shaking a little inside. She switches on the sat-nav for the last bit and follows the instructions. Brightlingsea. And eventually brings her car to rest outside his house. Lydia's house.

It sits in a small street, behind a high hedge. It is painted white and its roof is shallow and slated. The upstairs windows have their curtains closed – against the sun maybe? Or have they been like that since Lydia died? The hedge needs clipping; weeds grow along the outside edge of it. Parked at the side are two cars – a VW Golf, only two years old, and a battered Fiesta, white and rust, with an old S plate and an out-of-date tax disc.

Joan sits for some indefinite time looking at the house. It does not look like anything she ever imagined him living in. In spite of the weeds and the faint air of desolation it reminds her, as much as anything, of the house she and Martin lived in – solid, confident, prosperous, buffered by shrubbery, a family house. The afternoon sun shines squarely on the white render; the brick pillars either side of where the gate should be have the look of little sentry boxes, guarding the path from her, from her, the interloper, the invader, the uninvited.

Joan would like, at this moment, to be at home in her flat rather than sitting in her car looking at someone else's house. In her flat, contained and confined between her four walls, with no more than a potted bay tree on the balcony to take responsibility for. In there she sees herself in a box, boxes on either side, boxes above and below, like shelves in a shoe shop, or cells in a honeycomb. Whatever Martin would have said, Joan finds a sort of comfort in it – or hopes to, one day.

As sure as she can be that the house in front of her is empty, she gets out of the car and looks down at herself. Beige jeans, neat. A top with a faintly Indian print – was that maybe to remind him of those caftans of her student days? Flat sandals, nail polish on her toenails. She pushes her bag under the front passenger seat – though there is no sign that this is a high-crime area – locks the car and walks up the front path.

Even if he is at home, she can easily back out of anything. Have a cup of tea, say someone is waiting for her back at last night's B and B – who? Viv, Viv will do, she could say that if she needs to. He would never be in a position to know if she told a small lie.

Behind the hedge the front garden is paved, potted plants to soften the corners. The pots are raggedly weedy and uncared for – would have been Lydia's job, she supposes.

There is no answer to her ring on the bell, nor to the second one. She knocks with the heavy brass knocker. She goes to the side of the house, where the cars are parked, and on to the back gate. She peers through the window of the garage – garden tools, an old washing machine, a freezer, a tea chest, a deflated rubber dinghy. The back gate is not locked, or even closed, but the garden is empty. Tidier than the front, mostly grass (in need of cutting), a couple of wooden seats, a whirly clothes line with a peg bag hanging from it, a lop-sided faded plastic Wendy House leaning against the fence. She goes back to the road and leans against the warm car bonnet. That's all right, that's better really, gives her time to catch her breath. He's probably at his daughter's, or maybe – so obvious, of course – he's out sailing. Warm sun, light breeze, he'll be out there on the Creek, with some friends, as he should be.

She removes her handbag from the car, along with her jacket, locks it again, decides against leaving any kind of note, and wanders on down towards the harbour.

The town looks different to how she remembers it, from those days when she would come with him from London for a weekend with boats. That's what he used to say, Shall we have a weekend with boats? Not that she took any part in the boat aspect of the weekend. He would hang around, helping people get their boats off the trailers, making himself useful in the hope that someone might offer him a chance for a bit of sailing. Joan thought he might grow out of it – later that would be, when they were settled into adulthood, when he had a proper job and they had a house to occupy their weekends. For now, she would go along with it. She would read a book, or walk about the little town. It was quite scruffy in those days, little is the word for how she remembers it, little red houses in little streets going down to the sea, old women mumbling on doorsteps. A main road you could walk across most of the time without looking to see if there was traffic, because there usually wasn't. Some pubs with bar billiards.

Now, a surprising number of cafes. Jaunty blue-and-white, with bunting, and blackboard menus. There is a hotel – there was never a hotel, surely, in the old days. Not that they would have needed one, because there was always some old friend to stay with, someone who was doing graduate study, or who had just never left or gone away to find work. These were the ones he liked best. These were the ones who sat around smoking joints until it was time to start drinking. They were the ones who lived in a house with two staircases, where water from the upstairs toilet seeped through the downstairs light socket, and it had an unspeakably filthy kitchen, and an untuned piano that nobody knew how to play.

They would wander out, mildly high, mildly interested, and walk along past the beach huts to the swimming pool, which was filled by the tide and which Joan had never dared go in, because the tide brought in not only water but jellyfish and snails and other creatures she did not know the names of. She was a Sheffield girl and she was very unaccustomed to the sea and its creatures.

If you walked the other way, past the dark and derelict oyster beds, you reached the end of the world – only flat wet marsh under a wide sky. And back in the town, down at what they called the Hard, more mud, a muddy sort of beach, and people shouting as they hauled boat trailers out of the water with Land Rovers. Again, she knew nothing about what sort of boats they were, or how to work them. If I had married him, and ended up living here, would I have found out all these things? Would our children have grown up with a working knowledge of life jackets and cleats and tide tables?

Change has happened down at the harbour. She can't remember how it used to be, here, at what they call The Waterside, but it wasn't like this. Weren't there sheds? Maybe one that sold shellfish? And behind them, just mud? Now there is development. A marina? Is that what you call it? And apartments all around, three storeys of them, with pointy roofs and balconies with wicker chairs. Where did the mud go?

She is confident that he will have a boat – that was the whole point of living here after all, but she has no idea what shape or size of boat it might be. She looks at the boats on the beach, and the boats out in the Creek, white sails, coloured sails, like upturned bunting. He will be out there, not exactly battling the elements but feeling the pull of the tide, the swell of the waves, the movements of wind and water that you can only go along with, that you can't go against.

It's mid-afternoon. Joan will go and get a cup of tea, before the cafes close, and then come back here to wait for the sailors to come to shore. He will be one of them.

She has not booked her accommodation before she left home. It seemed like too solid a decision, and one that she would not be able to back out of. It is out of character, this. She is not a person who would normally leave things to chance. Having drunk some tea and eaten a piece of lemon drizzle cake – her healthy diet is going down the pan, as Viv would say – she goes in search of a bed for the night. And she is not anxious about finding one, or about how clean and comfortable it might be. Somehow she seems to have been transported back to her twenties, when such things didn't matter.

She ignores the hotel, from some sort of feeling that he wouldn't approve, and approaches the Seawinds Guest House, in Victoria Square. A substantial red-brick detached house, with more bay windows than one could reasonably design into a house. Its garden contains grass only, wall-to-wall grass, not even a flower border; but seeing the swing and the trampoline, Joan deduces children, who, after all, don't mix well with flower borders.

It is a child who opens the door. A boy, about ten years old. 'Mum!'

A young woman appears from the back kitchen. Blond ponytail, jeans, bare feet, big smile. Yes, she does have a room. How many nights?

'I'm not sure,' says Joan. 'It all depends. Two at least.'

'No problem,' she says. They all say that all the time, whether there is a problem or whether there is not.

After the first impression, Joan can see that she is older than she thought, or maybe just more tired. But no, there are lines at the corners of her eyes that are more than tiredness, she must be as old as Rachel, at least.

'I'm Tiff,' she says. 'That was Felix who opened the door. 'My son,' she adds unnecessarily.

The room she shows Joan is adequately nice. Clean, small – not one of the bay-windowed ones – single bed, tiny TV bracketed to the wall, bed covered in silver cushions. Why do they do that?

'On holiday?' She sounds very tentative, understandably.

'Sort of,' says Joan. 'I've come to see someone, but I couldn't get in touch first, so I'm just going to hang around for a day or two.' This sounds suspiciously feeble to her own ears, so she goes for a change of subject. 'Have you lived here long?'

'In Brightlingsea? All my life. But in this house, only three years. Doing quite well though.' She smiles, over-brightly.

She must know him, thinks Joan. If not him, his daughters. She tries to work out how old the daughters are, and how old Tiff might be, and then decides anyway not to ask. Not just yet.

'Can I park my car at the front?'

'No problem,' says Tiff. 'My car's put away, I've other guests, just one couple, but there's room for you both outside, so you can get off the road.'

The boy Felix appears, holding out a phone. 'It's Bea,' he says.

His mother listens, frowning. 'No,' she says. 'School tomorrow. You have coursework to hand in. No, come home and do it, you can stay at Miranda's on Friday.' She presses the button to cut short the discussion and smiles, wearily this time. 'Not even this term's coursework,' she says. 'Should have been handed in last July.'

As Joan parks her car Felix is hovering, approving. 'Nice,' he says.

*

The weather in Sheffield has turned autumnal. There is a cold wind coming over the Pennines and Viv pushes her hands deep into her pockets as she hurries to choir rehearsal. Summer seems to be over and it is time to search out her gloves from wherever she put them last spring. The heating has not yet been turned on in the hall.

'Keeping my coat on,' says Pamela.

'You'll warm up when we get started,' says Sandra.

Viv sits between them and they talk across her as she watches to see who comes in.

'That bloody "Let the Sun Shine",' says Pamela. 'I've had it going round my head all week.'

'I know.'

'You get to sleep eventually,' says Pamela, 'and when you wake up you think it's gone, but as soon as you listen to the weather forecast, or even just think it's gone, it comes back and before you know it's going round and round your head again like a bloody hamster in a wheel.'

Sandra nudges Viv. 'There he is, your favourite.'

She has seen him already. Tall, full head of grey hair, face still tanned from his time in Africa, nodding his head slightly to people he knows, but unsmiling.

'Thinks he owns the place,' says Pamela under her breath.

He acknowledges Viv, barely, and she smiles back her best smile. 'Evening Mr Fairlie.'

Pamela scowls. 'How come he gets called Mr, when nobody else does? You don't work for him now you know. He's no different from anyone else. He's got a Christian name, I take it?'

'We never used it at work,' says Viv. 'It wouldn't feel right somehow. Anyway, does he look like a Keith?'

'I don't care,' says Pamela. 'If that's his name, that's what I'll call him.'

'Oh look,' says Viv, 'there's that new man again.' This week, he is again the last to arrive, almost late, and goes and sits at the end of the tenor row, at the front, as near as he can to Richard. There is no time to discuss him though because Richard is calling them all to order, and getting them to do their warm up exercise.

'We'll have another go at "Sunshine",' he says. 'But first off we'll have a preliminary look at "Good Morning Starshine". You'll like this,' he adds reassuringly.

'You see what he's doing,' whispers Sandra. 'He's softening us up with the nice ones. Nothing rude, no sex or drugs. Then, when we're going along with it, bam, he'll pull out the heavy stuff.'

Halfway through the session there is a short break.

'What do we think then?'

'How old is this stuff?'

'1968,' calls Richard, overhearing. 'Ran in London 1968 to 1973. Caused a sensation. No one had ever seen anything like it before.'

'So what is it about?'

'Youth,' says Trevor. 'Politics. Hippy politics, that's what I remember.'

'I don't think we had them in Sheffield, only real ones,' says Joe.

'Bit of a departure from our usual range,' says Richard, smiling through his developing stubble. He smiles not as if he wants to be liked, but as if he is daring them to disagree with him.

'I was hoping for something like *South Pacific*,' says Christine.

'Give it a chance,' says Richard. 'After all, how many of us know the songs?'

'Exactly,' says Sandra. 'People like songs they know. We won't sell many tickets – I wouldn't buy one anyway.'

'And we like singing songs we know,' says Fiona. 'I can't be doing with learning a lot of new words at my age.'

'You're no older than me,' Pamela says to her. 'And I don't call myself old.'

'The words aren't difficult,' says Terry. 'Banal yes, but not difficult. *South Pacific* would have been more challenging.'

'There are different sorts of challenge,' says Richard.

'I've looked it all up online,' says Terry. 'I think there are people here –' he does not look at Keith Fairlie but Viv does – 'who might find there are

27

sentiments expressed which they find hard to go along with.'

'As there might be in *South Pacific*,' says Richard irritably. 'Can we try it for a month? Then see how people feel.'

'I've looked up some of it as well,' says Pamela, 'and I can tell you now, Richard, I will not be singing about sodomy and cocaine. So don't ask me to.'

'I won't ask you to sing "Sodomy".'

Terry is clearly not the only one who has looked it up online. There has never been so much discussion among the cups and saucers. People can barely eat their biscuits for wanting to say something.

'I don't like all that bad language. I know you hear it everywhere nowadays, but it's not what I want to sing.'

'No, it's not what we come here for is it?'

'Well, where shall we draw the line?'

'The problem will be in "I Got Life".'

'And you know even Nina Simone stopped singing tits and replaced it with boobies.'

'Boobies! I'm certainly not saying that.'

'Nothing wrong with tits.'

'Arse? Can we go with arse?'

'Well the Americans say ass.'

'Would that be better?'

'Do we want to sound American?'

'Have you seen the words to "Colored Spade"?'

'There's no way anyone could get away with that today. Is there?'

'We'd get some publicity if we did. End up on Look North I wouldn't be surprised.'

'The only way would be if we had a black man to sing it.'

'Well we don't do we.'

'I know. I wonder why we don't have any ethnic minorities in this group.'

Richard is standing in a corner of the room now, having been taken there by Keith Fairlie for a private word.

'There was nudity but it was only brief, and the lights were very dim. Blink and you'd miss it.'

'Anyway, Pamela, no one's asking you to take your clothes off.'

'I'd give him a piece of my mind, that Frank Mills, if he was anything to do with me. Borrowing money off a girl and buggering off like that.'

'But he's taken advantage of her being so soft, hasn't he. And she's so wet she doesn't even realise it.'

'Oh come on. She's only young, she's bound to be a bit wet.'

'They are openly advocating drugs.'

'Probably only grass or cannabis.'

'Aren't they the same thing?'

'And still illegal whatever they are.'

'They burnt the American flag on stage.'

'That must have gone down well.'

'And it was all to do with draft-dodging.'

'Well I would have tried to get out of it too. Wouldn't you?'

'Not patriotic though is it.'

'But it was a terrible war. Completely unjustified. Yeah, it's true, they didn't want to get killed, but they were also going with their consciences. People were demonstrating against the war.'

'Were you?'

'I was,' said Bill.

'Should we wear wigs when we sing the title song?' says Paul, keeping his face very obviously straight. 'I feel it would help the audience to understand.'

'We could whip them off at the end,' says Joe.

'Like at the end of *The Full Monty*,' says Sandra.

They all smile. The mood changes. The mention of Sheffield's iconic film, the reminder of something subversive, seems to soften them all, even Pamela, and they go in to the second half of the rehearsal in a better mood.

'Another new one,' says Richard. 'Originally this was an a capella solo, but I've arranged it for three parts. Tune and words with the men, altos and sopranos – you have oohs. No words. But you'll like it. We'll do the first half and see how we get on. Now, fellas, I'll sing this through for you – you've got the words, you might even recognise them, those of you with an education.'

He faces the left hand end of the group and sings:

'What a piece of work is man,
'How noble in reason,
'How infinite in faculties,
'In form and moving how express and admirable,
'In action how like an angel,
'In apprehension how like a god:
'The beauty of the world, the paragon of animals.'

'William Shakespeare,' he says. 'Hamlet.'

'Not much of a tune,' says someone.

'Just you wait. With your backing vocals it will be astonishing. Altos, you first. Sopranos, no chattering.'

Viv is an alto. She sits in the middle of the semi-circle, her hair escaping from its fastenings and her black eyes glistening like prunes She looks mostly to her right, where the men sit, and her eyes rest most often on Keith Fairlie and, this week, on the new man, Bill. It has been clear that as well as knowing Richard already, he would support him. He stood alongside him through most of the tea break, saying nothing much but being, somehow, on Richard's side.

They finish the session by practising "Let the Sunshine In".

'That's it then,' says Pamela. 'Morning noon and night, for another week.'

'You love it really,' says Viv.

She happens to be going out of the hall at the same time as the new man, Bill. She rather fancies him, his thin grooved face, his soft white hair that waves over his ears. His ears, she can see through the hair, are, at least the left one is, somewhat pointed.

'Well,' she says to him, 'what do you think of us?'

'Not for me to say,' he says. 'I won't be here for very long.'

'You're only visiting then? How long for?'

'Not sure yet,' he says. 'It all depends.'

'Where are you staying?'

'I'm on a camp site,' he says. 'Place called Hollin Clough. Do you know it?'

'Sort of,' says Viv. 'Isn't it a bit chilly to be in a tent?'

'It would be,' he says. 'But I'm in a campervan. Quite cosy.' He stops at the door to wait for Richard; Viv pauses too.

'What do you think of Richard's choice of music?' she says.

He chooses not to answer directly. 'I've known Richard for years. We were mates in London, when we were young.'

'But *Hair*,' she says. 'What do you think of it?'

He pauses to consider. 'I seem to remember' he says, 'that I saw it in the West End, many years ago. It ought to bring back memories but in fact I don't remember a thing about it.'

They seem to have run out of conversation. Viv, while waiting for Sandra, turns on her phone and sends a text to Joan. 'R U up 4 coffee 2morrow?' As she and Sandra walk towards their bus stop Joan replies: 'I am still in Paisley. I will let you know when I am home.'

*

In the evening Joan walks again to his house, but there are no lights on and nothing has changed. She walks again down to the Hard in the twilight, but cannot see any sign of him or of any boat that has something about it that would make her believe it was his. What a stupid idea, she thinks, what would Martin say, do I think his boat's going to be called the Joan Jones? She knows what Martin would say to any such extravagant fancies – Get a grip JJ, he would say, and he would be right. She orders herself to get a grip.

You would expect it to matter, she thinks, that there is no sign of the person she has come to see, but actually, it doesn't. She feels, in fact, released, free, almost invisible, in this place where nobody knows her. Relaxed, calm. If she finds him, if she meets him, that will be a different thing, but at the moment, the prospect doesn't disturb her. Time to myself, she thinks.

Although, these days, no work, no husband, when does she not have time to herself? She ponders. How to explain this? Well, what it is, is that at home she is conscious all the time of having no husband, no work, no structure. That's what it is. Moving out of her big house and into a flat was supposed to do away with that feeling. Getting out of the house that had been her home all her life, and hers and Martin's for all of their married life, for more than thirty years of it, was supposed to free her.

'But what about your garden?' Viv said. 'Won't you miss your garden?' and Joan replied that it took up too much time and she had stopped enjoying it, and that when she was in a flat she would be able to join groups and go to events and do voluntary work, as Viv did and was always urging Joan to do.

It is astonishing, thinks Joan, not for the first time, how much Viv crams into her days. Two mornings a week at the charity shop, one at the food bank; she collects some children (grandchildren of her ex-husband, if that makes any sense) from school twice a week. Then there is the choir, line dancing, some sort of craft workshop where she makes most of her Christmas presents, belly dancing and tai chi – something every day, some days two things, and she still goes for coffees and lunches and short strolls round the park with this or that friend. She is always trying, too, to get Joan to join in. 'You would get on really well,' she is always saying, of Maggie, or Lizzie, or Judy. 'You would be really good at it,' she says of any one of her hobbies. There were hints of this even before Martin died, and over the past four years not a week has passed without a phone call or text from Viv, a reminder of this or that occasion which Joan has failed to veto in strong enough terms.

Joan even used to think, herself, that once she had got over the shock of being widowed so suddenly, she might be ready to take up some outside activity. She put it off until she stopped working, because work was really all that kept her going at that stage. Then she put it off until she had moved house, because once she was in a smaller flat, with no garden, less house to keep, and fewer memories of Martin locked in every floorboard and doorway and shelf and curtain rail, when she was out of all that, she told herself, she would begin the rest of her life.

Viv doesn't really know about being widowed. He's dead, it's true, Colin, but he'd already been divorced from Viv and gone back to his previous wife, and lived apparently happily with her for at least two decades before dropping dead one day in a car park. That's what the men in that family do – continue in a perfectly normal way, healthy as you like, and then keel over without warning – her father Arthur on the golf course, his cousin Alec on a cross-channel ferry, Colin in Screwfix car park, Martin at the bottom of the garden. So Viv, of course, must have had some sort of feelings when, a couple of years before Martin, Colin breathed his last on the tarmac beside his battered van, but she was not truly widowed.

Joan knows about being widowed. It knocks it out of you. Oh god, the nights, and the mornings after the nights. The solitary meals, or not-meals – the meals of random items, stale bread, black bananas, half tins of soup from the back of the fridge, spoonfuls of jam straight out of the jar. She could tell no one about these things, they were too shameful.

Lying in a bath for hours, topping up the hot water with her toe, salting the bathwater with tears, afraid to get out and be assaulted by the air again. Wondering should she make herself stay here and die.

Howling. She never knew she could be a woman who howled, she didn't know she had it in her. One of her neighbours knocked at the door once, because she thought Joan might be injured. And she ignored her but she wouldn't go away, she kept standing there and knocking and calling through the letterbox, It's only Janet, are you all right? so that in the end Joan had to get off the floor and open the door and tell her she was fine. (Fine!) And then Janet was embarrassed because she'd intruded. She said that. 'Sorry, I didn't mean to intrude.'

As she returns to her room for the night, her phone jingles. It's a text from Viv – no surprise. In fact the only surprise is that she hasn't received one from her for at least two days – Viv loves to be in touch. Joan replies straight away. If it were done, she thinks to herself, it were better done quickly. Something like that anyway.

As she always does, Joan thinks about Martin last thing at night. It is one of the techniques that has helped her, after the first few months, when there was nothing else in the world, only that Martin was gone; but after that she learned to put it to one side, promising herself a good cry once she got to bed. These days she cries less often, but she still has a little think about him, a little review of a memory or two, most nights, and feels bad if she forgets.

Tuesday

Colchester is both familiar and changed. Joan travels in by bus, to save herself from having to find a parking space. The countryside on the way in is green and prosperous, containing, she can see from the top deck, some very nice properties.

The bus station, she is pleased to find, is in the same place, and on the way up the hill she passes the end of the road where she lived with her three friends in her second year. Trish and Bobbi and a third whose name she has forgotten. She knows that at the time she found Trish and Bobbi unbearably picky about washing up rotas and rules about turning lights off, more like landladies than students, but she remembers it fondly now, that house with the fridge in the hall and the back door that wouldn't lock.

Trish was the first friend she made when she came to Essex. After her first week in the south Joan was truly fed up with people asking her what she had just said, or mocking her accent – 'Eeh Bah Gum!' – or asking her where was her whippet and did she grow leeks. Trish was from Nottingham and that was a sort of comfort. She was also Christian – very firmly so – which was less endearing, and she took Joan on as a friend with the stated aim of converting her. She already had Bobbi, a pale and weedy version of herself, but she could appreciate that Joan was a different order of girl. She had striking good looks. She was tall and with a sort of presence that shone. At other times in her life – that is at times when she had not just lost her mother – she would have been – she had been – a social star. And soon became one again. She started going out with boys again, and staying out at night and if Trish had not organised her early in their first year into agreeing to share a house in their second she would probably have moved away from the other three even more quickly. She never heard from them after they all left university, but they remain vivid and unchanged, in her mind.

He – she rarely thinks of him by his name – he hated them, even though he hardly knew them. They were straights, they had nothing to say to him, they had no idea where he was coming from and they were too full of their own opinions. 'Get out from under, Joanie,' he said. 'They're stifling you.'

She wasn't that keen on his friends actually, particularly when they left Essex and went to live in Camden Town. She was working for her Civil Service exams and he took jobs on building sites, (Real work, he said.) and spent his evenings, while she studied, playing in a band with some other blokes, or practising, which usually seemed to mean drinking. She wanted to stay in London, he wanted to live on the coast. Any coast, he said, it doesn't have to be Essex. He grew up in Burnham-on-Crouch, messing about in dinghies as a boy, he wanted to go doing that as a man. Devon, he said, Brittany, Brighton, I don't mind, he said, as long as it's near the sea.

She wanders through the shops that have in many cases grown into much bigger stores, or else been bought up and changed by chain stores. She goes through the arch under the pub and out into the wide and handsome high street. She looks, and then turns back into the grid of lanes behind. She knows that she sometimes bought clothes here, and there was a bookshop, and one selling hippy knick-knacks – beads and chains and posters – but she cannot work out which of the present day shops are the same and which have changed. Not that it matters.

She visits the Castle and walks in the park, drinks a cup of coffee, feeling daring, and then takes the bus out of town, getting off at the university.

She knew it would have grown hugely bigger than it was when she was there. She remembers the construction that was going on all the time. But in the centre of it, it hasn't changed much. The concrete is greyer, that's all. And the faces are more serious, or is that her imagination. But the mass of students are still on vacation so it is not even as bustling as it was forty years ago. Forty? And the rest.

But as she stands in Square Four, in the intermittent sunshine, she can see him. Not really, and not as he is now. But she can see him as if he is there, as he was. Dark hair waving and falling in his eyes and over his ears to his collar, and a little fuzzy beard round his chin. He wasn't tall for a man, no taller than her – it was one of the things that didn't matter. He narrowed his eyes as he looked at you, she thought; he rarely changed his expression from one of weighing you up and reserving his opinion. Of course he won't be the same. She knows he will have changed – lined and wrinkled, with shorter hair, or none and creases and bags round his eyes. Fatter, maybe – though back then he didn't have a fat cell in his body; could he really have developed a paunch, a double chin, jowls? She doubts it.

She navigates past some new buildings and walks beside the lake. The ducks are still there. Somebody, so it was said, tried to cook and eat one once, but ended up poisoned. The grown up Joan thinks that probably it was not thoroughly cleaned.

The dark towers bracket the campus. When Rachel was little and making Lego towers as tall as she could Joan always thought of the Essex towers. They were an experiment in student democracy and the students often did their best to make the attempt fail. Ten residents in each flat, was it, or eight? and a further sixteen sharing the four study rooms. And there was often someone actually living in a sleeping bag in a study room, which was inconvenient for the other three. And anything you bought to keep in the fridge in the kitchen was fair game for any passing thief. And the doors were never locked, because if you locked them, someone had to get up in the middle of the night to let in people who had forgotten their key. And the lifts sometimes got stuck, if too many people crammed into them.

But also, there were parties, and evenings where people sat around gossiping, and a flow of people in and out – friends of someone or other, and friends of other friends, and random people who just happened to wash up there, drunk or depressed or tripping. And late night forays out to Maggie's van for a bowl of muesli – novelty food then – or chow mein if you had the money.

And in summer, water fights with the fire hoses, until the floors and the stairs were dripping and running and people were soaked and unable to stand for laughing. Did anyone get into trouble for that? She didn't know.

Those were the only wild times she ever had – and not very wild at that. A few – a very few, you could count them on one hand – acid trips. A considerable amount of smoking dope, – until her finals approached, when she gave up, and after that, never really bothered again. Some casual sex, some illicit sharing of single beds, some unwise choices perhaps. A little light shoplifting. When she thinks about it, which is not very often, it seems to be someone else she is remembering.

Now, she looks at the towers from a distance but does not approach. It is hard to imagine – why should she have to imagine? it was real – but it's hard to even know that she was once young, and here, and now she is not. Which is me, she wonders, Joanie then, tall, arrogant, sure of myself, sure of belonging to this place, knowing where I stood, opinions lined up and ready to go. I knew where I ranked in desirability, and it was pretty high. Is that me? Or the me that knows nothing, is that me?

Three years here, two years in London – they don't count for much against a lifetime of Sheffield and local government. But which was me?

*

'Do you know a Mrs Joan Jones?'

That was what the policewoman said to Viv on the phone. And of course she had to sit down suddenly because she knew at once that Joan must have had an accident on her way back from Paisley.

As if it was there in front of her own eyes she saw it, she saw her fancy grey BMW crushed by a lorry. She said a grey car was a risky colour for a car, and look, there it was, a lorry had failed to see Joan in the gathering dusk and pulled in too sharply – driver probably getting sleepy after driving all the way from Aberdeen – and caught her between the big front wheels of the cab, and the crash barrier. Of course it would have to happen where there was no hard shoulder for her to escape to, must have been on a flyover or a bridge, lorry driver suddenly finding himself in the wrong lane.

Poor Joan. Badly injured probably. Viv started worrying that she had never received Rachel's address, but the police would surely find it, as they had found her.

'Yes,' she said, cautiously.

'Riverview House, number 4?' said the policewoman.

'Yes,' she said. She was wondering how she could get to wherever Joan was. A lot of empty countryside lay between Sheffield and Paisley, she knew that much. She was worrying about taxi fares.

'There's been a –' said the voice.

'Is she all right?' said Viv.

'Was she at home?' asked the voice, a little puzzled maybe, Viv thought.

She started to say, Don't be silly, but stopped herself. Was this really a police officer? You hear about these scams. Maybe someone wanted her to open up Joan's flat, knowing that she had her spare key, and then what? Steal all her stuff and lock Viv inside with the phone lines cut maybe.

The voice resumed. 'It looks like her flat's been broken into. We're here now, me and my colleague, but we need someone, if not Mrs Jones, then a next of kin, or a relative at least, to authorise what we're going to do. We found your name and number on her list by the phone.'

'Oh,' said Viv. She was still not at all sure about this.

'If I come in the car to pick you up,' she said, 'could you take a look and be our contact for this crime. We'd take you back home again of course.'

So that is how Viv comes to be standing in Joan's doorway, at the back end of a Tuesday afternoon, giving her details to the young woman.

'Can you just spell that for me,' she says.

Viv sighs. This always happens. 'Vivienne – that's two ens and an e at the end – Flores – that's F, L, O, R, E, S – Jones, hyphenated. Yes, Flores-Jones.'

'So are you a relative of this Mrs Jones?'

'Sister-in-law.' Any further explanation gets too complicated.

Joan's front door has been forced open.

'Amateur job,' says the other policeman. 'Let this be a lesson to you. I hope you've got mortise locks on your house.'

'There's an entry phone on the main door,' says the WPC. 'I expect she thought that would be enough.'

Viv is peering through the door. She knows that she will see Joan's possessions strewn all over, as they look for her jewellery; she knows that wires will have been wrenched from walls as they cart away her electrical equipment. She sniffs carefully and hopes they have not left a pile of human excrement on her new carpet. 'Doesn't look like they took much,' says WPC Clark. 'Not really any sign of disturbance in here.'

She lets Viv in to look, warning her not to touch anything, as if she didn't know. Nothing has changed, as far as she can see, since the last, and only time she was here. Her TV, dvd player, all that stuff still in place. In the kitchen everything washed up and put away before she left. In her bedroom – well Viv has never been in there before, but a jewellery box is still neatly lined up on her dressing table, a little gilt ring tree still has rings hanging from its branches, even, Viv can see, Joan's wedding ring.

'Someone came in here, Barry,' says WPC Clark. 'Look, footmarks on the carpet.'

It is the sort of carpet – dark pink and new – that is deep and soft enough to hold a footprint.

'Trainer,' he says. 'About size nine.' Thinks he's Sherlock Holmes.

'So,' he says to Viv, 'Can you see anything obvious that's missing? Or changed? Any idea why someone would break into her flat and leave without taking anything?'

How should I know, says Viv to herself. Joan is about as forthcoming as . . . as that armchair about her life. Viv would know more about a person she sat next to on a bus than she knows about Joan. Secretive doesn't begin to describe her.

'This daughter,' says the man,' do you have her address?'

'You could look in Joan's address book.' But when they look by the phone it is no longer there. Viv's name and number are pinned (with a green drawing pin to match the décor) to a small corkboard – which is how they got hold of her, but the address book is gone.

'Well,' says the policewoman, 'she probably took it with her. People of her generation don't have everything programmed into their phones like we do.'

Viv thinks but doesn't say, That may be true of some, but Joan is perfectly well able to use her phone, if she so wishes, for every purpose it was made for. And so can I.

The policewoman hands over an official piece of paper with their names and a crime number. 'We'll send someone to secure her door,' she says. 'If you hear from her, ask her to contact us.'

So they are ready to go back to the car. The whole business has taken until late afternoon and Viv is going to be too late to get to her line-dancing evening. They hear the door downstairs open and someone coming up the stairs. It's another of Joan's neighbours, not the one who reported the open door, but Marion, home from her school with an armful of exercise books and a shopping bag of cardboard folders. She is alarmed at the sight of the police, and has to be told what has been happening, and is duly shocked.

'I feel bad now,' she says. 'I knew I should have told someone, but it felt like something and nothing, you know.'

Someone has been hanging around the building for a couple of days. Outside, mostly, sitting on the garden wall, but once or twice inside, been seen on the stairs, been seen reading the names on the bells, and also peering through the glass door at the post boxes.

Viv listens as she gives a description. Male. Medium height, slight build – well, anyone is slight compared to Marion – wears a hat so hair colour unknown.

'Age?'

'Can't be sure, with the hat, you know. Over fifty certainly. Very suntanned face though, hard to tell.'

'Suntanned? Do you mean foreign? Asian?'

'No, no. I don't think so. Just suntanned.'

'Let us know if you see him again, would you.'

'Oh I certainly will,' she says. 'And I'll go round all the residents and tell them to be careful about letting people in. You know, sometimes if you're going out and there's someone coming in, you'll hold the door open and then they can get in without putting in the code or ringing someone's bell.'

'What's the point of an entryphone system?' grumbles PC Barry when they are in the car, 'if people are going to let in all and sundry just because they don't wear a label saying serial killer.'

Later in the evening, Viv is looking at her tomato plants in the back garden when she hears knocking on her front door. This in spite of the notice that tells people to use the back door.

She goes through the house and shouts through the letterbox. 'What is it?'

A man's voice answers. 'You won't know me. I just wanted to ask you about Joanie.'

Joanie? Does he mean Joan? 'Who are you?'

'Can you open the door?'

'Not this one,' says Viv. 'There's furniture in the way. Come round the back.' She is not scared. It's still daylight, the students next door, just returned in plenty of time for their new term, are throwing a frisbee back and forth down the jennel between her house and theirs. Anyway, his voice sounded nice. And above all, she wants to know what he has to say about Joan.

She meets him as he emerges from the passage.

'You.'

'Do I know you?' he says. He does not smile. Viv wonders if he ever smiles.

'Come in,' and he steps into her kitchen. She does not even think of thinking twice. Maybe she should do, but it feels as if she knows him well enough. Bill. Bill from the choir, Bill of the campervan and the slightly-too-long white hair and the pleasant tenor voice.

As she closes the door behind him she hears Marion's voice again. Male, medium height, suntanned face.

'I've been looking for Joanie,' he says, before she has decided what to say.

'Did you break into her flat?'

'It was me,' he says. 'But I've been waiting weeks and I couldn't think of any way to move it forward. I mean, I can't stay here for ever. I didn't intend to make such a mess of the door. I was hoping no one would notice.'

'What for?' she says.

43

'I don't know,' he says. 'I didn't mean to do her any harm. I wasn't going to steal anything. I don't know really, I just couldn't think of anything else to do.'

Viv thinks he looks mournful, making excuses like a small boy. 'Coffee?' she says.

'Have you got anything stronger?' he says. 'I've had quite a difficult day.'

'Have you eaten anything?' She switches off the kettle, passes her only bottle of wine to him, and a corkscrew, and starts to put together a cheese and chutney sandwich. Then she notices that the wine bottle is a screw top and reaches past him to take the corkscrew away so that he doesn't think she's a complete idiot, and then finds she's put marmalade on top of his cheese instead of chutney.

'Don't waste it,' he says. 'I'll eat it.' She hears the resignation in his voice and it makes her mad.

'Bollocks,' she says. 'You don't need to be a martyr.' And tips it into the bin and starts again.

'You must think,' he says, 'that I'm a total dickhead. I really appreciate this by the way.' His sandwich is almost gone, his glass of wine nearly finished.

Viv sips hers cautiously. It would not do to get too drunk, and whatever happens she will not open a second bottle, even in the unlikely event that she could find a forgotten one lurking at the back of the cupboard.

'Tell me first,' he says, 'if you don't mind, how you are connected to Joanie? I mean, have you known her long?'

She never knows what order to put it in, her connection with Joan. This time, she starts at the most recent end.

'She's a friend really. We were work colleagues and we retired at the same time and we just kept on seeing each other once a week or so.'

'You worked together. Where was that?'

'For the Council. Hold on. You're not a detective or something are you?' Maybe, she thinks, one of those agencies looking for subversives, maybe Joan was mixed up in something, but no, she wouldn't be; but maybe Keith Fairlie is and she was his PA, so –

'If I was a detective,' says Bill, 'I think they would have sacked me by now. I don't think I've been very competent so far, do you?'

'I don't know do I? So far you've been asking all the questions.'

'Sorry,' he says. 'Ask me, go on, ask me anything you need to know.'

She's thinking. She doesn't know where to start. And does he maybe want her to ask questions so he can find out what she knows about him?

'While you're thinking,' he says, 'just tell me a bit more about you and Joanie.'

As if she can tell him things and think at the same time.

'You worked at the Council?'

'She were senior to me,' says Viv. 'I were only an admin assistant, in the big office you know, running backwards and forwards between the officers, sending out minutes, booking rooms, you know the sort of thing. Well over the years I had several different jobs there, I were there before Joan actually, but she – well, you know Keith Fairlie don't you – in the choir, tall, sings the bass part, very distinguished looking.'

'Oh yes, I think so. Bit starchy. Quite pleased with himself.'

'I suppose so. If you don't know him. You'll find he's quite an important person round here, even now he's retired. He does a lot of good you know, very good man.'

'And his connection to Joanie is –?'

'She were his PA. For years. So of course that made her pretty important too. She controlled his diary, she could make you an appointment with him or not. He were involved with so many aspects you see, that he needed someone to keep it all organised and in order. Not that she's ever really discussed it with me. She's very discreet, always has been.'

'Just his PA? Nothing more?'

What is he getting at? What is he implying about Joan? And about Mr Fairlie, come to that? (Should Viv be looking out of her front window at this moment she would see Keith Fairlie walking up to the front door of her new neighbours and putting a large brown envelope through the letter box. But she isn't.)

'I don't know what you want me to say. I'm sure they were both very professional. They were both married.'

'Were?'

'Well, Joan's husband died about four years ago. She were still working then, and she kept right on working. I think she needed some structure to her life. It's not easy always, is it, being retired. You have to fill your days and I think she didn't want to have to figure out how to do it, so she just carried right on working. Till Mr Fairlie retired. About two years ago, that were.'

'And you and she kept in touch?'

Is he thinking that they are so different that they could not be friends? Is he thinking that Joan is a cut or two above Viv?

'Well, we did have a connection outside work. Her husband, when he were alive, were my husband's brother. That is, my ex-husband. Though he's dead too now.'

He nods slowly. 'I knew,' he says, 'that she married a Jones, even though she was born a Jones. Why did she do that? She hated her name and yet she went and did it again. When she could have married someone with a different name.'

'When did you know her then?' Because it's clear that he did.

'Long ago. Before you did I expect.'

Then how come, thinks Viv, that I have never – *never* – heard of anyone called Bill?

'Where have you come from then?'

'Essex,' he says. He sighs.

'And you've what? You've come here looking for Joan, just on the off-chance? Or you were coming here anyway and you thought you'd just go and burgle her flat while you were here?'

'I've been here nearly three weeks,' he says. 'I've been to her old house, that one in the street with the stupid name –'

'– Stumperlowe.'

'Curtains shut, as if she's on holiday or something. So I think maybe she's gone away for the weekend and I think I'll try again on Monday. So I do. No one at home so after a couple of tries through the day I ask a neighbour, and find out she's moved house. How long ago did she do that?'

'Just back there in the summer. July.'

'Anyway, no one's home, whatever time I try –'

'I think maybe they –'

'– and this neighbour must think I'm up to no good, she won't tell me anything, not where Joanie has gone, nothing, so then I get hold of a phone book – nice woman in Stannington library lets me photocopy the page – do you know how many J Joneses there are? And how many M Joneses?'

'– Martin's dead. Didn't you know that?'

'I did know,' he says, 'but I thought the phone might still be in his name. So I started working through them.'

'You went knocking on their doors?'

'I phoned them. I mean, what a tedious job that was. Bloody stinking phone box, pocket full of ten p pieces –'

'For fuck's sake,' cries Viv, slightly surprising herself. 'Haven't you even got a mobile?'

'No.'

47

'Even if you had,' says Viv, 'you wouldn't find her that way, she's not in the book. So how did you find her, in the end?'

'You might notice,' he says, 'that I haven't found her yet. But I found her flat. It was an amazing coincidence. I called more than forty people, some of them twice, when I got mixed up where I was on the list. I heard I-don't-know-how-many bloody answering machines asking me to leave my number, which of course I don't have. And then, day before yesterday, Sunday that would be, one of the M's, she says to me, Well, she says, there's no Joan at this number, but actually, there's a new person moved into our block, she's called Jones, because I've seen her name on her post box in the lobby, and I thought to myself, I wonder if our mail will get muddled up.

'And I thought to myself, well it's a long shot, but I go round, yesterday, and, I don't know, it just felt like I was in the right place. Obviously I haven't got a photo of Joanie, not as she is now, so I couldn't ask anyone, Have you seen this woman? But then I had another stroke of luck because I saw the postie and I asked him – pretending to be Joanie's husband you know – I asked him was there any redirected mail for Flat Four, and he said no, not since last week, he'd put a postcard in last week, and I wondered if that was the one from me, and I went round to her old house and there were the new people, moved in, so they must have sent it on.

'But she was still never there, and I can't stay here for ever. I've got to get the van back to my mate, and I want to get back to my boat, and of course it's costing me, in food, this is. All this eating out and buying sandwiches, and sitting in the pub in the evenings.'

Viv is laughing. 'No, you're right, you wouldn't make a detective would you? You've been to the choir, what? twice? And I've been there both times, and I could tell you anything you want to know about Joan. Why didn't you say something?'

'Go on then. Tell me where she is.'

'Scotland. Her daughter lives there. My niece. Rachel.'

'And you're sure about that?'

Viv takes out her phone and scrolls through her texts. 'There.'

'Yesterday. How long was she staying?'

'Well, she's hasn't come home, has she? And anyway, now I come to think of it, how did you find me?'

He reaches into his canvas bag and pulls out an address book. Holds it out to Viv, who takes it. It's almost new, the cover is still stiff, unmarked by cup rings or sticky fingers. Inside there are no corrections or amendments, no crossings out where people have moved, or died. Addresses, all written with the same pen (black fineline), all in Joan's small, firm handwriting. Viv can see her, having moved into her new home, buying a new book, sitting down for a whole evening, transcribing addresses from her old book, rewriting history it could almost be said, then throwing away the old book, anything connected to Martin disposed of, all the old addresses gone and forgotten. Starting again, Viv can see it.

'Joan's,' she says. She finds where Joan had put her in – twice, once under F for Flores and again under J for Jones, below Rachel's address. She turns back to page F. Yes, she was not mistaken – Joan has Keith Fairlie's address in her book, and his home phone number.

'I knew she wouldn't have took it with her,' she said. 'She'll have all these in her phone.'

'I sent her a postcard you see. That was our arrangement, from way back – a card at Christmas, just to touch base, as they say, and nothing else until we were both free.'

Viv tries not to show how shocked and thrilled she is by this piece of knowledge about Joan.

'When Lydia died I phoned her. I said we should meet. She wanted to, I am sure of that, but she said, not yet. Wait till you're ready, she said. Let me know.

I sent her a postcard. Nothing threatening, just a date and a place. Halfway between us, Rutland Water I suggested, a day out, that was all it was going to be. Never turned up. Didn't I feel a dick, sitting waiting in the car park, thinking I must be in the wrong place, scared to move in case I missed her. Found a phone box, phoned her home, no answer.

'Stayed all day, numb. Stunned. Bewildered. Went home, no message. Borrowed my mate's van and here I am. On another wild goose chase. What does she think she's doing?'

He says nothing for a while. Then he fidgets a bit, shifting as if he's getting ready to leave. Viv feels the need to hang on to him. Between them, the bottle of red wine is nearly finished. 'You have the last bit,' says Viv. 'I'll put the kettle on. Tea or coffee?'

'No thanks,' he says. 'Is there an off-licence? I could go and buy another bottle.'

'No,' she says. There actually is an off-licence, plus the Co-op which stays open till ten o'clock, but she is reluctant to drink too much these days. She finds that getting older does not stop her getting giddy under the influence of alcohol.

She makes a pot of tea for two, and brings it in on a tray, with slices of cake.

'I've been thinking,' says Bill. 'I'm going to go and find her. I can't wait around here any longer. Only take a day to get up to Paisley – not sure where it is, but how far away can it be? It's still in Britain. I'm going to go tomorrow, crack of dawn.'

Viv has a picture in her head of Paisley, conjured up by its name. It will be pretty, with coloured houses and streets that curl like the patterns on the cloth. It will be tucked away in a valley, with mountains on the horizon. She has never been to Scotland.

'I could come with you,' she says. 'Rachel doesn't know you, it will be easier for you if I'm there. I can help with the driving.'

'You won't be insured,' he says, 'so no.'

'Why don't we phone Rachel now?' says Viv.

'No,' he says.

'So you're going to turn up unannounced. Is that a good idea?'

'All right,' he says, after a pause. 'If you want to come, why not. I'm leaving early though.'

'No problem,' says Viv. 'Tell me what time and I'll be ready.'

'Eight.'

'No problem,' says Viv, again.

Wednesday

So here is Viv, now, watching the M1 unroll before her and wondering if this was a sensible thing to do. She hasn't even told anyone where she is going and who with. Bill keeps the van in the inside lane, chugging along behind a scrap metal lorry. Neither of them has said anything for quite a while. A few trees are just beginning to change colour, piecemeal. Odd leaves of mustard and saffron spice up the dull green.

'See those sheds,' says Viv, waving to the left. 'That's where they grow the rhubarb.'

He does not reply except to make a noise that she thinks means, You're having me on and I'm not in the mood.

When they planned last night to travel to Paisley to look for Joan, it sounded like fun. She could see Rachel opening her door and laughing in a delighted sort of way, and calling her Auntie Viv (which she never does any more), and then Joan coming out of the kitchen, maybe with a paintbrush in her hand, and looking pleased to see her, and trying to work out who is this person with her? And she would get out her phone and find that she had switched it off and so missed all the calls and messages Viv is planning to send, and she and Bill would work out how their communications had gone astray and everything would be easy and joyful and – well, after that her imagination failed rather, but that was enough for her to say to herself, Go for it Viv. What's the worst that can happen?

So far the worst that can happen is that Bill is grouchy. He told her eight o'clock but did not arrive till after nine. Viv was packed, dressed, breakfasted and waiting from seven forty-five, standing at her front window looking for the campervan turning into her road. By eight forty-five she had given up and was in her kitchen, putting the kettle on and unpacking the food that she had prepared for the journey. She hung her coat back up on its hook at the bottom of the stairs, now that she wouldn't be needing it, put the radio on and wondered what to do with her day, that had been cancelled and was now seemingly un-cancelled, when Bill appeared at the back door.

'Aren't you ready yet?'

'I thought you weren't coming.'

'Fifteen minutes late is all. I got a bit lost finding your road again.'

Forty-five minutes late actually.'

'I said half past eight.'

'You said eight o'clock. I've been waiting over an hour.'

'I'm here now. Are you coming or aren't you?'

Viv seriously considered staying at home, but why should she – she has called Maggie to cancel their lunch date, swapped her school pick-up with the other granny, emailed to say she won't be at belly-dancing – why should she miss this little adventure too?

She grabbed her bags and some of the food, forgetting the fruit and the chocolate and leaving her coat on its hook, followed him to the van and climbed into the passenger seat.

'You told me eight,' she said again. 'I don't mind you being late, but you could apologise, it wouldn't hurt you.'

But apparently it would. He hasn't spoken since then, and now they are passing Wakefield.

'The other thing about Joan and me,' says Viv. If he won't talk she will, and she'll stick to his favourite subject and see if she can soften him up a bit. 'The other way we're related, that I didn't tell you about, is that she is my step-sister.'

He briefly lifts his foot from the accelerator, so she knows this is a surprise to him. She waits, to see if he will ask for more. He waits to see if she will continue, and eventually she does.

'My mother,' she says, 'married Joan's father.'

'Joanie's father died,' he says.

'Of course he did. But before that, he married my mum.'

Her mother had been widowed for many years when she married Arthur Jones. Viv tells Bill this. They worked in the same company, a smallish engineering firm on Penistone Road, her in the canteen, him as something high up – chief draughtsman or something like that. (The social gap between them was about as big as the gap between Keith Fairlie and Viv, bigger even, though this is a fact she doesn't mention to Bill.)

Every day he went to the canteen for his dinner at half past twelve. Every day she saw him. In the early days from a distance, while she was in the kitchen, draining potatoes or ladling the custard from the great saucepan into jugs. Later, she would often be on the counter, asking people did they want roast or mash, telling them to put their own gravy on from the jug at the end. Later still, she was running the whole operation. When the workers started to come in at twelve she would take off her overalls and her hairnet and stand where she could see all that was going on, making sure the kitchen was keeping up with the counter, the tables were being cleared as soon as people finished.

He must have seen her every day of his working life. But when they met by chance one day at the castle in Scarborough, where she had gone on a day trip and he was staying with his sister-in-law, on the second anniversary of his wife's death, he did not recognise her. She approached him. 'Hello Mr Jones,' she said. And he said, 'I know you from somewhere, don't I?'

'I met him once,' says Bill.

Viv waits to see if he will say more. Yes he will.

'He brought Joanie down to Essex once,' he finally says. 'I think, actually, he wanted to take a look at me, you know, check out who his little girl was hanging around with.'

Well, she has already guessed – it wasn't difficult – that this Bill was an old boyfriend. She wonders how long it is since his wife died. Not long, she would be willing to bet.

'Did he approve?'

'I shouldn't think so,' he says. 'Long hair, Afghan coat, pockets full of dope – though he didn't know about that. I saw him whispering to Joanie, I think he was asking who I was, you know, was I actually the boyfriend. I think she told him I wasn't.'

'He were a nice man,' says Viv. 'It were a pity he died so soon. I mean, he were a lot older than my mum, but it were still a young age to die, too young, not much past sixty.'

She would go on to tell him about her mum, if he seemed interested, but he's gone quiet again, just driving through the intermittent drizzle, windscreen wipers going, lorries passing, the engine growling away. It doesn't actually sound that good, this engine.

'How long have you had this van?'

'It's not mine,' he says. 'I borrowed it off a mate. Actually, it's a sort of swap – I'm using this for a month, he's taken my boat and should be in Spain by now.'

'My father were Spanish,' Viv tell him, but there is no response, and after waiting for one, she picks up the battered old road atlas to look at their route.

She's not familiar with this road, now they are past the A64 turn off. She's been to Scarborough many times, she's been to Whitby. York Races on a workplace outing. Leeds for the shops. But if she wanted a holiday she would go south, in a plane, to a place where the sea laps gently on to a beach – not crashing over rocks and sweeping innocent teenagers off the promenade – and where the summer evenings are dark and warm. The North, the road signs are telling her, and she's thinking Gales. Frost. Inclement weather. Why has she done this?

It's a slow journey too. Ordinary cars – red, white, black, silver – cruise past them at astonishing speeds and diminish into the distance. Vans and lorries and National Express buses pull out and pass them, throwing quantities of water off the road on to them. At this rate, she thinks, they will not be in Paisley by nightfall. And where are they going to sleep? It would be asking a lot for Rachel to have two more spare beds.

Something called Scotch Corner is now on the signs, which is encouraging. They turn off into the services and make use of the toilets and the rather nasty cafeteria. He fills up with diesel, and while he does so Viv sends a text to Joan, deciding the time has definitely come to warn her of what is approaching.

'Let's see the map,' says Bill.

'We must be in Scotland,' says Viv, but when they look there is still a long way to go to the border.

'Have you been to Scotland before?'

'Not by road,' he says. 'I've sailed there. A bloody long way and when you get there the weather's shit.'

Quite like this then, she thinks.

'So this daughter,' he says, 'Joanie's daughter – what's her name?'

'Rachel.'

'And what does she do? Married? How old?'

'Late thirties. Nearly forty, now I come to think of it. No not married. She's an engineer, like her dad were, only he were civil and she's structural.'

'So why did she move to Scotland?'

'A job I suppose. Well yes, it were, something about listed buildings, that's what she's doing. They have a lot of them up there apparently.'

She can see him forming an opinion of Rachel as a tough builder-type figure, in butch shirts and big boots, and she smiles to herself.

They discuss which road to take. He is all for cutting across country on the A68, Viv favours going west and picking up the M6/M74. A motorway will be quicker, she says.

'If you want me to be in a filthy temper,' he says. 'I hate motorways. I hate cars, if it comes to that, but at least on a little road you have more contact with the land you're travelling through. I mean, motorways are just alienation made concrete.'

Viv doesn't know what he's talking about. 'If you hate driving so much,' she says, 'why not go the quickest way?' And he looks at her with a look that makes her realise that the same wavelength is something she and he will never be on. So he gets his way and off they go, up hill and down dale, toiling up great slopes with a queue of cars behind them, trundling down the other side as they all flash past, cursing. High moors stretch away in all directions, insignificant villages appear and are left behind, wind turbines turn steadily, in groups. It takes over two hours and a half to get to a place called Corbridge and they are still not in Scotland.

*

'I think I'll be leaving today,' says Joan to Tiff, as she brings her scrambled eggs.

'Not found your friend then?'

'Not at home,' says Joan. She is shy about referring to him as 'he', as if it's somehow a bit too risqué. This gives her speech a somewhat telegraphic flavour. 'Must be on holiday.'

'What did you do yesterday?'

'Oh, lots,' says Joan. 'I went to Colchester on the bus and looked around the town centre. It's changed a lot, I think, but I could recognise some of it. Went round the castle – much more interesting than it used to be, if I remember rightly, unless it's just that I'm older and more interested. Then in the afternoon I went up to the university. So much bigger than it was when I was there. So much more business-like too. Many more foreign students – well, that's true everywhere I think, certainly in Sheffield. But of course the bits I knew are still there, the towers, and the squares, and the lakes.'

'So today,' says Tiff, 'are you going straight home? Have you decided?' There are no other guests this morning and the children have gone to school. Tiff pulls out a chair and sits down.

'I'll check out,' says Joan, 'so that you know I've gone and you can let the room if someone else comes. But I'd like to see Clacton again before I go home. I lived there for my third year, with my boyfriend. I'd like to see it again.'

'You might be disappointed,' says Tiff. 'It's gone downhill, Clacton. The visitors don't really come any more, it's all a bit sad.'

'Everything's changed,' says Joan, 'but what can you do? I still think I'll go for a quick look, and then head home.'

'Clacton won't take up much of your time,' says Tiff. 'You'll be home before it gets dark. What happened to the boyfriend though? Did you marry him?'

'Nearly,' says Joan. 'But no. It didn't work out. And it probably would have been a disaster. At the time I didn't realise, but we wanted different things out of life.'

Tiff sighs. 'Did you get what you wanted?'

'I suppose I did. I got what you'd call a very normal life.'

'Comfortable.'

'Exactly. It was comfortable. In all sorts of ways.'

'And then?'

'Martin died. My husband. Quite suddenly.'

Tiff smiles the sort of smile that screws up a person's eyes in an attempt to stop them leaking tears. 'You know I wake up every morning wondering will this be the day I get the visit. If he gets killed, of course it's likely to be sudden, but I've been dreading it for so long that it will feel like I've been waiting for it.'

'Army?' says Joan. Not a surprise, with Colchester so close.

'Sergeant Instructor,' says Tiff. 'Sometimes I even wake up and think it has happened – like while I was asleep. I just have these feelings all the time, if I let myself think, like, now, maybe he's being blown up right this minute.'

'Don't,' says Joan – feebly, she thinks. 'You'll drive yourself crazy.'

'It's all very well,' says Tiff, standing up and taking away the teapot and the toast rack, 'saying don't. Tell me how to stop and I'll stop.' But she goes out of the room without waiting for an answer.

Joan has paid her bill, put her belongings into the car, driven, via Lydia's house where nothing has visibly changed, out of Brightlingsea and turned right towards Clacton. She has parked near the sea front and walked along to the shops to find a cash machine. Removed a hundred pounds from her account, after checking the balance as she always does. She checks her phone and finds a text from Viv. 'Surprise. On our way. See you soon.' It makes no sense and Joan considers that it has probably been sent to her in error; it is probably intended for Maggie or Judy. She does not bother to reply.

Did she, she wonders, really think of marrying him? Certainly they seemed to assume they would always be together but marriage was not necessary between two people who loved each other. The state should have nothing to do with relationships between people. Both of them said so. They talked about the children they might have – those children were going to be free spirits, free of neuroses and hang-ups and they were not going to be brought up to join in the respectability rat race.

'We don't need to belong to the bourgeois system,' he said.

'It's a patriarchal institution,' she said. She felt strongly that she did not want to take his name, but that could have been because she didn't like it; she was beginning, belatedly, to be more attached to her own name.

She wanders by a different way back to the sea front. Tiff was right, there is really very little here.

And not many people about. The North Sea stretches away without anything to break the expanse, shades of grey, and where the cloud has broken, glinting with sharp points of light. Joan leans upon the green-painted railings. Herring gulls perch nearby, no doubt hoping for bread crusts, or chips.

But when we lived here, she thinks, we hardly ever looked at the sea. I caught the bus into uni every day – we never called it 'uni' did we, that's a more modern thing, I never heard it until Rachel went. Anyway, I took a bus, and he went to work. He had a 2.2 in Economics and a job as a binman. His parents were mortified. And we lived back there, quite a way from the sea. Once the winter started there wasn't much incentive to come down here to the front. Windy, Essex. Not a hill to stop the wind between here and Siberia, so we used to say. I wonder if it's true.

We shared that flat – top half of a house – with that other couple, who we never saw. Nocturnal. She was called Sheila, what was he called –?

Joan feels a sharp jerk to her shoulder. She feels her bag going away from her. She turns, she grabs. She misses, and then someone pushes her hard in the back and she, already off-balance, feels herself falling towards the concrete, sees the concrete rushing to meet her. She looks, can see only legs, feet, running away, puts her hand out to save herself. Feels the shock run up her arm, feels the bone break.

It is a couple with a dog who are first on the scene. Joan has sat up, leaning against the railing, holding her right arm at the wrist. She knows clearly that it is broken and she also knows clearly that her bag has gone. She knows what it contains. Her purse, with a hundred and some pounds – which she would gladly give them now if they would give back the other items. Her credit card. Her debit card. Her phone with all her numbers and addresses carefully entered. Her car keys.

The lady with the dog escorts her to a nearby bench. The man gets out his phone and dials 999. The dog sits down and pays attention to its bum.

'Did you get a look at them?'

Joan shakes her head.

*

Viv and Bill have eaten their sandwiches – more cheese and chutney – and decide to stop for a cup of tea. Viv takes the map into the teashop.

'If we go back to the A69,' she says, 'we can pick up the M6 here, at Carlisle.'

His finger traces the A68. 'Look at that,' he says. 'Jedburgh. Carter Bar. Don't they sound enticing?'

Well no they don't, not to Viv. Paisley, and Joan, and Rachel, are what she has in mind, it's gone half past three o'clock and they are still far from their destination. She thinks he's got cold feet.

'Bill,' she says, and she is trying not to get his back up. 'Bill, are you feeling a little nervous about this expedition?'

He does not answer. He does not say anything until they are back in the van and he has turned it towards Scotland. On the A68. His choice. This is one stubborn man.

'Does the radio work?' says Viv. 'It would make it go quicker if there were something to listen to.'

He does not reply. A little further on he begins to speak. She listens. At first she does.

'I met Joanie at university. They were strange times – when you look back now they were strange times. My parents couldn't work it out at all, why people didn't want respectable jobs, why would they want posters of Karl Marx and Che – not that they knew who he was anyway. They were a bit taken aback that I was even going to university – I don't suppose you did, did you?'

'No,' says Viv. 'I didn't get any exams. I left school as soon as I could, when I were fifteen. You learn things as you go along, though, don't you?'

'Strange times,' he says again. 'We thought there was a revolution going on. We thought the world was changing.'

'Like Flower Power?' she says. 'I remember that.'

He makes a noise to dismiss flower power. 'That was just pussying about. There were proper causes to fight for.'

'You told me yesterday. Like a war between two other countries thousands of miles away.'

'Not just that. Civil Rights in the US, the war in Biafra, apartheid in South Africa –'

'So what did you do about all that?'

'I closed my Barclays bank account,' he says. 'I went on some demos.'

'So you said. You got arrested.'

'Well, nearly. But we were aware. We talked about all these things. We knew we didn't want to be part of that world. We wanted a better world.'

'That's reasonable,' says Viv. 'I still want a better world. But what can you do? Shit keeps on happening, over and over, on and on.'

Outside the van the moors and the road over the moors go on and on. The lowering sun shines in through the windscreen. The rain has stopped. They have crossed the border.

'We took over the university,' he says. 'They tried to expel some students for a protest, and the students went on strike and took over the whole place.'

'And?'

'They backed down. It was great. It was people power. Joanie must have told you about it. She was there.'

'No,' says Viv.

'The lesson was,' says Bill, 'that they're scared of you – of us I mean. If we stick together and stand up to them, then it's possible to win.'

'Yeah,' says Viv, 'like the miners did.'

'I never really followed that story. It was a busy time for me and Lyd. Two kids and the house and everything, and the business taking off. God, the hours Lyd and me worked, paperwork after the girls had gone to bed, up early, planning the day, take the kids to school, back to the jobs, fetching materials, or phoning up to find out where the deliveries had got to, and people changing their mind and wanting something different, something they've seen on the telly and all of a sudden they think you can alter the whole thing without them having to pay for it. They've got something to answer for, them on the telly making it look as if you can do the whole thing in a weekend. But Lyd was good at all that, she could make them see sense, but nicely. A lot of them knew her anyway, the local ones, grown up with her obviously. They would never take as much notice of me.'

He has begun to talk as if she is not there, as if he is justifying himself to himself. Viv is not that interested in his excuses; tell me more about Joan, she wants to say.

'She was a good wife, Lyd, and a good business partner, good business head on her shoulders. We did well, and most of it was down to her. She was the brains. Good mother as well, our kids don't know how lucky they were, having her for a mother. Always made time for them, not too strict, not too easy. They could have managed without me, the whole family could have, I was a passenger a lot of the time, off sailing, whole weekends sometimes. I mean I tried to pull my weight but it was like they didn't need me for very much. I seem to have spent my life surrounded by women. Grew up with three sisters, and then a wife and two daughters – no wonder I needed to get away sometimes.

'And on top of that, we were renovating our own house, more or less back to the brickwork and start again. With the kids underfoot. But it's a great house. It was all worth it in the end. I'm thinking of selling but it all depends –'

Viv wakes with a jump. Bill has stopped talking, that must be what woke her. The light has nearly gone now. The moors are gone, there seem to be buildings around, complicated road junctions.

'Sorry,' she says. 'I must have dropped off.'

Bill pulls the van to the side of the road, picks up the map from the floor where it has slid.

'We should have turned off this road,' he says. 'We've come too far. We'll be in Edinburgh if we keep going.'

Viv says, irritated, 'I said to take a left before Jedburgh.'

'I didn't hear you,' he says. 'Or if I did I forgot. I was thinking.'

'Give me the map,' she says. 'I'm awake now.' She's not going to say sorry again, not after she gave him clear instructions that he totally, wilfully ignored.

'Look,' she says, 'continue towards Edinburgh, then we can get on to the M8 and go across to Glasgow. We'll be fine.'

'I think we should stop for the night,' he says. 'I'm tired with all this driving. I really don't want to start on a motorway now.'

'Where would we stop?'

'Oh anywhere,' he says. 'So long as it's off the main road. A lay-by would do.'

'What about facilities?' she says. 'You know, toilets. Food.'

'There'll be a pub somewhere. That will do.'

'I hoped we would be there by now,' says Viv, but her protest is muted. It's as if she's been carried along like a stick in a stream, and there really isn't any point any more in arguing, or trying to have things her way. He's the one driving, he has all the power, she is helpless.

They pass a place called the Muirhead Hotel. Very welcoming it looks, light shining in the dusk, cars pulled up outside, hanging baskets beside the doors.

'Too fancy,' says Bill. 'Too posh.'

But he pulls into the next one, which is called The Wee Howff, sideways on to the road, trees screening the car park. 'With a bit of luck and a bit of sweet talking, ' he says, 'I reckon we can park the van here all night.'

There isn't much in the way of food, only an all day breakfast, but the landlady promises them some chips with it.

'So,' says Viv, 'you knew Richard before?'

'Who told you that?'

'You did,' she says. 'But anyway it was obvious. When you came to the choir you were stuck to him like glue. Is he another old university friend?'

'Friend from London days,' says Bill. 'We played together in a band. Hung out a lot. You wouldn't think it to look at him now, but he was this long skinny bloke, hair down past his shoulders, he was a pretty boy in those days. I was best man at his wedding, or a witness or something, it wasn't a big do. Joanie wasn't there, it was a week day, she was at work.'

'I didn't know he had a wife.'

'Oh it didn't last, don't know why. I sort of lost touch with him when I left London, then found him – or he found me, can't remember which – a few years back. More than a few probably, time kind of gets away from me.'

'Friends Reunited? Facebook?'

'Something like that I suppose. It was my daughter who did it all. I don't have anything to do with computers.'

'I think,' she says, 'that he's barking up the wrong tree, with these songs, don't you? I don't think people are taking to them. What do you think?'

He does not answer, does not even appear to hear her.

'What I'm thinking,' she says, '*Hair*, it's not mainstream enough. It's a bit weird. Our choir – Pamela and people like that – they like something they're familiar with. All this hippy-dippy stuff – it doesn't suit them, we've moved on since those days.'

'If you ask me,' says Bill, 'which you did, I'd say the ideas behind *Hair* haven't ever taken hold up here in the North. Haven't even touched down. I mean, personal freedom, being anti-war –'

'We were anti-war,' says Viv. 'Nobody round here wanted their boys killed in Iraq and Afghanistan. You won't find people round here –'

'I'm talking about the Vietnam war,' says Bill. 'That's what it was about.'

'Exactly,' says Viv. 'It's over. It were America's war anyway, nothing to do with us.'

'It was to do with us,' says Bill. 'We protested against it. I got arrested in Grosvenor Square.'

'So you said. And I suppose that had the Yanks quaking in their boots.'

'You have to stand up and be counted.'

'We had our own battles to fight,' says Viv. 'We had miners' strikes and pit closures. Steel.'

'Not exactly the same, is it? Anyway, I mean, *Hair* wasn't only about the war – it drew everything together, drugs and feminism and anti-racism. It was –'

'It weren't the real world.' Viv, like the rest of the choir, has been reading about it online. 'Ordinary people won't connect with it, not then and not now. That's all I'm saying.'

'Look at me,' says Bill. 'I was as ordinary as – as anyone. But when I left home I came across new ideas, and – and experiences, and things like that, and –'

'And now you're not ordinary?'

'I'm more aware than I might have been.'

'Very tactfully put,' says Viv. 'But I think the choir is perfectly aware of what they do want to sing and what they don't. That's what we're talking about. The trouble with Richard, he's restless. He does something, it's successful, does he do something similar next time? No, he's off on some wild idea. This is not the first time. One time he wanted us to sing a Kate Bush song. Sounded like hyenas mating – not when she does it, obviously, but when we did it. Another time he wanted to put together a programme called an evening with Elvis – well there were no soprano parts in that, only the odd ooh and aah, so we told him we wouldn't do it. He's good, Richard, and we like him, but we have to keep him in check. This one won't be a goer, you wait and see.'

Bill smiles. This is the first smile Viv has seen from him. 'Anyone would think,' he says, 'that Richard's asking you all to take your clothes off. It's a pity, these days, we've gone all prudish again. Nothing wrong with the human body, if you ask me, nothing to be ashamed of.'

'I'm not ashamed,' says Viv. 'I don't mind a bit of nakedness, but what I don't like, I don't mind admitting, it's the drugs that bother me. Not nice, drugs aren't.'

'It's about opening your eyes,' says Bill. 'Opening your mind and seeing the world afresh. Expanding your consciousness, we said in those days. Sounds a bit pretentious now, I know.'

'And did you?'

'Oh yes.'

'And Joan, did she expand her consciousness?'

'Of course she did. We all did. Didn't you?'

Viv shakes her head. Her hair comes loose from its grips and she holds it back again with a scrunchie she has been keeping on her wrist for the purpose.

'You're talking to a working-class Sheffield girl,' she says. 'Never lived out of Sheffield. Expanding consciousness weren't on the agenda. Getting drunk were, I did that. Losing consciousness I suppose that were.'

'In all honesty,' says Bill, 'we did that too.'

Viv sips her drink and looks round at the shabby brown bar, where they are the only customers.

'So, did you tell him – Richard I mean – what you were doing? I mean, looking for Joan?'

'No point,' says Bill. 'He never knew her. She kept well clear of the band, as I remember. She had all this studying to do, for her exams. Civil Service. I may have mentioned her name to him, but that's as far as it would go. If he knew her he would have said. And he didn't, so he can't do, can he. She would never have liked him anyway, he wasn't her sort, not serious enough. Actually, now I come to think about it, it was at that performance of *Hair* that I met Ricky – Richard I mean, obviously. I went outside to smoke a little joint and there he was, doing the same thing. And we got talking, you know, as you do, about the orchestra – it wasn't an orchestra, it was just a band, and not a very good one –'

'And about the play?'

'Not really. I'd never been to a theatre before. People said it was ground-breaking but I wasn't to know was I. We went with a bunch of people from Essex, me and Joan. I only went to impress her I expect.'

'So your wife?' says Viv. 'Lydia. When did –?'

'April,' he says. 'Poor old Lyd. We had our ups and downs but she was a good sort really.'

'Did you tell her about Joan?'

'Well,' he says, 'sort of. I mean, she knew, obviously, that I had girlfriends before her. I mean, everybody has haven't they. You don't get to about twenty-five without –. But she didn't now how much Joanie meant to me, that wouldn't have been fair on her.'

'So those Christmas cards – didn't she ever ask?'

'Who looks at Christmas cards? Though, I have to say, I never put my name on the one I sent to Joanie. From Lydia, I put, and a note inside saying things like, what the children are doing, that sort of thing, just to keep in touch.'

'But without your name? Isn't that a bit odd?'

'Touching base, that's all. Just so she knew I was still there and I knew she was.'

'But Lydia didn't know?'

'There wasn't anything to know.'

'You can't have it both ways. If it were entirely innocent you might as well tell her. If it's going to upset her that's because it's not entirely innocent.'

'It was entirely innocent.'

'Then why not tell her?'

'Because,' he says, 'she might have been as illogical as you are being.'

In the offended silence the woman from behind the bar brings over two large plates of unhealthy food.

'Tell you something,' says Viv, shaking brown sauce over her chips, 'Joan wouldn't be seen dead eating this. She'd have something to say if she could see us now.'

'Healthy eater?'

'Completely. Salad. Vegetables. No cakes, no chips.'

'Hm,' says Bill.

'But why didn't you let her know you were coming to see her? Or did you? Is she trying to stay out of your way?'

He stops chewing for a second, looks down at his plate. Then takes a breath, cuts a sausage in quarters. 'I never thought of that,' he says. 'What I mean is, I have never for one moment thought that she would do that.'

'So she didn't know you were coming? Wouldn't it have been sensible to –'

'What I did,' he says, 'was what we arranged. I sent her a postcard. That was the deal. When Lydia died, what she said, what Joanie said, she said, wait a bit till you've got everything sorted out, then just drop me a line. Tell me where and when and we'll meet up. And that's what I did. What she never said was that she had moved house.'

'So you sent it to Stumperlowe Close?' says Viv. 'That were stupid.'

'Stupid address,' says Bill. 'How was I to know? So I guess she never got it. You'd think people would redirect it wouldn't you.'

'Oh those people who bought her house,' says Viv, 'we know who they are, they're always on holiday. They moved in, then turned round and went to the States for six weeks. So you turned up and she never did. Why didn't you check? Why didn't you text her to make sure?'

'I refuse to have a mobile phone,' says Bill. 'They are one of the curses of the world. Along with computers and virtual reality and the internet and all that crap. We got on fine without them, we should go on getting on fine without them.'

'Fine,' says Viv. She finishes her last chip, mopping up the last trace of brown sauce with it, and pushes her plate away. 'That were all right,' she says. 'I were ready for that.'

He grins at her suddenly. 'At least you're not a fussy eater.'

'Never have been,' she says. 'Never been thin either.'

'Tell me about Joanie's husband,' he says.

Viv looks at their glasses which are nearly empty. She has been rather hoping this is his treat, but he is making no move to go for a refill. 'Another half?' she says.

When she brings them back from the bar he says it again. 'Joanie's husband. What was he like?'

'Martin. Solid. Big, cheerful, reliable, you know the sort. Matey, liked a drink. Plenty to say for himself.'

'Happy together, were they?'

Viv considers. 'He had some old-fashioned ideas. He thought if he bought her things – you know, jewellery and state of the art food processors – she was short of nothing I can tell you – but then he thought it as all right to ignore her all the rest of the time. I mean, ignore what she might want to do. Like, when they went on holiday, it were always where he wanted to go, he liked Greece and Turkey and she hated places like that. And he liked to do things like water-ski and that, and I know I were there once when she said she'd like to go to Paris and he said it were all just art galleries and he couldn't be doing with it.'

'Not happy then. I mean, she wasn't happy?'

'I wouldn't say that. When he died she were like a zombie for a year or more. I saw her every day at work of course and she carried on, everyone said she was wonderful, but it was like there were nothing there behind her eyes, you know? It would have been better for her, in my opinion, if she'd fell apart, or if she'd made a fuss and got some sympathy – from me for instance – but no, she said she were fine, she held herself together and she's been like that ever since.'

'Ok,' says Bill. 'One of us can go up in the roof, one down here. But the one in the roof gets the sleeping bag, because it can get cold up there. There's a blanket for the one who stays down here. Which do you want?'

Viv considers the bunk which has been behind her seat all day but which she never counted on actually having to sleep on. 'I think I'll take the roof,' she says. The sleeping bag sounds better than a blanket, even though Bill – or, worse, his mate Pete – has probably been sleeping in it for decades and never thought of washing it. 'How do I get up there?'

He pushes back the hatch. 'Stand on the edge of the sink. Now, get your arms through and push up on your elbows.'

She is standing on the edge of the sink, nervously because she's not sure if it will take her weight, and it's not her van. Not even Bill's van. But she's too short to get good leverage with her elbows, or maybe just not strong enough to lift her own weight. And – let's face it, she has a big bosom which, though squashy, doesn't seem to want to squeeze through the hatch.

'I'll take the bunk,' she says.

So Viv lies, in her clothes, wrapped in a blanket, an inadequate cushion for a pillow, on the edge of cold and far from the edge of sleep. She thinks with longing about her leopard skin – fake fur – jacket, hanging uselessly at home on its hook at the foot of the stairs, and with resentment about Bill's lateness which caused her to leave it behind. She unwraps herself and gets off the bunk, stumbling against Bill's guitar in the dark, and gets her cardigan – not a very thick one – to put round her feet, then wraps herself up again.

There are sounds from up in the roof. Something – two things hit the floor – Bill's shoes no doubt. A grunt or two – that will be him bending to take off his socks. Viv has been without a man for a long time, she can't help being aware of him, such a very few centimetres away. Well, there has been the odd fling since Colin died, but nothing that ever amounted to anything, and lately, nothing at all. She misses a man, she would not deny it. However much she likes her life the way it is, she misses the chance of a bit of romance. It was a sort of yearning, after all, that prompted her to accompany Bill on this daft expedition; a sort of yearning for romance, even if it was Joan's rather than hers. Give over, she says to herself. Go to sleep.

Sleep still will not come. Viv's bones are well padded, but even so her hip bone is feeling the unyielding quality of the bunk. Breathe, she says to herself. Keep still. What is it they tell you do to these days? Mindfulness. I'm *too* bloody mindful, that's the trouble. I can't help thinking where am I and why did I get into this. She is conscious of there being metal all around her. It feels wrong. Bricks, bricks and plaster are what should surround you as you go to bed at night, not sheet metal as if you were a sardine or a pilchard. Pilchards, her grandmother's favourite. Sunday tea, pilchards on toast, Sing Something Simple on the wireless, Viv and her brother bored out of their minds.

Maybe she is close to sleep after all, thinking about her brother. Roland. A vague, quiet, studious boy, he was called Florrie at school by the other boys but never seemed to take it amiss. She likes him still, as she always has, but thoughts of him do not often intrude into her days or nights.

She will think about all the dead people, that usually sends her off to sleep. From the beginning – her grandmother, Nannan. No before that, the grandfather she never knew, a Frenchman. Where did Nannan – Mary-Ada were her name – wherever did she pick up a French man in Rotherham? She never said, at least, not to anyone who is still alive. She lived a few doors down from them, Nannan did. Viv and Roland always went there for their breakfast because their mum started work early. Nannan got up early too, put on her crossover pinny and began cleaning something. Whenever you saw her she was cleaning something. Then she'd stop and have breakfast – porridge and toast – with the children, and send them off to school and then go round to their house and clean that. She died shortly before Viv's mother married again, without, as far as anyone knew, ever a word of complaint about her life.

And Viv's own father – he died long ago too, she can only just remember him. Another foreigner, Spanish this time, as if Viv's mother was trying to replicate her own mother's story, and with some success. Himinez was his name but he was called Jim by everyone in England. Viv can only just remember him – a pair of boots and a stubbly chin. Tickling. 'You're just like your father,' her mother used to say to her, usually when she had done something foolish or something that necessitated unscheduled cleaning. Why did that matter so much, wonders Viv, when the whole house was scrubbed every day.

Viv tries to turn over on the hard bunk but the blanket threatens to come unwrapped and she gives up on the attempt. Listening hard she can hear Bill's regular breathing, up there in the roof. Selfish bastard. She is nearly off when she is brought back to wakefulness by remembering that she is due at the Age Concern charity shop in the morning, and hasn't let them know. Nothing to be done about it now, except try again to get to sleep.

So, three down, how many more to go. Her stepfather, Arthur Jones. All the men in his family seemed to go early and suddenly – him, his cousin, Martin and Colin. It should have brought us closer, Joan and me, she thinks, being married to brothers and then both of them dying within a year or two of each other. Or maybe we were never meant to be close.

Colin – feckless, reckless Colin, with his womanising and his hand-to mouth business arrangements. Very different from his brother, Martin, steady-eddie Martin, with his nice cars and his nice friends who were all the same as him, and his boring conversations about rugby or bridges or, in later life, blackfly and where to acquire horse manure.

Poor Colin. How daft, to make such a mess of a perfectly decent life, how lucky that Carol set out to get him back, and that she had a steady career of her own to support him and the children without relying on him for an income. They managed to retrieve the situation, with only a little damage done, and that mainly to her, Viv, who could most certainly cope. Couldn't she? Hadn't she? Yes she could, and had. By then, anyway, she was ready for a change. So, bruised but not scarred, maybe down but certainly not out.

Her feet have warmed up, she slips into sleep.

Thursday

Joan wakes again in the bed at Seawinds, in the bedroom from which she checked out the previous morning. This, thinks Joan, is so stupid. Just as I was going home. Just as I made a decision, this. Because the doctor at the hospital has wrapped her wrist up in a temporary plaster, told her to come back in two day's time to the fracture clinic, and – this is the real bother – no driving for six weeks.

'But I live hundreds of miles away,' Joan said to her, panic making her exaggerate. 'My car's here, I'm on my own.'

'Sorry,' said the doctor. 'Maybe you can call someone to come and get you. Or leave your car and go home by train.' She could tell that Joan is not so poor that she couldn't afford a train fare.

The couple on the sea front were wonderful, the policeman was wonderful, the man from the BMW garage was wonderful. The couple stayed with her until the policeman came, the policeman drove her to hospital and on the way, over his radio, he contacted her bank and cancelled her cards, and arranged for her car to be towed away to the dealer to have a new lock fitted.

She has given a statement to the police and received a crime number. She is a statistic.

The people at the hospital, though under some pressure, were wonderfully calm and calming, and once her wrist was in what Joan called a pot and they called a plaster cast, the woman behind the glass window looked up the number of Seawinds and phoned to ask if Joan could go back there. And Tiff was wonderful too, driving into Colchester and taking Joan back, and being so kind that Joan, on seeing her bed, still there, freshly made and ready for her to lie down in, began to cry, in a helpless, slow dribbly sort of way.

Now, awake early in the morning, she considers her plight.

She is not going to leave her car, unless she can find a lockup, secure garage to leave it in. You don't go away and leave a BMW on the street for six weeks, and come back and find it still there, undamaged. And it wouldn't be fair to expect Tiff to take responsibility for it in her off-road parking space, because she will need that for other visitors. She considers who she might call to help.

'Aren't you in the AA?' says Tiff.

But she's not. Rescue services are for old cars, Martin always said. And old people, he sometimes added.

There's Viv, but Viv gave up her own car ages ago. It must be five years since she has driven anywhere, and Joan certainly does not fancy the idea of sitting in her own passenger seat while Viv crunches the gears and has little panics about overtaking – or worse, gets properly into the mood and starts to behave like one of those boy racers.

Rachel obviously is out of the question. So far away, how would she get here, how would she get the time off work, how would she even respond if Joan were to ask her? Besides, Rachel or Viv, either would want to know what she was doing there.

'You could get a transporter to take it back,' says Tiff. 'You could sit in the lorry.'

But the cost is enough to make a person gasp, even Joan. Not to mention the prospect of sitting in a lorry cab having to make conversation with some taciturn driver for a whole day. He would want to talk about football, or computer games.

I really don't trust anyone else at all.

It is still too early to get up when she has a brilliant idea. She smiles to herself in the dim dawn light, with relief and triumph. She will get it organised first thing in the morning, as soon as she can be sure that people will be up and about.

*

Viv is wakened early, and unwillingly.

76

The bunk was hard, the blanket inadequate and her sleep was disturbed by unusual noises in the night. But by now, as Bill descends from the roof, she feels comfortable and warm and does not want ever to get out of bed. He stands next to the bunk with a mug of something hot. She sits up, clothed, with her clothes twisted round her, her bra undone, her hair straggling over her face.

'Tea,' he says.

But it's not tea, not as she knows it. The teabag is oddly speckled and the smell is wrong. No milk.

'Haven't you got coffee?' she says.

'Poison,' he says.

She takes the tea and sips it. It's hot liquid after all; and no more wrong than any other sort of tea to a person who has to start her day with coffee. She knows that she will be able to laugh about all this one day, maybe even today, once they have caught up with Joan.

'Let's get going,' says Bill. 'We don't want her to go out before we get there.'

'We don't want her to be still in bed either,' says Viv, looking out of the window and seeing the sun just edging over the horizon.

'Once you're awake,' he says, 'there's no point in waiting around.'

'I weren't awake,' she says, but he pays no attention.

She makes him stop at a café – just a truck stop really – where she can go to the toilet, and also buy a coffee and some toast. He won't let her stay there to eat and drink though – she has to have a cardboard cup and sit in the van with her toast. She would like to be able to change her clothes and clean her teeth but he is in too much of a hurry for that. I'll laugh about it one day, she thinks.

He's in better spirits today, singing.

'I haven't heard that song since I were in junior school,' says Viv.

'Did you have it too? They used to play it to us in Assembly. Why though, when we had no idea what it was all about?'

It feels like the first time they have agreed on anything. She joins in the song. 'Oh the blue somethings are pulling me away as step I with m' something to the sea.'

They are not the same words he is singing and she stops.

'Sure by Tummel and Loch Rannoch and Lochaber I will go,' he sings, and then he stops. 'I don't know the words either.'

For maybe a quarter of a mile he is quiet, as if chastened, but then starts again. "Let the Sunshine In". Viv joins in, singing the tune, and he switches to the harmony, as Richard has taught them. And it is a sunny morning.

'You like music,' she says. 'Are you in a band?'

'Not any more,' he says. 'But I still strum a bit.'

They sing it through again.

'See,' he says, 'the counter-culture – what you would call the hippies – they believed in the power of drugs to change people's perceptions of the world. I mean they weren't in favour of having smackheads dossing down in stairwells, it was more acid and dope and peace and love.'

'Well, they let the genie out of the bottle didn't they,' says Viv. 'At least, that's how it's always seemed to me.'

'I'll tell you how I met Joanie,' he says. 'I don't care what you think.

'She saved me, that night I met her. I was in a proper state, should never have been there. Ever had a bad trip? You won't have done if you've never even touched acid. As you've said yourself, you were never part of a drug scene. Well, take my word for it, an end of term disco is the wrong place to have a bad trip. She pulled me out of there, she talked me down, she walked round and round that campus with me, telling me it was all right, like she was my sister or my mother, or something. She took me back to my room and she made me coffee – not that that's the best thing – and she stayed with me. Sat up nearly all night with me, until I went to sleep and then she crept out.

'You have no idea how terrifying it can be, watching the walls melt. Things come to get you, the floor becomes slime, you've no idea. You shut your eyes and it gets worse. You know those people who jump out of windows and their friends say, He thought he could fly – I've never believed that. What it was – he thought they were after him and he was trying to get away, that's what he was doing.

'Anyway. You wake up next morning with a headache, things look a bit weird, you get the odd flashback. I could remember some bits and not others, I knew there'd been a girl, I knew it wasn't my girlfriend, I somehow had it in my mind it was my sister, but I worked out that couldn't be right. One of my flatmates says to me, Who was that brought you back here last night? Someone else says, She's in second year sociology. They piece it together, who she goes out with, where she's from even. Sheffield, they say. Where the hell is that? we all say.

'What does she look like? I say. They all laugh at me. Listen to him, they say, Listen to Oggy – What does she look like? Don't you know? I gather that I've been in my bedroom with the most desired girl on campus and then I know who she is. God, she was a looker. I suppose you didn't know her then.'

Viv is thinking, 'Oggy?'

'And actually, though, her nose was too big, and her feet were big, and she wore a lot of flowing dresses, kaftans and such, so her figure was a bit of a mystery, but even so – she had those dark, dark eyes, that auburn hair, that smile. I wandered back in my head through the events of the previous evening but I couldn't see the smile. It was her though, the boys convinced me, it was her, and they all wanted me to tell them what had happened, i.e. did I screw her? I let them think I did. Well, I mean, who wouldn't?'

'That's not very nice,' Viv says, startled into speech. But he seems not to hear her.

'Then we all went home for Christmas. My mum thought I looked terrible. She thought I must have been working too hard. I sat and watched telly for three weeks – all that Christmas stuff, Morecombe and Wise, you remember all that stuff, and rolled myself joints after my mum and dad were in bed. They had just got a colour telly – they were a new thing then, and I sat and got stoned all on my own and I came to the conclusion that materialism was evil and that I should abandon my studies and go and live in a tent by a lake.

'But I never did it. Not because it would have upset my parents, not even because I was scared to do it, not for any reason except inertia. And because it was winter. And besides, I had to get back in January to find her. I knew her name. I was going to find her and explain to her that we were prisoners of the system and we had to go off to a Scottish island or a Welsh hill and live off the land, authentically, both of us, together.

'We used to laugh about that, later on. But it wasn't so stupid. I took my finals. I got a degree, which I never used. I can tell you the difference between macro-economics and micro-economics, if you want. If you want any more, then no.

'I can see how it was possible for us to think like that. It was all given to us, on a plate. I was the first baby in our town born on the NHS, first NHS baby in Burnham-on-Crouch, that was me. Everything was free, orange juice, school milk, teeth, glasses, everything. University was free. I didn't have to do anything. My dad worked but my mum didn't and I was the eldest of four, so there it was, full grant, enough to live on. No loans, no fees, no debt – you weren't allowed to get into debt – handed out like we deserved it.

'So of course we despised it. We knew all about the evils of capitalism and the influence of advertising and planned obsolescence. We weren't going to have lives full of material goods, or sell our souls to some big corporation. We were going to float around like clouds, or flowers, or something, and bring our children up to be anarchists. And we know how that turned out don't we.

'If I had married Joanie, not Lydia, I don't suppose it would have been any different, they'd still be children of Thatcher.'

He pauses. Viv is surprised by the fluency of his account – it is as if he's rehearsed it, more than once. Has he really been this obsessed, with Joan, for this long? 'Turn off here,' she says 'We're going on the M8.' He obeys without any argument.

'So, back to uni I came, to find her. I was scared shitless. What if she laughed at me, what if she'd forgotten me, what if I dumped my girlfriend and couldn't get Joanie to dump her boyfriend? What if I dumped my girlfriend and she dumped her boyfriend and then it didn't work out with her? What if I couldn't find her, what if I could find her but she was different from what I remembered? Even, what if the lads had been winding me up and it wasn't Joanie Jones at all who I'd been with?

'She wasn't hard to find. I just hung around outside sociology lectures. You ever see that film, The Graduate? Dustin Hoffman is standing outside her classes, practically stalking her. I'd seen it, I think I was consciously doing it, I was showing off to myself. Anyway, I think I only had to do it twice and then she came out and I said was she going for a coffee and we went off to the coffee bar in Square Four.

'She had a boyfriend and I had a girlfriend. In fact I was staying at my girlfriend's most nights of the week. One of the reasons I got so off my head at that disco was that she'd gone home to her parents early and left me to it. So I dropped her ration of the acid as well as mine. Anyway, she was called Rosemary, perfectly nice girl, absolutely right for me if you know what I mean. Same league, you know. But I'd been telling her about the evils of the world – cars and colour tellies, they were all evil, and people telling you what to do, and banks –

'– Ha, listen to me, I knew bankers were evil before anyone else did. Did they listen to me? Did they fuck!

'So Rosemary was thinking that I'd gone off my rocker just a bit. She was a bit, Whoa, tell you what, let's get these finals out of the way and then we'll think about it. All the women in my life, they've never understood what I was on about, not even Joanie. Especially not Joanie. Thinking back, Rosemary would have been my best bet, bit of a Girl Guide type, country girl but still into the stuff I was into. I don't know what happened to her in the end.'

So this, thinks Viv, this scrawny boring old bloke, he must be the one that Joan was so broken-hearted about that time just before she went and married Martin. Good call, Joan.

'I played it pretty cool with Joanie to start with. I said I wanted to buy her a coffee to say thank you for looking after me. I wanted her to say she hoped I was feeling better and had I had a good Christmas and take it from there. Well it never turns out like you think. We get into the coffee bar, juke box turned up really loud that day so certainly no possibility of a nuanced conversation. We've no sooner sat down than these three girls turn up, friends of hers.

'Who's this? they say, and she says, This is him I was telling you about. And two of them fall about laughing and the third one – who looks religious to me, or so I've always said – starts laying into me about dropping acid.

'You don't know what it might do to your brain, she says. Well, obviously not, that's part of the point.

'What if it damaged your unborn children? she goes, and naturally I pay no attention to that.

'Don't you read the papers? she goes and I say No I don't actually, they are full of capitalist lies, and of

82

course they don't want us to open our minds and see through the garbage they've been selling us.

'My father's a psychiatrist, she says, and at that I just laugh and turn my back on her, and all four of them, Joanie too, get up and walk out of the coffee bar.

'The juke box was playing "All Along the Watchtower".'

Viv considers he's made that last bit up, just for some sort of effect. 'See how groovy I am' – that kind of thing.

'I was going to give up on it. I couldn't see how a girl with friends like those could ever be someone I wanted to be with. So I left it. I didn't see her again, except in the distance, for two or three weeks. By then though, someone – and I bet I know who – told Rosemary that I spent the night with another girl as soon as she went home for Christmas. Me and Rosemary split up.

'The next time I saw Joanie was one evening, late, after the bar closed. A bunch of people said they were going up to this room someone had where there was a record player. Not many people had record players and this person, so it was said, had an LP called *Alice's Restaurant*. It wasn't something you would ever get on a juke box, I'd heard of it, but never heard it, so I tagged along.

'Yeah, it was always someone else's room where you heard music. All the girls had Leonard Cohen, the boys would be more likely to go for Led Zeppelin. So we get there, it's packed, it's standing room only, and after a bar or two I've given up on this because it's not my kind of thing. I never was interested in that folky kind of stuff. So I wander into the kitchen and there is Joanie, laying out a hand of Patience on the table and blowing her nose quite a lot.

'So I sit down nearby and she just looks at me briefly, you know, and then ignores me, and so I roll up, and light up, and after a bit I offer it to her, and she takes it and drags on it and nearly coughs her insides up and I fetch her some water from the tap, and after that it seems like we're ok again.

'So I ask her what's up, and she tells me that her dad is getting married again. This doesn't sound so bad to me, but she's really upset about it, her mum has been dead a couple of years but it doesn't seem long to her and she thinks her will never be the same with her again. And I ask her about this woman and she tells me she's all right, quite kind, probably will look after her dad ok, but – well – common, not her dad's sort. Much younger apparently, from the other end of Sheffield.'

'That was my mum,' says Viv, but he doesn't seem to hear her.

'She goes on a bit, sniffing a bit, and then she says, Oh I'm probably being unreasonable. If it stops him being lonely . . . And then I walk her to the bus stop for the last bus and give her a little kiss, just a little kiss, and she doesn't stop me, she accepts it, and the bus comes and she gets on, and off she goes back to her house that she shares with the Poison Pals, and I think that's it.

'It's like I was always thinking it was over, or never going to start really. I always thought someone else would get to her before I ever got my act together. But I kept on seeing her, more and more often. In the bookshop, in the bank, just walking backwards and forwards between the Hexagon and the tower blocks. I got to know where she would be. I gathered that she and the boyfriend weren't together any more, she seemed to be with the other girls less and less, more and more on her own.

'And eventually it just happened. We were walking in the same direction – it was blowing a gale I remember – and I said come up to the flat and have a coffee, and she did and we went into my room and sat there all afternoon just talking, and after that day we were never apart again, day or night. Hardly ever.

'So we got together because her dad was getting remarried, and we broke up because he died. Not the whole story, that isn't, but it's a way of looking at it.

'We were remarkable. We were inseparable. I didn't love her more than she loved me, she loved me just as much as I loved her – are those two statements the same thing? Never mind. We were in it together, really in it together. We would probably have got married some time in the future, but we didn't need it, I mean, not with a ring and all that bourgeois crap. We just knew we'd be together for ever. It was perfect, everything was perfect.'

'So perfect,' says Viv, unable to stop herself, 'that you haven't seen her for however many years. Why's that then?'

'Her dad died. As I say, I only met him once. She knew my parents, we used to go there quite often on a nice sunny day, get a bit of sea air, you know, but she never took me with her when she came up north to see her dad. There was always some reason. Oh like, he wouldn't want us to sleep together in his house, or else, it was going to be really boring for me, just family you know, and I'd feel left out. I didn't feel bothered. I figured I've got all my life to go visiting old relatives, it didn't matter to me if she nipped up to the grimy north for a day or two.'

'Well I remember when her dad died,' says Viv. 'Course I do. She were, well, devastated is the only word for it. I don't remember that she ever mentioned you though.'

'We were on holiday, in Greece. Corfu, 1972. It was wonderful. She had this black bikini on white skin. All the other girls were pink, or red, and some were tanned, but Joanie was as pale as if she was newborn and she smothered herself in stuff and she was all sticky when I put my arms round her. We were staying in this minute room they called a studio – just four walls, and a bed, bathroom two floors down. We were set to have a brilliant time, just dossing around, doing nothing, you know, swimming, drinking, making love in the afternoon.

'Tour rep turns up one afternoon, takes her aside, next thing, floods of tears, absolutely distraught, and she says she's got to go home. I say, What for, we'll be back before the funeral, what can she do by going back? She says I don't understand, I say, I'm sorry, but I don't.

'She went home without me and let me tell you, there is nothing that spoils a holiday so much as the person you went with suddenly buggering off and leaving you. I mean, I was sorry her dad had died, but I was seriously pissed off about his timing. If she had stayed I would have been extra specially good to her, I'm not an insensitive sort of person but I'd been looking forward to that holiday, I was tired, I needed a break, she needed it too.

'That's the last time I saw her, getting into a taxi that was going to take her to the airport. About two in the morning, that was, I can never hear those bloody cicadas without thinking of it, and she looked out of the taxi window at me and tears were just flooding down her face and I would have jumped in beside her, but I didn't have my passport on me, and besides I was still hacked off at what she was doing. But I went round to the driver's window and he wound it down, and I said, Can you wait a minute, and he just fucked off, just roared away and that was it.

'So the last time I saw Joanie Jones was in 1972. I've thought about her every day. Never met her again, never in the flesh. That's a lot of years of waiting.

'Sent her a postcard. Should have known it would all go wrong. Where the fuck is she? What is she playing at? Come all this way, as promised, no sign of her. No message. 1972 all over again, is that it?

'I let her down, then she let me down, then – well, I thought we'd got over all that. She wouldn't still be holding it against me, surely not. I mean, I'm not the best man in the world, I haven't been the best, but I'm surely better than some. I'm not the worst.

'Not like her to run away. Or is it? Marrying that Martin – she did that just to run away from me, just to show me she had her own life, I didn't own her. Does she want me to chase her, is that it? Well I am doing, so I hope it's what she wants.

'All the time she was married to someone else, all the time I was married to someone else, all that time she was still with me, locked away, in my heart. Listen to me sounding like an old fool. It was like – I tell you what it was like – it was like these people who believe in an afterlife, and one of them dies and the other one says, We'll meet again in heaven. That's what it's like.

'Losing her was like death, at least I thought so at the time. Now maybe I'm not so sure. But it was bad, it was the worst time of my life, at the time. Devastated they would be saying now. "How devastated are you?" they could say to me, they'd be poking a microphone at me, and I could have sobbed into it. "Utterly, absolutely, irretrievably devastated." Laid waste, that's what it means, that's what she did to me, wasted me, to use a metaphor from the cop movies.

'Wasted me. I've been wasted on drugs in my time, drink too, recently, but never like she did to me. No hangover has ever been a hundredth of what I felt like then, and it went on and on. On and on.

'No one can have any idea how much we loved each other. Epic, that's what it was. And I'd seen her around for a year, more than a year, before we got together. A year wasted, when I could have been with her. Would have made five years together instead of four. Nearly four.'

He stops. Viv is delighted to know this fragment of Joan's history, but she's not going to let him know that. Sentimental, she thinks he is. Self-dramatising, looking for sympathy. She's not going to say anything.

As the light gets stronger the traffic gets busier but they make good time.

'It's not actually so far,' says Viv. 'And it's actually not that grimy, the North, is it?'

*

Joan, at Seawinds, puts in Viv's number with her left hand and then puts the phone to her ear. She hears it ringing just as it should do. She imagines Viv running down her steep stairs to answer it. It keeps on ringing, and then the answering machine cuts in. 'I'm sorry,' says Viv's voice. 'I'm not able to take your call at the moment. Please leave your name and number and I'll get back to you as soon as I can.'

Where can she be at this time? Joan has called early in order to catch her before she goes out. Also because it's so urgent. Surely, even if Viv is still in bed she would have heard the phone ringing. She'll try again at ten o'clock.

*

Viv consults Joan's address book and there is Rachel's new address. It is just after nine and they have gone round the north of Glasgow and there are signs for Paisley. Bill turns off the motorway and into the town. Paisley is not as Viv imagined it at all, not pretty and clean and small but shabbily imposing; high red sandstone buildings line the streets and gardens are in short supply. Rachel's road is one back from the High Street, lined on both sides by three storey buildings. The sun has not yet reached this street. Maybe it never does.

It is not Joan who answers the door. Nor Rachel. After a longish wait it is a youngish man, apparently just out of bed, from the way he is zipping his jeans and pushing his hair out of his eyes.

'We're looking for Rachel,' says Viv. 'Or, actually, Joan, her mother.'

'Rachel's gone to her work,' he says. 'There's no one else here.'

Bill comes forward. 'She's been visiting here, hasn't she?'

'I had a text from her,' says Viv. 'Joan, I'm talking about. She said she were in Paisley. She told me she were coming here. To help Rachel decorate her new flat.'

He shakes his head. 'Come in if you like,' he says. 'Search all you want, there's only me here, and Rachel when she's not at work. There's no room for anyone else, right enough. We've only got the one bedroom. And it doesnae need decorated, it's a refurb, all done already.' He stands back to let them in and because there seems nothing else to do, they step into the flat.

'Have we got the right place?' says Bill to Viv.

She points to the shelves, where there are photographs. 'That's Rachel. There's a little one of Joan too, see.'

He peers at it, suddenly intense. 'That's her.' Maybe a question, maybe not. 'She's cut her hair.'

'Of course she did,' says Viv, impatiently.

'Here,' says the young man, holding a phone towards Viv. 'Talk to Rachel.'

'Hello Rachel.'

'Who is that?'

'Viv,' says Viv.

'Is something wrong? What's happened?'

'Everything's fine. At least – well – I think it is. I'm a bit confused. We're at your flat.'

'What do you mean? Who is? I'm not getting this. And I've got to go into a meeting in ten minutes. Eight.'

'I'm sorry,' says Viv. 'This is all a bit daft really, but we came here, to your flat you know, looking for your mother. She told me, honestly she did, a couple of weeks ago, that you had moved house and she were coming up to visit you. But then this old friend of hers turned up – What? Oh, Bill he's called.' She turns to him. 'Bill who, she wants to know?'

'Badger,' he says.

The young man laughs, a trifle wildly. 'Surreal,' he says.

'She says,' Viv says, 'Rachel says she's never heard of you. Do you want to talk to her?'

'Ask her,' says Bill, 'if she knows where her mother is. Tell her she's not at home.'

'Haven't you seen her at all?' says Viv into the phone. 'She sent me a text on Monday saying she were in Paisley, and what is it now? – Thursday. So where is she?'

'Wait there,' says Rachel. 'I'm on my way.'

Viv and Bill stand awkwardly in the room. Viv looks round appreciatively at the pale grey sofa and the glass shades over the table lamps. Stylish, she thinks.

'Want to sit down?' says the young man.

'No,' says Bill, abruptly. He has been looking at his watch, and now, suddenly, he makes for the door. 'We need to get on our way. This has all been a waste of time, we need to leave.'

'Wait,' says Viv. 'Rachel said to wait. She's on her way. We need to discuss it with her. What's to be done. Should we go to the police?'

'Not here,' says Bill. 'If she's never been here – do it in Sheffield, they can ask people who know her.'

Viv's phone jingles. 'Hi Rachel. Yes I know, yes so am I. We're still at your flat. OK. Five minutes.'

'She's on her way,' she says to Bill. 'She's working close by. We're waiting here for her.'

'If we must,' says Bill. 'But we'd be better off getting on our way. I'd like to get back to Sheffield by nightfall, then on my way home for tomorrow.' He opens the door and is outside again, impatient to get into the van.

'So all of a sudden there's a big hurry? What's that about?'

'I know where she must be,' he says. 'I can get there today, if I hurry.'

Rachel is hurrying towards them, trying to run in high heels, arrives, breathless. Except for the darkness of her eyes she does not look like Joan. She is smaller, skinny and boyish where Joan is elegantly slim, her hair is ordinary dark brown, her face is mobile and pale.

'I phoned Mum,' she says, before she's even reached them. 'There's no reply, it seems dead.'

'When did you last –?'

'Saturday,' says Rachel. 'I usually speak to her on Saturday. She was fine, she was at home.'

'So she said,' says Viv.

'Well that's a point,' says Rachel, 'I called her on her mobile so she could have been anywhere.'

'Try her landline now.'

Rachel presses buttons. Viv puts her ear close to Rachel's. They can hear a phone ringing, but no one picks up.

'This is Bill,' says Viv. He opens his mouth to speak but she does not seem to notice.

'Come inside,' says Rachel. 'You've met Ryan haven't you.'

'No,' says Bill. The women look at him. 'No,' he says again. 'I want to be out of here. It was a mistake, it was stupid. Come on,' he says to Viv. He walks round to the driver's door. 'Let's go.'

She shrugs at Rachel. 'I'll call you when I get home,' she says. 'Best to go now, she may be home by the time we get there, you never know. I'll call you tonight. Don't worry, there'll be some explanation.' Behind Bill's back she indicates that he is a bit crazy.

Bill is already in the driver's seat. Viv clambers in. Before she has her seat belt on he has started the engine. Rachel stands on the pavement, blank, baffled. Her young man appears beside her, they stand watching as the van pulls away.

*

Joan has sat by the phone for nearly two and a half hours. It has rung twice but each time it was for Tiff and Joan has had to go and skulk in the breakfast room so as not to appear to be listening to a conversation not meant for her. (One from Tiff's father asking if she wanted anything from the big Tesco in Colchester. One from a friend – or at least the mother of one of Bea's friends; this took a long time as they tried to pick apart some bullying issue, while Joan fretted that Viv would at this moment be trying to get hold of her.)

At last Tiff hangs up the phone. Joan cannot wait until ten, cannot hold herself back any longer.

Dials. Rings. Machine. Damn. Missed her. She'll be – what day is it? Thursday. Joan thinks it's her food bank morning. Could she access the number of a food bank, when she doesn't clearly know the name or location of it? Do they even have phones? I'll try again at one-thirty, she decides.

*

'So that was Rachel,' says Bill. 'Not a patch on her mother, if you ask me.'

They are hammering east on the M8. Viv looks out of the passenger window at road signs and slip roads, at tower blocks of different colours and configurations, at gas works and power stations. This is the first time Bill has spoken since they left Rachel standing on the pavement watching them drive away.

'She's all right, Rachel,' says Viv. 'Very career-minded, like her father, but she's all right.'

'Close to Joanie?'

'As close as anyone I suppose. They talk every week on the phone but she doesn't often come back to Sheffield. All her friends have moved away by now I expect.'

'My daughters have moved away,' says Bill. 'One down in Somerset, one in Cardiff.'

Viv is surprised to hear he has daughters, or any children at all. 'What do you call them?'

'My girls? Laura, she's the eldest. And Emily. That's their names.'

'And what do you think of you dashing off to look up old girlfriends?'

'Well,' he says, 'I haven't actually discussed it with them. It's not really anything to do with them, is it.'

'I just thought,' says Viv, 'that they might be a bit – put out. Given that it's not that long since their mother died.'

'Which is,' he says, 'not your business in the slightest. Is it?'

They travel in silence for a good few miles. There's some services coming up,' says Viv. 'How about we stop for a coffee?'

'No,' he says.

She looks at him, sees how his jaw is clenched and stiff, his hands gripping the steering wheel so that the tendons stand out on his skinny wrists. She waits.

*

Joan sips her weak tea and watches Tiff emptying and shaking out the washing from the drier. Joan has gone from paying guest (though she will still pay her bill of course) to friend who is allowed in the kitchen.

'Did Bea get off to school on time?' She has been here long enough to have heard the daily drama of getting the kids out of the house.

'For once,' says Tiff. She flaps a pillowcase right side out. 'I know fifteen is a difficult age. I remember being fifteen myself. My dad still tells me I was a monster. But I don't remember arguing about every little thing like she does. I give in to her just because I'm so tired of it. I know I shouldn't.'

Joan has found it interesting, being in a house with a teenager. Though Rachel had been a dark and little gnome while Bea is big and blonde, there is something about the set of her mouth, the roll of her eyes that brings back the time that Martin used to refer to, with sarcasm, as the best years of all their lives. 'My daughter was like that,' she says. 'I think it's the worst age. After that they grow up a bit, so you're not quite so worried about them.'

'Just the one daughter, have you got?'

'That's right.'

'See, I've still got Felix to get through his teens. Though they do say boys are easier.'

'Maybe by the time he gets to thirteen his dad will be home. He can share the load.'

'Oh god I hope so,' says Tiff. 'If I thought this was going to go on for another three years – well, I don't know what I'd do.'

*

'What is the big idea?' Viv has waited for miles before she trusts herself to speak. They are a long way the other side of Glasgow, pressing on as fast as the van will go down the M74. No mention now of his aversion to motorways, though it is true he seems to be in a ragingly bad temper. He has not spoken a word to her, his eyes are fixed on the road, he mutters to himself, not this time, that soothing stream of reminiscence but swearing caused by other road users, by signposts, by the fuel gauge, by – Viv is sure – her.

'What?'

'What's the rush? Will another day hurt you? Calm down for goodness' sake. You're driving like a maniac, you'll get us both killed.'

'Shut the fuck up,' he says. 'What do you know about driving anyway?'

'More than you, from the way you're doing it,' she says. 'I want to get back in one piece, if you don't mind.'

'Moron,' he says, whether at her or at a car which has speeded up as he's pulled out to pass, she doesn't know.

'Look,' says Bill. 'I'm already having to go the long way round – I could get back quicker if I didn't have to take you home first. That's going to put a good hour on the journey.'

'Sorry,' says Viv sarcastically, like a teenager. 'Aren't you going anyway, back to Sheffield, checking to see if she's turned up?'

'She won't have,' he says stubbornly.

'She might have. She's bound to be back by now from wherever she went.'

'Why should I listen to you?' he says savagely. 'You haven't got anything right yet. It's your fault we've come all this way. For nothing except to waste my money on diesel.'

'*My* fault.'

'I should never have listened to you. I don't know why I did. You know nothing, do you. You're useless.'

'And you're not I suppose.'

'If I am,' he says, childishly, 'then you're worse. You're fucking useless.'

'Just drop me at a train station, why don't you. If I'm so fucking useless. I wouldn't want to hold you up, not after you've been hanging around just waiting for about three weeks, doing nothing.'

'Fine,' he says. 'We're nearly at Carlisle. I'll drop you there.'

'Don't trouble,' she says. 'Drop me here. Here will do. I wouldn't want to put you to any more trouble. In fact I wouldn't want to breathe the same air as you for a second longer. Pull in, go on, there's a lay-by, let me out, I don't want to be in here with you. Do it now.'

He pulls over, at speed, braking hard. He stares straight ahead as she pushes open the door, and slides out. Closes the door and gives it a kick, just to show him.

Takes a deep breath, seeing in front of her a peaceful green hill, with sheep. This will be all right. She moves towards the sliding door, to retrieve her handbag and overnight bag, but the van moves away from her, fast, she feels it brush her fingers as he thrusts it into gear and pulls out again into the traffic.

'I'm going no farther than Moffat, I'm afraid,' says Viv's rescuer.

'I'm very grateful,' says Viv.

'New car,' he says. 'You're my first passenger.'

No wife then, thinks Viv. She believes she is good at detecting the existence of wives.

'I'm grateful,' she says again. 'People don't pick up hitchhikers these days, do they?'

'Well,' says the man, 'you don't look like your typical hitchhiker do you?'

'I'm not,' says Viv. 'I wouldn't be doing this if I hadn't been chucked out of a van by a bastard.'

The man says nothing.

'I can't believe what he thought he was doing. The man's a total bastard. I came all this way with him to help him – I had to rearrange umpteen things to do it, just to be of assistance to the friend of a friend, I didn't have to, and he just goes off and abandons me. I'd better not see him again, I tell you, he'll be sorry if I do.'

'Why would he do a thing like that though?' says the man.

'We were having words,' says Viv. 'He stopped, I got out – that was all right, but then he drove off before I could get my bag out of the back. Just because I gave his van a bit of a kick.'

The driver looks quite alarmed. 'He must have thought you meant it,' he says, tentatively.

'I bloody did mean it,' says Viv. 'And if I didn't, I do now.'

'Do you want I should take you into the town?' says the man. From his accent she thinks he must be local, older than he seemed at first sight, maybe someone who grew up with the idea of hitch hiking being a normal and undeviant behaviour.

'Trouble is,' says Viv. 'My money's in the van. In my handbag.'

'That's a wee problem,' he says, as if it's only a minor one.

'Do you think,' she says, 'that if I went into my bank and told them, that they would let me have some money?'

'Do you not have your bank card?'

'No.' Of course I don't, she thinks, what a stupid question.

'Do you not know your account number?'

'Won't they be able to find it?'

'Do you not have anything that would identify you? A photo? Bus pass? Driving licence?'

'Not on me.' That's the whole point, stupid.

'Is your account with the Bank of Scotland?'

'No. Yorkshire Bank.'

'There's only Bank of Scotland in Moffat. I think you'd be out of luck there.'

She waits, not very hopefully, for him to offer a loan to get her home, but he does not.

'Then, could you drop me at these services coming up. I'll have to see if a lorry driver will give me a lift.'

'Mostly,' he says, 'they're no' allowed to. Insurance.' But he takes her right through to the car park, with its view of the bare, pale green hills, wishes her good luck, and drives away.

Why, she wonders, did he pick her up in the first place. If he was so keen to help a person, then why not help? One of those people, she decides, who dip no more than a toe into the lives of others. She is grateful to him anyway.

And he was right about the lorry drivers. She looks for English lorries, hoping for one from Sheffield, or at least Yorkshire, but the few that are in the lorry park – it's not midday yet – mostly seem to be Dutch or Polish. She approaches an elderly driver of a smallish truck. He takes off his baseball cap and scratches his head like someone in a bad sitcom, before telling her what she feared, that he's not insured to carry passengers, and if caught, would lose his job.

'Best bet's a private car,' he says. 'Make sure there's a lady in it. Don't want to read in the paper about your body being dumped in a ditch.'

Nasty suspicious, untrusting mind, thinks Viv.

'I could phone someone for you,' he offers, but there is no one whose number she knows by heart, except her mother who lives now in Devon, with Roland, and doesn't drive, or go out at all very much.

'Thanks for the offer,' she says, 'but all my numbers are in my phone, and my phone's halfway to England.'

He digs out a handful of change and gives it to her. 'Here. Get yourself a cup of tea. And take care of yourself remember.'

'You're a gentleman,' she tells him.

It takes twenty minutes, and several approaches to people who look as if they might be able to find a space in their car for a distressed elderly woman. Some are sympathetic but going north, not south, some make what is clearly an excuse about having too much stuff in the back of their car, or turning off at the next junction, but finally Viv is on her way again, sitting in the back of a Toyota Yaris, looking at the backs of two women of her own sort of age, who are obviously enthralled at their own daring.

*

As Bill approaches the A69 junction he becomes aware, above the grumbling of the engine, of a phone ringing, a nasty, tinny, jangling noise. It continues for several rings and then stops. Starts again. He glances behind the passenger seat and sees what he was hoping would not be there. A large red bag from which the phone is ringing, and a jute shopping bag which, he recalls, yesterday was packed with sandwiches. He sighs, and sighs several more times before he reaches the next junction and resigns himself to heading north again.

Bill crosses the border again, back into Scotland again. On cue, a small rain begins to speckle the windscreen. He presses on, looking to his right to locate the lay-by where he left Viv. There it is, at last. He distinctly recalls the litter bin that has clearly felt a side-swipe from a lorry and never straightened again. Behind the grass verge, a two bar fence, and behind that, three horses. He does an illegal U-turn and pulls in.

No sign of the woman. He sighs. He turns off the engine and rests his head on the steering wheel. He feels as if he has been driving for a day and a night, and still it is not even mid-day. After a while he raises his head and looks around once more. No sign. He gives a few blasts on the horn. No one will be able to say he didn't try everything to put right whatever wrong he has done. But no sign of Viv. She has, though he did not see her nor she him, passed on the other side of the road going south in a car with two women.

He turns on the engine, engages first gear, checks his mirrors and pulls out. South again, then.

*

'There,' says the driver woman. 'We're over the border.'

Does it look more English? Not really, but Viv is pleased with the proof that she is getting nearer home. It is not going to be as bad as she feared. She realises that she will definitely miss her Tai chi class, and there's no money back if you don't go. Nothing can be done about it and she puts it out of her mind.

'I should have known he was an idiot. I should never have trusted him to wait while I got my bag. But really, he must be stupid to drive off like that, without checking. Just pulled out into the traffic as if it was a race.'

The passenger woman passes the road map back to her so that she can plan her route, but Viv's reading glasses, like everything else, are in her handbag, and she has to admit as much, making them all laugh. These two ladies have come to the clear conclusion that Viv is a chaotic and bohemian creature. They have given her an apple, a sandwich, a packet of polo mints and plenty of advice.

'We'll take you to the junction with the A66,' says the passenger.

'I was thinking,' says Viv, 'if there's a services before that, of doing that again. So that I can approach people. It feels a bit safer than just standing on the side of the road, more likely to get a result too, I think.'

'You'll be better off at the junction,' says the passenger woman, but Viv feels able to insist, and after goodbyes and thank yous, she finds herself at Southwaite services, where she visits the toilets to try to make herself a bit more presentable.

It worries her, that she looks like she feels, having slept in her clothes and having been unable to clean her teeth. She sniffs her underarms in the privacy of the cubicle – could be worse – and when she comes out washes her hands and face, at least. Her hair is always unruly and she claws at it and bundles it back into its scrunchie. It's an improvement – maybe only a five per cent one, but an improvement and maybe she won't scare off her prospective targets.

But something does, or else they are sincere when they tell her they are going north, not south. After thirty minutes of standing at the door attempting to engage the sympathy of likely-looking drivers Viv is feeling desperate. She can see herself spending her whole life here, like that person she read about once who lived in an airport. She can see herself eating the little hard chips that people leave on their plates and finishing up the milk left in their little milk jugs, and getting more and more smelly and less and less likely to appeal to anyone to take her away from there. She can see herself being a news item on Look North, or whatever the equivalent programme is called in these parts. She can see Maggie, or Judy, or even Joan reading about her in an old copy of the Metro and wondering, Can that really be Viv, who disappeared all those months ago?

She sits down at one of the outside tables, under an umbrella, next to a group of young men that she would certainly not consider asking for a lift. She puts her arms on the table and her head on her arms. A few tears squeeze out of her eyes but no one would see them. The sun warms her shoulders. At least it's not raining, she thinks. People are always kinder when the sun's shining. She falls – not quite asleep – into a dozing state.

Next thing, someone is shaking her shoulder. Before she lifts her head, she has the wild idea that it is Bill who has somehow found her. It is in fact the manager of the cafeteria, a woman as plump as Viv is, as brisk as Joan would be, asking, Is she all right?

'I'm sorry,' says Viv. She manages not to cry. 'The person I was travelling with drove off and left me, but I left my bag in the back of the van. He drove away too quick, I didn't get the door open in time.'

'I can't have people soliciting lifts at the door,' says the manager. Her badge tells the world her name is Arlene McLeod.

'I have to get home,' says Viv. 'Do you see, there's nothing else I can do.'

'Isn't there someone you could call?'

'All my numbers are in my phone. I only know my brother's – he's in Devon, and my friend's, but she's the friend I went to Paisley to look for, and she wasn't there.'

'Mightn't she be home by now?'

'It's possible, I suppose.' Viv does not see what Joan could possibly do. Is it really feasible that she might get in her car and drive almost to Scotland to save her? Well, Viv will say, I would do it for you.

From the manager's office she dials Joan's landline number but there is no answer, except from the machine. Viv cannot even feel disappointed, she is resigned to it by now.

'I tell you what,' says Arlene McLeod. 'I've someone finishing their shift in about ten minutes. I'll ask if she'll take you to the junction with the road to Scotch Corner. That will be a start, and you'll know at least that the folk will be going in the right direction for you. Would you like a cup of tea while you're waiting for her?'

So Viv travels the few miles to Penrith and the big junction, arriving there a good hour after she would have done if she had stayed with the two ladies.

Her driver this time is a girl who looks barely old enough to drive and who looks, moreover, scared half to death to be given the responsibility of moving on a vagrant.

'Don't worry,' says Viv. 'I'm not usually like this. I'm quite civilised really.' Which makes the girl smile, wanly.

It feels strange to get out of a car without being encumbered by anything like a handbag, an umbrella, a bag of shopping. It reminds her each time she does it how lacking she is in any sort of life support. Robinson Crusoe, she thinks. Bilbo Baggins. But they were stories, this is real, a real cool breeze blowing, real clouds in the sky that might turn to rain, a real grass verge under her feet and, inches away, real lorries, cars, vans, coaches, motorbikes swooping round the roundabout, accelerating away too fast to stop for her even if they wanted to.

She pulls herself together and walks a little way on until there is a lay-by. There are some vehicles there which she can solicit. That's what Arlene said she was doing. If there is no joy from them she can stand near the opening of the lay-by which will at least give people a chance to pull in if they want to. Though why would they want to, she asks herself.

It is a Dutch lorry she finds herself in. Too late to be picky now, she tells herself. He's not an old man, maybe thirty-five, with a pink face and a beer belly, just her idea of what a Dutch man would look like.

'Scotch Corner?' he says. 'No problem. Even I can take you to Darlington.'

'Scotch Corner,' she says firmly. She is pretty sure Darlington is not on her route.

He is going to Middlesbrough, he tells her – pronouncing it with some difficulty – and then on to Hull to return to Rotterdam. 'And where do you go?'

He does not show any surprise at finding a lone woman of her age hitching a lift.

'Sheffield,' she says. It seems very far away.

'Steel,' he says. 'You like football? Your team?'

'I don't really know about football,' says Viv.

'Your team? You have to have a team. What team is yours?'

'Sheffield Wednesday,' says Viv. She knows where their ground is of course, and has a sort of tribal loyalty to them, as her brother has always supported them, as did everyone she went to school with. She suspects though, that he will ask her now for the names of their players.

'Good team once,' he says. 'Since a disaster, no longer a good team.'

'I suppose so.'

'It is fate,' he says. 'Karma.'

'Maybe,' she says.'

'Sure.'

Viv looks out of her window at the pretty scenery. This is not the worst thing that has ever happened to me, she says to herself. People will get me home. I can go to a police station if need be, but it's not going to be necessary. This is a good and helpful man, all I need to do is let him talk about football.

'Which team do you support?'

'Feyenoord,' he says. 'You know it?'

'Say again.'

He says again.

'Is that a town?'

'Rotterdam,' he says. 'Rotterdam is my town. Feyenoord is my team.'

'Good team?'

'The best,' he says. 'In England, Chelsea, Manchester City, in Nederland, Feyenoord, Ajax.'

'I see,' says Viv, wishing she did. 'Good players?'

He tells her some names – a confusion, to her, of Ks and Vs and Rs. She nods, hoping to give the impression of wisdom, if not actual understanding.

When he drops her at Scotch Corner she is cheered by the thought that she is in Yorkshire again, and simultaneously alarmed by the thought that where she needs to get to is at the very farthest point she could get to and still be in Yorkshire.

*

Bill, since Lydia died, has talked to himself. Even before that, since she started going into hospital for longer and longer stays, he has had conversations with himself. It has made the house less quiet, it has given the illusion that someone might just answer him. He tries, consciously, because he does not want to be thought of as crazy, to keep the habit under wraps when someone might be near enough to hear him. Sometimes at home he puts music on, but then finds himself talking to other dead people. 'You see Jimi,' he might say, 'you had to burn out one way or another, it was always going to happen. You wouldn't want to fade away, now would you.'

In his own car he can listen to music but in this van there is no operational radio. He should have known better than to borrow a vehicle off a deaf person. There is only the sound of his own voice to accompany him on the long drive south. South and east, from one coast, almost, to another. He talks as if explaining himself, or as if he's being interviewed on Desert Island Discs.

'Of course I miss Lydia. There was never anything wrong between me and Lydia. People think I married her just because I worked for her father – there's something in that, I suppose, but only that it's the way I met her. Really it was mostly her idea anyway, I wouldn't have dared I don't think if she hadn't invited me to. Not that she was posh or anything, no posher than Joanie, or Rosemary, or a hundred girls I knew. Or knew of, I don't mean I knew them in the biblical sense – not a hundred, not a chance.

'Poor old Lyd, she'd had a hard time of it, losing a baby and then her marriage falling apart, why she took me on I couldn't imagine, unless it was a project to take her mind off things.

'It did work. It really did work. She made it work. She made me work.

'God, what a stupid woman, that Viv. All over me to start with, sandwiches and wine and everything, then thought better of it I suppose, once we were on the road. Was it something I said? Maybe – did I say something about her mother? Well if I did it was only what Joanie said to me, not my fault.'

He approaches Southwaites services and is tempted by the thought of a bacon sandwich and a cup of tea, but decides to press on as far as Scotch Corner.

'After Joanie ran out on me I was wrecked. Intoxicated most evenings, snivelling down the phone, hoping she would weaken and cry too, and it would all be back where we were, then after that I got my head together and packed up my stuff, and the things she had left behind – obviously didn't want them – and I moved back to the coast. I am always better by the sea; I am a better person there. Sheffield, and those moors – quite impressive – little streams, very pretty, but I can feel that the sea is far away, too far away. There's no smell of it at all, no feeling of edgeness, no margins.

'I could have gone back to Burnham, where I grew up, but I chose to come back to where I still had mates who had never left university, or at least had stayed in the area. Colchester. Not that I wanted to live in Colchester, but I had friends there in Brightlingsea, on the estuary and I moved in – where Joanie and I used to spend weekends – and I've been there ever since.

'I had to get a job. The building trade was nothing like it had been in Camden, but I got taken on at the nursery – that's what it was then, before Lyd and I turned it into the garden centre. At least she did, if I'm honest it didn't have much to do with me. I suppose I can take some credit for the landscape gardening we set up later. You get all these City types around there now – they all want a low-maintenance garden with paving and concealed lighting and sitooteries. I hardly ever had to lift a finger myself, but I could organise a bloke with a digger, and a brickie who could lay York stone and a couple of lads who could lift and carry. We got more adept as time went on – both at doing it and at getting the customer to pay more. Lyd found this nice woman who was a dab hand at drawing plans, and of course Lyd's dad, even after he'd given up nursery growing, was good at telling us what to plant. Though a bit too keen on heathers and evergreens. Too sixties for people nowadays, but if you want low maintenance they can't be beat.

'We sold the business when Lyd started with her illness, for a nice sum of money – not that it ever did her any good because she didn't live long enough, or well enough to enjoy it.

'I should sell the house as well. My girls don't want me to. Emily would like to buy it herself and live there, but they can't afford the market price and if I let them have it for less, I'll have to do something for Laura to make it fair. I wouldn't mind if they both lived in it together, but that would involve Loz coming back from Taunton and probably they'd both have to get rid of their boyfriends – partners, whatever you have to call them these days. I can't see any situation – or any house – that could contain both of those characters.

'Something will work itself out.

'I wonder where that idiot of a woman has got to. I just hope nobody's run her over, or raped her, or anything that will get in the papers. Someone, surely, will pick her up and see her home. It wasn't all my fault. Someone gets out of your car, screaming abuse, and slams the door, you think they've gone. They don't want you around any more. She should have said. Wait, let me get my bag, she should have said. I would have waited. I'm not a monster.

'She'll be thinking I am though. She'll tell Joanie. I'll have to get my story in first.

'I know what has happened. Joanie never went to see that Rachel. That was just a cover story for nosy old Viv. She's gone down to Brightlingsea, somehow, my postcard has caught up with her, she's made a decision, she's feeling bad for standing me up, she's on her way down there now. She might be there already. I must have just missed her.

'Oh god, we could be criss-crossing the country like this for years, never meeting. Maybe I do need to go via Sheffield, if she's not there, put a note through her door. Stay here, do not move, I will be back. Love from – who? What name shall I put? There's another thing.'

Bill is two people. Or rather, not two people at once, but two people sequentially.

Until the age of twenty three he was, as he was christened, Aughton John Badger. Why, he never knew. As a small child he did not think to question it. It took him all his time to learn how to spell it to people who found it unusual and difficult. His mother said it was a name from her family and she thought it lent a bit of gravitas to the frankly amusing surname. She didn't put it in those words, but that was what Bill thought she'd intended.

He was Aughton Badger, but everyone called him Oggy. He didn't mind. Other boys were called worse things. His best friend was known throughout his schooldays as Ear'ole. Oggy was quite a nice name. Matey.

Joanie never liked it though. She called him Aughton though she didn't like that either. Sometimes, if she was feeling jocular, she called him AJ, but it never took off as a name for him. Your name was your name and there was nothing to be done about it. He never thought for a moment of changing it. For one thing his mother would have been upset. Then, when he came back to Brightlingsea, washed up there with his broken heart and his P45 someone called him Bill. Lydia's father actually.

When he employed Aughton to dig some new beds at the nursery he thought it was funny to have someone called Badger digging earth. 'Well, Bill Badger,' he would say, coming round to see what he was doing, 'and how's Bill today? Where's Rupert Bear then?' And laugh. He introduced him to Lydia as Bill. 'Bill Badger,' he said. At first she thought it was the Badger that was made up, until she had to make out the slip for his wages.

*

Joan and Tiff have shared a tin of soup in Tiff's kitchen. Afterwards she tries Viv again. Still not home. Is it the wrong number? But Joan has had this number in her head for decades, it has never changed – well, the dialling code was changed once, but so long ago that it is neither here nor there. And although she doesn't often phone Viv – it's usually to call her back and say No thank you, I'm busy doing something else – the number remains like a little lifebelt. Except it hasn't been.

She'll leave it until eight o'clock, it's not a choir evening and after being out all day Viv will surely be at home.

*

Viv has been thinking about her technique. She will now ask people first which way they are heading, to save them from having to lie – or to make them search for another lie – to avoid helping her. She will not smile, she will look as downcast as she can without looking like a total victim. Fortitude in adversity, is the look she is aiming for. Also respectability. Distressed gentlewoman. Joan could do this better, she knows.

She doesn't visit the coffee shop, but even if she did, she would not find Bill – he has already bought his bacon roll and taken it to the van to eat while driving.

The afternoon is drawing on. They have passed schoolchildren getting out of buses on their way home from school. It must be around four o'clock, she reckons, as she revisits the toilet she used yesterday – really? only yesterday? – on her way north with Bill.

A husband and wife are going to York and take her as far as the junction with the A59. The wife drives.

'It were my own stupid fault,' says Viv. 'I bet when I kicked the door he thought I were letting him know I were standing out of the way – that's what people do, don't they.'

The couple seem to find the story funny; they catch each other's eye and laugh heartily as if they have a similar story in their own past. The husband lends Viv a pair of glasses with which she can just make out the road map. Sheffield still looks a long way away.

'You should be all right,' he says. 'Or we could take you into York, drop you at the police station.'

'What would they do?'

'No idea,' he says.

'Well,' says Viv, 'if there's a risk that they'll just send me away I might as well stay on the road. I've done ok so far, all things considered.'

But standing at the junction she sees that people by now are on their way home from work, in too much of a hurry to notice her, let alone stop for her. Large grey clouds are rolling in front of the sun now; it could turn into a dark rainy evening.

Indeed it begins to rain, and just then a car slows and stops. A lone woman this time.

'Thank you,' says Viv, breathless from running to catch the car, scared it will start up again and leave her. 'Thank you so much.'

'Where are you headed for?' The driver is dressed in grey, with heavy-rimmed glasses, and would look severe if it were not for her abundant grey-blond curls. 'I'm Jane.' This is the first time any of her fellow travellers have introduced themselves.

Viv tells her story. It sounds sillier each time she has told it, sometimes she thinks it puts her in a worse light than Bill. This time, believing from very little evidence that this woman will be on her side whatever, she softens Bill's part. 'I could kill him of course, but it were my own fault. I should have made him wait while I'd got my stuff. In fact, I should have got back into the bloody van.'

'Why would he even stop there?' says Jane. 'What did he think you were going to do? How could you possibly get home from there?'

'I guess,' says Viv, 'that he thought I would at least have my money, and my phone. If I had just bit my tongue and put up with him I'd be home ages ago. Cup of tea, feet up, and all my stuff with me as well.'

'What an awful man though,' says Jane. 'I would take you home if I could,' she says, 'but I have to get to Hull by seven. What I'll do though – I can't drop you at the M62, it's a nightmare if you're in a car, never mind being a pedestrian – I'll take you as far as the next junction. I hope you'll be all right from there.'

Viv feels a burst of tears coming on and manages to change it into a sort of laugh. 'People are so kind,' she says.

'I wish I could give you some money,' says Jane. 'But I really only have enough on me for the evening. I'm meeting my son at the airport, and he'll need to eat, and I'll need to pay for parking.'

'It's all right,' says Viv. 'I wouldn't have took it anyway. Look, I'm nearly home now, past Leeds and Sheffield's the next stop. Don't worry about me.'

Jane pulls off the motorway to let her out, and scribbles her name and number on a piece of paper. 'Let me know how you get on,' she says. 'As soon as you get your phone back, let me know you're safe.'

'Thank you,' says Viv again. 'Thank you for everything.'

*

Joan's arm is aching, Her head is tired with the problems that are going round and round it. Being away from home is fine, she thinks, as long as it *is* fine. The moment you want to be back in your own place, being away becomes torture. Nothing pleases. Tiff's kindness is not felt any more, she is a nuisance, offering too much help, too many solutions. Too kind.

Joan wants to go to bed and sleep until morning, but she knows that her thoughts will pace up and down like a wolf in the zoo, and she will be miserable and the night will be one of those that last a year. It is a strange feeling, to be needing Viv, of all people. But who else is there?

She leaves another message. She thinks later about other things she might have said that will make Viv get in touch. She begins to wonder if she has upset her in some way, but that makes no sense. It is just possible that Viv has a sensitive side but she has never yet shown it – not to Joan anyway. Viv doesn't let people upset her. And she loves to help people.

No, she is just not at home. It occurs to Joan for the first time to wonder if she should worry about where Viv is. But she has enough to do worrying about herself. Tiff will surely not want her around all the time tomorrow and the next day. Maybe she'll have to grit her teeth and get her car towed back home. Maybe she can go by train. It feels like a nightmare waiting to happen.

*

Bill has never used a mobile phone. Never had one, never used one. Of course his daughters have them, but they are unable to contact their father, except when he is at home. Lydia had one when she was alive but Bill ignored it, as if it was something only women had, some feminine item that he could not be expected to take notice of.

Several times on his journey he has been startled by the jangling noise which comes from Viv's bag behind the front seat, but each time it is short-lived and hardly bothers him except to remind him of her. At about four o'clock he hears the phone ringing again – well, not exactly ringing, it's actually a tune, "Don't You Want Me", so off-key as to be unpleasant, and he hates this sort of music anyway. It goes on and on, but there is no way Bill can answer it, because for one thing it is still in Viv's bag behind the front seat, and for another thing he would not know how to begin.

It stops and he tries to sing something else out loud, to remove the taint of awful synthpop, but nothing drives it away, and then it begins again. He thinks it is probably Rachel, unless it's Viv trying to locate him by somehow ringing her own phone. He doesn't want to speak to either of them, but it makes up his mind for him. He is on the A1 now (not far past where Viv is looking for a lift at Scotch Corner) and he has been trying to work out a way of going straight on to Essex, without a detour into Sheffield. But if Rachel and/or Viv are going to be making that noise every half hour or more, to say nothing of all or any of Viv's friends wondering where she is, then it will be better to drop her things off at her house. It will cost in time and diesel, but save on postage and hassle.

He hits Sheffield at the rush hour – or maybe it's always rush hour in a big city. As he turns west off the motorway the sun breaks through the dark grey cloud, as if to welcome him back. Don't bother, he thinks, I'm not stopping.

He calculates that Viv is unlikely to have reached her home before he has, even allowing for his double journey across the border, but he knocks on her back door just for form's sake – she won't be able to say he didn't try. He hesitates about leaving her things on the doorstep, and as he does so, the next door neighbour comes out of her back door.

'I think she's gone away,' she says. She is about his age, with smooth dark brown hair – dyed probably – and round blue eyes. She is wearing cut-off jeans and an old shirt splashed with paint, just as Lyd used to do when she was decorating. Bill feels a small pain somewhere – something to do with this woman being still here while Lyd has gone. He ignores it.

'I've got these things of hers,' he says. 'But I've got to go. I'm in a hurry. Can I leave them with you?'

'No problem,' says the woman, and then, a bit suspicious maybe, 'Where is she?'

'She's on her way,' he says. 'Just a bit of a mix-up, and she forgot her things.' He thrusts the two bags at the woman and heads off. As he retreats down the passage between the houses he can hear that Viv's phone has started ringing again.

Before he heads out of Sheffield – it will be at least five hours until he reaches home – he goes once more to try Joan's flat. She could so easily be home by now and it would be beyond crazy if he missed her yet again. But the residents have been warned about intruders and are taking it seriously. He presses several buzzers but no one will let him in. Joan's buzzer is unresponsive. He looks up at her window but there is no light on and no sign that she has returned from wherever she went.

'I know where you are,' says Bill under his breath. 'I'll see you soon.'

*

By eight o'clock Viv is at the tram stop at Meadowhall. Her last lift was in a van so noisy that there was no need to speak at all, which was quite a relief in itself. He was going to Rotherham but kindly detoured enough to drop her off, after she had checked how much change she had from the lorry driver at Abingdon. How long ago that seemed. And how grateful she was to him now, finding that she had enough – just – to get a tram to within a mile of home.

That last mile – she was to tell everyone – is the worst mile of all. Uphill all the way. 'I'm not made for walking,' she will say, later when the exhaustion and anguish has worn off. It rains all the way too, not hard, but cold, and she worries all the way too, about how she will be able to break into her house. She tried Joan's landline again, from a call box at Meadowhall, and was not surprised to find that there was still no reply. She should be worried about Joan, she feels, but is really too tired to be.

Uphill, steeply uphill, like the foothills of the bloody Alps. Too tired to hurry, even if she were fit enough, too cold to take it slowly. Dying for a cup of tea, she says to herself, and feels as if it is literally true. The issue of having no door key now becomes uppermost in her mind. Could I kick the door in? Break the lock like Bill did to Joan's door? Smash the kitchen window? If I ask the lads next door, could they get in? Would they know how to? If they know how to, will that worry me for ever? Suppose they're not in?

At last – stitch in her side, shivering and footsore – she turns the corner into her road. It is too soon to feel the relief that she should.

The student house next door is in darkness, and her heart sinks.

However. By the light of her neighbours' new security light she can see a piece of paper stuck to her back door. 'Knock at number 24,' it says, in big reassuring letters. So she does.

The new neighbours stand at their back door together. They stand back and invite her in. They apologise for the disorder, as if it could possibly matter to her. 'Still decorating,' says the woman.

They give her tea. They offer her food – Toast? Boiled Egg? Soup? – and she accepts a piece of cake. She hardly knows what she can say, she sits in their front room in a daze, in a sort of trance.

'How did you manage?' says the man, and the woman says, 'Not now Frank, she's worn out.'

'I need to get in my house,' says Viv, reviving a little.

'It's ok,' says the man, Frank. 'We've got your bag and everything. Is your key in it?'

And Viv realises that one of the shapes in the room in fact consists of her overnight bag and her handbag, neatly piled in a corner out of the way of the stepladder and tins of paint.

'Can we do anything else?' says the woman. Viv still does not know her name. 'Do you just want to go home to bed?'

'That's about it,' says Viv.

They escort her the four yards from their back door to hers, watch as she opens her door and switches on the light, assure her that they will see her tomorrow to make sure she's all right. The man puts his arm round the woman's shoulders as they go back to their own kitchen door.

Friday

Viv wakes next morning to the phone ringing. She is groggy, thirsty, sticky, deflated. Her joints ache. She went straight to bed last night, without a shower – too tired – without listening to the messages on her answering machine – too tired – without letting Jane or anyone know that she was home. She fell into bed and as soon as she closed her eyes the road started unwinding again in front of her. Grey road, windscreen wipers backwards and forwards, hedges and fields, engines drumming like a headache, grey road, white lines, going on ahead of her for ever. She sat up, she lay down again. She turned over, she put the light on. She waited. She put the light out, she lay down. The road appeared in front of her. She was still and it was moving. It seemed like hours before she fell asleep.

Before she is awake enough to answer the phone it stops and there is the indistinct sound of a message being left. It will wait. Viv takes a luxuriously long shower, puts on luxuriously clean clothes and sips her strong coffee while she listens to her messages.

Two from Wednesday – one from the dentist reminding her that she has an appointment for her six-monthly checkup. One from the step-grandchildren's other grandma, asking if she will pick them up on Friday – which by now is today. Then three, all from Joan, from yesterday.

7.30 a.m.: 'Hello Viv. This is Joan. I'm sorry if I've woken you up. Could you call me back on this number please. As soon as you get this message.'

9.53 a.m.: 'Hello Viv. Joan again. Look, I'm in a bit of a fix. Could you call me, not on my mobile, use this number. As soon as you can please.'

1.26 p.m.: 'Viv, I thought you'd be there at this time. It's Joan. Look I really need some help, you're the only person I can call, please call me back, it's really urgent.'

Then there is one from Rachel. 'Hi Viv. I guess you're not home yet. I've been trying your mobile but there's no reply. Maybe you haven't got a signal in the Borders. Let me know as soon as you can what's going on. Still haven't been able to contact Mum.'

7.54 p.m.: 'Viv, I've been trying you all day. I hope you haven't gone away. It's Joan and I'm getting desperate. Please get in touch.'

And then one this morning, much the same. Viv's imagination has failed. Joan is obviously in trouble – has she come home and found her door sealed up by the police? Has she been sitting in the corridor for a day and a night unable to get in her flat? But the phone number she's been giving isn't a Sheffield number, nor a mobile, but a completely unfamiliar code.

Viv gives up thinking and dials the number. 'Seawinds,' says a chirpy voice. Not Joan's voice. Viv feels like a computer must feel when someone presses unfathomably random keys, and finds she cannot think what to say.

After a pause, 'Oh,' says the voice. 'Are you the lady who Joan has been phoning? Shall I call her?'

Seawinds? Viv has time, in the few seconds before Joan's voice speaks to her, to run through all Joan's acquaintances that she has ever heard of, and to discount the possibility that any of them live on the coast.

'Viv?'

'Joan?'

'Where have you been?'

'What's going on?'

'I'll tell you in a minute. Look I want you to do something for me. Please. Can you go round to my flat? I want you to get my address book, it's near the phone on the shelf in the hall. If you could do that – get a taxi, I'll pay you back, and then ring me again, here, then I'll tell you what's happened. Ring me from the flat, it will be quicker.'

'Hold on,' says Viv. 'There could be a problem.' Which one should she tell her about, that fact that her flat door has been secured by the police, or the fact that Bill has driven off with her address book?

'Are you busy? I'm sorry Viv, but this is really, really important. I'm stuck here and I can't drive, I've had an accident –'

I knew it, thinks Viv, but she must have had the accident on her way *to* Paisley. But – Seawinds? 'Are you badly hurt?'

'It's not bad. I'm going this afternoon to the fracture clinic. They'll put another pot on and then I'll be able to come home. I just need someone to drive the car –'

'You see, something's happened –'

'I wouldn't ask you to do it, I know you don't like driving these days –'

Only because I can't afford a car, thinks Viv, but there is no time to say it. At this point her neighbour – the woman – knocks at her back door and Viv waves to her to come in. She stands quietly inside the door, waiting.

'I want to ask Keith Fairlie if he'll come and get me. I need his number.'

'Haven't you got it in your phone?'

'I've lost my phone. Or rather, it was stolen.'

'No,' says Viv, 'you had it with you. It wasn't in your flat, you texted me, remember.'

'Of course I had it with me,' says Joan. 'It was stolen on Wednesday.'

'But you said you were in Paisley.'

There's a pause. 'I'm sorry' says Joan. 'That was a bit of a fib. I'll tell you all about it, really. But I want to get hold of Keith as soon as I can.'

'I don't know Keith Fairlie's number,' says Viv. 'Why would I?'

'There must be someone who does know,' says Joan. 'What about that singing group? That man who runs it – he must have contact numbers.'

'Ok,' says Viv. 'I'll see what I can do and I'll get back to you. Where are you though?'

'You can get me on this number,' say Joan. 'If I'm not here – because I've got to go to the fracture clinic, as I said – leave the number with Tiff. I'll call you later anyway.'

'But where are you?'

'Essex,' she says.

*

Bill also has woken up. He was so tired when he got in that he hardly remembers opening the door. He must have been asleep before he even got up the stairs and into bed. Bashing through the night, leaving the North behind, wiping Joan – and Viv and Rachel – from his mind with every stroke of the windscreen wipers, he was longing to be home. He would not be so stupid again. He would go back to being an intelligent, sensible retired man, himself. For the last few hours of yesterday's journey, through the dark and intermittent rain, he held it in his mind, the house, lit and welcoming, warm and familiar. By the time he gets off the A14 he is so tired that he can even believe that Lydia will be there waiting for him, placidly watching TV as he found her so many late evenings when he came in off the boat. Or with the sound turned off, talking on the phone to one of her friends, or her sister, or one of the girls. And she would have left him something to eat under a plate next to the microwave. (He never liked the idea of a microwave but he had to admit its usefulness on these occasions.)

Now he sits up slowly in his bed and looks around. He is bewildered by his room. It is not, somehow, the way he has remembered it. His clothes – most of them – are on the floor. He never closed the curtains last night and he can see the top of a tree in a garden across the road – silver birch, leaves yellow and thinning like old men's teeth – and the red of the roof behind it, just catching the sun. The bed itself seems unfamiliar, though in fact nothing has changed except that Lydia is no longer in it, ever. He lies down again, but it doesn't work, he can't send himself back to sleep; hunger, and a full bladder, compel him to get up. He has a shower, relieved to find that it works as normal – though why wouldn't it? – and finds some clean clothes in a drawer feeling as he puts them on as if he has been away so long that nothing belongs to him any more, nothing is recognisably his. He goes down the stairs.

There is a strew of envelopes and junk in the hall, scattered where he kicked it last night. The light on his answering machine – Lyd insisted that they have one – is blinking incessantly. He finds it difficult to know what he should do first. Or second. Breakfast first. He goes to the kitchen, switches on the kettle and opens the fridge.

The fridge emits an unpleasant smell. There are plastic bags in there which feel nastily squashy when he touches them and turn out to contain sausages and bacon, both stinking and green. He pulls everything out, into the kitchen bin. 'Sorry,' he is saying, 'sorry, I know I've wasted all this food, but it's too late.' He doesn't even hold back the plastic packaging for recycling. Now the kitchen smells. He takes the bin outside to dispose of its contents.

He makes himself a cup of tea – black, for there is no milk of course. The kitchen still smells. So, right, get rid of the smell, that's Job One. Maybe if he runs a wash through the machine that will do the trick. If he brought his dirty clothes out of the van that would do two jobs at once. And getting the van back to Pete might be a priority. And seeing his boat, and finding out where Pete went in it and how it behaved and whether there are any little snags that need sorting out.

But a load of washing – that's what Lyd would want him to do. He goes to the van and retrieves the bag of dirty clothes. 'Look,' he says quietly to whatever ghosts might be listening, 'look, it's only one week's washing. I did go to the launderette while I was away, I'm not a complete slob.'

As he closes the van door he sees Joan's address book on the dashboard, and retrieves that too. He could call her, to see if she's home yet, call her before that Viv gets hold of her and tells her everything and puts him in her bad books. Yet he suspects that he won't.

He opens the door of the washing machine. The smell grows much stronger. He pulls out a very grey, very stiff dishcloth and wonders whether to wash it with his clothes or if they will come out smelling of it. He hates to throw away a perfectly serviceable item – one that Lyd will have bought as she bought so much stuff before her death to keep him going and civilised after her death. 'Sod it,' he says, and takes it outside to the dustbin.

He summons up his idea of himself as a competent man. He *is* a competent man. Largely due to Lydia, it's true. But he knows that he has to get the place cleaned up – at least smelling better – before one of his daughters comes to visit, which, he realises, they might well do, as he has not been in touch with them for more than a fortnight. Probably the messages on the machine are them – since their mother died they have been calling more often from their faraway homes. Even, it's possible, they have been talking together about what to do about him.

He picks up all the post and stacks it in a pile on the dining room table for later. The washing machine is whining and swishing as it is meant to do and Bill feels strengthened. Then hungry.

A fresh wind is blowing as he walks into the town. He intended to go only as far as the Spar to buy some milk and eggs, but the sun and the wind draw him on to the Hard, where he hopes his boat will be.

*

'How are you?' says Viv's neighbour. 'Did you sleep all right?'

'Fine,' says Viv. It feels so good to be home that she has decided to forget her disturbed night.

'Good.' The woman hesitates. Then, 'I'm sorry, I shouldn't have been listening, but I heard you say – on the phone just now – someone wanted Keith Fairlie's phone number?'

'A friend,' says Viv. 'My friend Joan. She used to work with Mr Fairlie. She's in some kind of bother.'

'I've got his number,' says the woman. 'I can go and get it for you.'

'That's amazing,' cries Viv. 'That's unbelievable.'

'Well, you know what Sheffield's like,' says the woman. 'Everyone knows everyone.' Which Viv knows – and everyone knows – to be flagrantly untrue, but it's what everyone says.

She goes back to her house and returns with a piece of paper on which she has written two phone numbers and an email address.

'I hope it helps your friend,' she says. 'Keith loves to help people.'

*

Bill cannot see his boat lying in the estuary, but as Pete said he might be away for a month he is not too surprised. He orders a breakfast at the café and reads the Essex County Standard. One assault, not fatal, several road accidents, a planning dispute, an attempt by some bored teenagers to drive a tractor away in Elmstead Market. None of it matters to him and he feels peaceful and ordinary once again.

He finishes his breakfast and walks back up to the Square. He buys some bread and some milk, cheese and pasta sauce, sausages and potatoes, apples and bananas. He can look after himself better than this, but at the moment he is on autopilot, doing the basics. He passes in front of Seawinds on his way back home but does not look at Joan's car parked on the forecourt. Even if he did, he would not have known it was hers.

His house still smells of several sorts of decay, but less strongly. He hangs his washing on the line in the garden, feeling that he will live a wholesome and rational life from now on. He looks at the lawn and wonders if he should cut it. He thinks of his phone messages and thinks he should listen to them. He compromises by clearing out Pete's van.

He finds more washing to do – the sleeping bag for a start, towels and a pillowcase. He sweeps out the living space with a dustpan and brush. He imagines Pete's surprise at seeing it so spruce. He finds a pair of earrings on the floor next to the bunk. He holds them in his hand, confused for a moment, thinking they must be Lydia's. But no, Lydia wasn't there, not at all.

This whole expedition – to Sheffield, to Scotland and back – is something that will be in his memory but never in Lydia's. It will never include her. He will never be able to say to her, Remember that journey in that clapped out old van of Pete's, remember that campsite where you could see towards the Pennines, remember Richard and that choir of his in Sheffield, and that thing he did where he told them they were going to sing all the songs from *Hair*. It all had nothing to do with Lydia. Except that he had been thinking of her, not all the way, not all the time, but some of it.

He fetches the vacuum cleaner and gives the inside of the van a bit of a going over. He removes his detritus from the cupboards. He gives the steering wheel a cursory wipe with a cloth. It will do.

The earrings are still in his pocket and he realises they must be Viv's. Will she miss them? Do they look valuable? No, actually they don't – dangly and glittery, but probably not valuable. But he will be virtuous and put them in the post for her, to show there are no hard feelings.

Post. He will go and read it all now, while virtue is still his middle name.

Much of it is flyers and junk. Party politicals and pizza takeaways. A couple of catalogues addressed to Lydia. Charity appeals and an estate agent wondering if he would like to sell. He piles it up to put in the paper recycling. A postcard from Pete from Quimper. Nothing from Joanie.

*

Joan does not move away from the phone. She clenches and unclenches her left hand. She taps her feet alternately on the floor. She twists her left earring round and round. She looks – again – at the pictures on the wall, reads the things that people have written in the guest book, peers at the fire notice on the wall, and the insurance certificate, moves her head from side to side to see the effect of the stained glass in the front door at different angles.

When the phone rings she has to leave it of course, in case it's for Tiff, but Tiff passes it straight over to her. Joan leans against the sideboard with relief.

'I've got it,' says Viv triumphantly. 'Am I quick, or what?'

Joan – with her clumsy left hand – writes the numbers on the paper she has had in readiness for more than a day. She reads them back to Viv to make sure.'

'Now,' says Viv, 'tell me what's been happening. I've got things to tell you as well.'

'I will,' says Joan. 'I promise. As soon as I've got hold of Keith. As soon as I've sorted myself out – no, when I get back from the hospital – I might not have time this morning. I'll call you this afternoon.'

*

Viv has things to do. She sends a grateful text to Jane. She replies to Other Granny. She goes to the food bank and spends two hours unpacking, noting, stacking and putting things on shelves.

She comes home for a snack at lunchtime, and does not call Joan. She intends to wait and see if Joan will call her, and besides, she is probably at the fracture clinic. Viv doesn't even know what bone she has broken. She potters around in her garden. The tomatoes are not going to grow any more now the nights are getting colder. She picks them all and puts the unripe ones in a bowl on her kitchen windowsill to see if they will ripen. If not, chutney.

At half past two she puts her jacket on and makes her way through the cemetery to the infants' school to meet the two children. They are Colin's grandchildren, sons of his son, two more Joneses. Viv knows that some people find it peculiar that she has any dealings at all with her ex-stepchildren, but it seems natural to her. If you know someone – and Colin's children, for all the five years they were together, used to come and stay for entire weekends – if you know someone, says Viv, you don't stop knowing them just because you don't know their father any more. In a biblical sense, she says then, and cackles.

On Wednesdays, she takes Daniel and Callum back to her house until their father comes to pick them up; on Fridays they go straight home, where their mother will be waiting, having slept for most of the day after her night shift at the hospital. On Wednesdays they are polite, and Callum at least is more subdued. On Fridays Viv is allowed to buy them sweets and they are giddy and giggly, whether because of the sugar or because they are looking forward to the weekend, or because they do not have to walk through the cemetery back to Viv's house, she has never found out.

Daniel runs to her, dragging his coat on the floor. Callum wears his coat with the hood over his head and the sleeves flapping loose, and walks backwards across the playground towards her. Viv is very fond of them, as she was of their father when he was small. Sometimes she feels she would have liked children of her own, but she would stop short of saying she felt deeply sad, or even moderately sad, that she hadn't. It was one of those things. She knew plenty of people who had had more sadness than joy from their children, when you added it all up over the years. Who could know how hers might have turned out?

By the time she gets home again, having had a coffee with Asha (her step-ex-daughter-in-law, if such a designation exists) and having called at the Co-op for some salad and chocolate – Friday night is balanced diet night – it is gone five o'clock. There is no message on the machine. If Joan has taken the trouble to call she hasn't taken the trouble to say anything. Viv will wait and see.

*

Joan puts down the phone after talking to Keith Fairlie, wondering what she has done. Their relationship in all of the preceding thirty five years or so has been simply professional; they have never been part of each other's lives even in the narrow sense of having met the other's partner, knowing their names, going to the same events and parties. She cannot believe she has called him out of nowhere and asked him – made him, really, because what could he say except yes – to travel the best part of two hundred miles to the edge of the country to pick up the pieces of her life.

He sounded willing enough to do it. He sounded polite enough to be not even surprised to be asked. It only shows, thinks Joan, how few people I have in my life. What will it be like when I am really old? Will Rachel have to come and look after me? Somehow she cannot see that happening.

Joan has an afternoon to fill, after returning by bus from the fracture clinic. Her arm is no longer in its temporary cast, but in a neater and more long-lasting one. The motherly woman in the plaster room offered her a choice of colours.

'A lot of ladies like the pink,' she said.

'Black,' said Joan.

'We do a lot of the black,' said the woman, 'but mostly for teenagers.'

Joan could spend the afternoon in her room at Seawinds, or chatting to Tiff in the kitchen, or sitting reading magazines in the breakfast room, but decides instead to take a last walk by the water. The afternoon is soft and golden, only a slight breeze is up and about and only a couple of boats are on the water. She walks along past the beach huts towards the paddling pool. If I had married him, this is where our children would have grown up. Here, where it's flat and windy, no hills, no rocks sticking through the ground, no cliffs and moors, no heather. A little town, not a city. Would Rachel have flourished here? Would she have been encouraged in her maths and engineering? Something about this place feels twenty years out of date. Thirty even.

But then, would she even have been Rachel?

She thinks of Keith Fairlie, even now on his way to her. A place this size, he could have run the whole show single-handed, she thinks. She worries about what he will think of her, getting into a scrape like this.

As she walks back she passes the Sailing Club. She pauses. She's come all this way, and maybe given up too soon. Maybe he's not living at his old house any more, he could have moved into a flat, for instance, just as she has. She hasn't even asked Tiff if she knows him, she has been half-hearted about the whole expedition, cowardly even. She decides that she will ask someone. She will ask the first person she sees going into the Sailing Club.

The first person she sees is a youngish, smoothish sort of man, very neatly dressed, somehow giving the impression of a person playing at being a member of a sailing club. But the first person is what she said to herself, and the first person is who she must approach, or else it will never happen at all.

'Excuse me.'

He stops.

'I was looking,' she says, 'I mean, I was wondering – I'm looking for a friend of mine and I wondered –' she indicates the sailing club.

'Name?' he says.

She almost gives her own name, as if she was still at the hospital, but remembers in time. 'Aughton,' she says.

'Mr Aughton,' he says. 'No, I can say with some certainty that we don't have a Mr Aughton here.'

'No no,' she says as he begins to move away. 'Not Mr Aughton. It's his first name. People used to call him Oggy sometimes.'

'Sorry. Never heard of an Oggy.'

He goes, she's been brushed off, she can tell he had no intention of going to any trouble for her. She feels chastened, as if she's tried her best and even so been found inadequate. Tears come to her eyes. 'Still in shock,' she says to herself. She wonders how long she must wait for Keith to arrive; she wonders if he will also dismiss her as a stupid woman. Not that he ever did in the past.

By six-thirty he has arrived, by train and taxi, at Seawinds. He is tall and distinguished-looking. His skin is improbably shiny and unwrinkled for a man of his age and he is dressed quite formally, with a jacket and tie.

'I didn't expect you to drop everything and come today,' says Joan. 'I know how busy you must be.'

'Nothing that won't wait,' he says.

'I am so grateful,' she says.

He wrinkles the corners of his eyes, which is his way of smiling. 'Just think,' he says, 'of all the years you've been my right hand. Think of this as my turn.' It sounds like a speech he has rehearsed.

Tiff has been hovering by them, ready to offer him tea, to take his bag to his room – because of course they are not going to set off tonight. She is obviously impressed by him, as who wouldn't be. His whole demeanour says he is competent, and capable and will know what to do. He is polite to her, and adds his gratitude to Joan's for looking after her so well, in a way that suggests that she is valuable to him. Even though Tiff has been told that they have not seen each other for nearly two years, and to be honest, that Joan has been putting off seeing him. Not avoiding exactly, just putting off the day.

Tiff recommends a pub and that's where they go. They are early enough to get a table in the bar. Joan has a glass of white wine and Keith a half pint of beer. Although she has rarely been in a social setting with him – unless a Town Hall staff buffet would count – she is somehow sure that he is not a big drinker.

It is awkward. Joan feels it is awkward. She probably spent more hours in the course of her life with Keith than she did with Martin but they were never what she would call friends. He was an attractive man but she never felt attracted to him. He was married but his wife was never in evidence, never part of any conversation, and events where she might have been invited took place without her. After he retired he went to Africa for a year, doing some sort of voluntary work – that's all Joan knows about it – but it appears his wife did not go with him. Viv says she heard a rumour that they are no longer living together, but rumours mean nothing, Joan said and Viv agreed.

He is not at ease either. After his little show of gallantry in Tiff's hall, he seems at a loss for any sort of conversation. Is he waiting for even more gratitude than she has already shown? Is he wondering if she will pay her share of this dinner bill? Maybe it's just that a pub is not his natural milieu. The little round table they are sitting at pushes them too close together; the noise of so many people talking means they have to look at each other to understand what the other is saying. He would be less uncomfortable taking his place at the end of the big committee table in the big meeting room at the town hall.

They consult the menu. They order. Now, until their food comes, there really is nothing else to do but talk to each other.

'I really am very grateful,' says Joan. 'You must let me buy dinner. And obviously, I'll pay you back for your train fare and your room tonight. As soon as I have been able to get money out of my account. When we get home. Is that all right?'

He nods – Joan has asked him so many questions in their life together – questions about times and venues, about attendance at committees, about decisions, about minutes and spelling mistakes and unreadable abbreviations. About delicate questions of who to contact and when, about who to tell and in what order, about omissions and commissions and lost agendas and mislaid files (never by Joan), and priorities and budgets and virements and surpluses and overspends (more of the latter than the former) and many times she has received that nod in reply, that curt nod, without eye contact. It means, she has got it right, she knew already, she didn't need to ask. It also means that she has to look at him, to see what he is doing, while he does not have to look at her.

'I mean it,' says Joan. 'I know it might look – ungracious, but I'm going to keep count of what you are spending and pay you back. All of it.'

'There's no need,' he says, still without looking at her.

'We'll discuss it another time,' says Joan – though why not discuss it now, when they seem to have nothing else to say? She makes an effort. 'How did you enjoy Africa?'

'It was interesting,' he says. 'Though in many ways just like being at home. Same problems – you know, lack of funding, deciding where to put resources for the best outcome, working out how to evaluate work that was going on.'

He makes it – the bush? the savannah? Joan has no idea – sound really no different from Sheffield. Children's centre in Hackenthorpe or three playgrounds and an after school club? How many youth support workers can be employed for the cost of sending children outside the city to specialist foster care? Weigh. Balance. Judge. Decide.

He was on so many boards of trustees, so many working parties and evaluation panels. His fingers were in so many pies – never in a bad sense – that no one in the city had had such a broad overview of statutory and voluntary support programmes for a whole range of different problems. Children and old people. Disability, mental health. Drugs, alcohol, domestic violence. Nearly everything the council did could be attached in some way to one of his projects. Transport, education, health centres, mobile libraries, policing, even bins – they could all have a bearing on one or more of the groups of people Keith was there to provide for. He was Mr Fairlie, trying his best to behave as his name dictated.

'I see,' she says. They are two inarticulate people all of a sudden, unable to cope with a social situation. Viv, thinks Joan crossly, would have no trouble with this. She would make him laugh about it. I ought to take lessons from her, she thinks.

'What about you though?' he says. 'How did you get into this fix?'

'As I told you on the phone,' says Joan, 'I had my handbag stolen, and I fell and broke my arm. Only a minor crime, in the scheme of things – I mean, I don't think they intended to injure me – it's just that being so far from home has made everything difficult. I couldn't think of anyone else who would be able to come and get me.'

'Don't you have a daughter?'

'She's in Scotland. She works. I don't think she could get the time off, and it would take her for ever to make her way here.'

'Is that what she said?'

'I haven't actually told her.'

He says nothing to this piece of information and it sounds to Joan's own ears a feeble explanation. 'I don't have her number,' she says, 'all my numbers were in my phone.' This is true but she knows she would not have told Rachel anyway unless she was forced to. And that was because she wouldn't want her to know the reason for her journey. Her wild goose chase.

After a while he says, 'But why, though, did you come here in the first place?'

Bizarrely, this is a question Joan has not imagined he would ask. 'I suppose,' she says, speaking slowly, thinking quickly, 'it was a nostalgia trip. I wanted to see the university again. Just out of interest.'

'So you don't know anyone who lives here?'

'Not as far as I know. There may be people still around, but I don't suppose I would recognise them these days. And they wouldn't recognise me.'

'You haven't changed much since I've known you,' says Keith. Joan knows that is not true.

As they walk back to Seawinds – the wind has dropped and it is still warm – Joan feels all at once an arm round her waist. A tentative arm, is how it seems to her.

'Thank you,' she says, after a pause, 'but I can manage, really.'

The arm goes away. What was that about? Only being helpful because she's injured? Does he fancy her, after all these years? Does he think that's why she has called him here? Is there some obligation on her to repay him by sleeping with him?

As they arrive at the front door, she makes the mistake of looking at his face. It has on it an expression she thinks she has never seen before, not on him anyway. Sort of wistful? Sort of yearning? Definitely uncertain. Anxious. That makes two of them.

She looks away so that when he leans forward to kiss her, she is not expecting it. The sudden feel of his moustache makes her jump with surprise, and she moves backwards and bumps the door. It opens immediately and Tiff is standing there.

*

Viv puts down her phone, after a long conversation. Joan was all right this morning, she has told Rachel, but has not called her back, although she promised to. She has explained about Joan's plan to contact Mr Fairlie to come to the rescue. She has had to tell about the break-in to Joan's flat and her own, rather foolish, expedition with Bill, omitting the details of her journey home. She and Rachel have wondered to each other whether Joan has really defied all their past experience of her by running off to Essex to meet a man. Viv has promised to keep Rachel in the loop.

She leans back in her chair and closes her eyes. Tonight, she hopes, she will sleep well. She will do a little of her tapestry in front of something pleasant on TV and have an early night. Maybe Joan will be home tomorrow.

Now Viv realises that of all the things she has been waiting to tell Joan, there is one that really has to be told before she arrives home. She cannot let Joan arrive home to find that her house has been secured by the police. She imagines Keith Fairlie dropping her at the outer door and Joan pressing the buttons to get in and then finding a strong metal front door and no way in. And her with no phone to call the police. She would just sit down on the landing and sob, thinks Viv. Well, some people would, she does not really know what Joan would do.

Viv calls the number Joan gave her and is told that Joan is out with a man having dinner. Which one? wonders Viv.

'Tell her,' says Viv, 'that when she gets back to Sheffield, she's to come to my house. Someone has broken into hers.'

'No,' says Tiff, aghast. 'Do you mean, using her keys? From her bag?'

'Oh no,' says Viv. 'In fact I know what happened but it's really too confusing to tell you. Tell her to come to my house. As soon as she's here we can contact the police and they'll let her in.'

*

Bill has had a long day. He has kept up his house-cleaning campaign. He has dealt with the items of post that needed dealing with. He has spoken to Laura and left a message for Emily, explaining that he has been away but he is back and he is fine. He has made a list of things to do for the following day. He has walked down to the sailing club and had a single pint in the bar. He is now on his way back home to retrieve a frozen ready meal from the freezer and doze in front of the TV.

As he passes the Brewers' Arms he is tempted to go in for another pint, but the Friday night hum repels him. It will be full of young people shouting at each other and showing each other their phones. There will be no one there he knows. Another night, a weekday night, will be more congenial.

He is finding it hard to get used to being in a house again. Sounds are muffled by the brick walls, instead of being amplified by metal ones. The carpets and cushions and soft furnishings seem to him too lavish all of a sudden, too padded and stifling. He briefly considers sleeping in the van but it would be too eccentric even for him and anyway, sooner or later he has to become reconciled to being civilised again.

He leaves his dirty dishes – one plate, one mug – for tomorrow and picks up Joan's address book. Her handwriting has not really changed from what he remembers. Imagine that, he thinks, all the changes a person goes through, all the experiences and events, all the griefs and emotions, all the thinning and thickening of skin and bone and tissue, and yet her writing is recognisably hers. He looks through the names, and recognises none of them, except his own, his sister's and Rachel's, and Viv's. No one there that he recognises from the days when he knew Joan. No mutual friends.

He knows he should call Viv. He ought to make sure she is safely home. He could even bring himself to apologise, mildly, for leaving her at the roadside. He has been putting it off all day, making up reasons for leaving it until later. Until now.

He dials. 'Viv?'

'Is that Bill?'

'Yes it is. Are you all right?'

She makes a snorting noise, a bit like laughing, but not quite. 'I'm fine thank you. And you?'

'I'm ok.'

She waits for him to say something more. He says, 'You got home all right?'

'No problem.'

'And you got your things back?'

'Of course.'

'All right then.'

'Right then.'

'Goodbye then.'

'Goodbye.' She puts the phone down.

Bill tries to imagine what she is doing. Laughing at him? Punching the wall in anger? Is there someone there with her? Is that why she had no more to say? He could have said that he would post her earrings to her. Should he phone her back to say it? But no, he is not brave enough.

He turns the TV on and opens a can of Guinness.

Saturday

Keith drives Joan back to Sheffield by a more direct route than the one she took nearly a week ago. 'What a very comfortable car,' he says. 'I don't have one at the moment. When I came back from Africa I never got round to buying one, and I've found I can do without it.'

'I sold my car when Martin died,' says Joan, 'and used his. But it was getting on a bit so when I sold the house and moved into a flat I sold it and bought this one.'

'Very nice,' he says, but she knows he must be thinking badly of her green credentials. She could have bought a small hybrid for the same money. But Martin always had BMWs, they were what she was used to. She would like to defend herself but holds herself back. Why should she mind what he thinks after all?

She wishes she were more ill so that she could be excused the task of making conversation for two hundred miles. She wishes she could tell what Keith was thinking. Of her, of this expedition, of anything at all.

She glances sideways at his profile. Nose, strong and slightly beaky; lips, fuller than you might think. His hair, though grey, is still a full head. She remembers when it was blond, and much longer, touching his collar and clothing his ears. That would be when she first worked for the council, before Rachel was born. It was Viv who told her about the job. Viv was an office assistant by then, quite a lowly job, and was studying secretarial skills at night school, in a bid to progress. Joan, with her Civil Service exams behind her, went in several pay grades above her step-sister.

'Are we still step-sisters?' said Viv to her one day, as they walked together down Fargate to their respective bus stops. 'I mean now that your father's dead?'

'I suppose we are,' said Joan, without enthusiasm.

'Well,' said Viv, with an air of knowing some secret, 'I suppose there's more ways than one of being sisters.'

But Joan did not ask her what she meant.

'I've been wondering,' says Keith now, smoothly overtaking an articulated lorry, 'How did you get hold of my number? Not that I mind, of course.'

'Viv found it for me. You remember Viv? Flores-Jones? From the general office?'

'Maybe,' he says. 'Well I expect I would know her if I saw her. So you keep in touch with her?'

'We're sort of related,' admits Joan. She braces herself to explain, but he doesn't ask any more.

She had not wanted to go to her father's wedding. She did not want to leave her boyfriend, and he was too new for her to take him with her. She did not want to believe in this marriage at all. She wanted her father to stay the way he was, keeping his house unchanged, as her mother had left it when she died. She was sure she would be uncomfortable and she was.

There was her new stepmother, Vicky. That was what everyone called her, though her proper name was Victorine. She was bright, busy, efficient. She had produced the wedding buffet single-handed, and when they came back from the registry office – Joan, Viv, Viv's brother, Arthur's cousin Alec – who Joan always called Uncle - one of his sons, Colin, and a handful of friends – there was the spread of food, piled on platters and interspersed with posies of spring flowers, so neat and pretty that you could tell it was professionally done, all laid out on the big table in the dining room, with two of Vicky's work colleagues ready to pour champagne and hover helpfully. Vicky, in her cream suit which was only a little too tight, took off her hat, laid down her flowers (pink roses) and began tweaking at the tablecloth –

one of Joan's mother's cloths, but now indubitably Vicky's.

'Vivienne,' she said. 'Fetch the ice buckets.'

Joan thought, If she starts ordering me about, I'm gone.

Her father and Vicky posed for photographs, taken by Uncle Alec. On the sideboard sat the cake, made and iced, naturally, by Vicky.

'I made the rosebuds,' said Viv, next to Joan all of a sudden, carrying a silver bucket half full of ice. Joan looked at the cake with new eyes, having assumed that sugar roses were something you could only acquire by buying them from a shop – the sort of specialist shop that she had no knowledge of, and didn't want to have. She looked at Viv, and the silver bucket.

'Where did that come from?' she said. 'My mother never had one of those.'

'Mum borrowed them,' said Viv. 'She has loads of contacts in catering.'

'Are you going to live here with them?' said Joan. This was the first time she had thought of this, now, having seen with her own eyes these strangers in her mother's house.

'Not a chance,' said Viv cheerfully. 'I'm moving in with some mates. As long as the landlord don't find out. I'm going to sleep in the front room, help em out with the rent. Have a laugh.'

'Well, that's what I do,' said Joan. 'I share a house with three other girls, in Colchester. Where's yours?'

'Walkley,' said Viv. 'On the bus route, straight into town.'

'Where do you work?'

'Cole Brothers,' said Viv. 'In the office, ordering. I used to be in the shop, on toys, but they moved me. Not on my feet so much now.'

'Can you type then?' said Joan. 'Shorthand?'

'Not a bit. Wouldn't know where to start. No, all I have to do is count what we've got, look up the stockists, fill in an order form, sometimes have to phone to see what's in stock. Then check it when it comes in, phone them if it's wrong.'

'Do you like it?'

'We have a laugh,' said Viv. 'Office manager, she's all right, lets us talk as long as we get us work done. I might look around though. I wouldn't mind a change.'

'Vivienne,' called her mother, 'where are you with that bucket?'

'Right here, mother dear,' sang out Viv, with noticeable irony and grinned at Joan and was gone.

Later Joan was talking to her cousin Colin's fiancée. She was at the College of Education, training to be a science teacher.

'My parents are teachers,' she said. 'I never really thought of doing anything different. And the holidays fit in so well when you have a family.'

'What, are you going to have children soon?' said Joan. The idea of having children had not yet come over her horizon.

'No point waiting,' said the girl. Her name was Carol. 'Teaching is a career I can always go back to.'

'I just didn't think Colin was a very parental person,' said Joan. She looked over to where he was talking to Viv. To her eyes it looked like flirting.

'He'll be fine,' said Carol confidently.

Later still the young people – Joan, Viv, Roland, Colin and Carol – were sitting outside in the cold garden, drinking and smoking.

'So where is your brother?' Joan asked Colin.

'Didn't Dad tell you? Martin's away working. He's laying a pipeline in Saudi Arabia. Getting paid squads of money, lucky bugger.'

'Language,' said Carol, not loudly but firmly.

Joan is worrying, sitting in the passenger seat of her nice car, where she has never sat before, about the message from Viv. Can it be true that her flat has been broken into? How can it be, when there is a security code on the downstairs door? Have they got in

139

through the balcony window? But wouldn't they be seen from the street? She has not yet told Keith about this further complication; she wants to think it through herself first. And she certainly doesn't want him to suggest that she puts up at his house tonight. Things are awkward enough already.

Anyway, it serves her right for breaking her promise to phone Viv. She found ways of putting it off though it nagged her all through the day. And she had to speak to Rachel who called late in the evening, after she and Keith were back from the pub. In fact she was in her room, having told him she was too tired to talk any more, when Tiff came tentatively tapping at the door, already in her dressing gown and holding the phone out. After that it really was too late.

But what excuse can she give to Keith for not going straight home, when she distinctly remembers telling him how eager she is to be back in her own space. Oh what a tangled web I've weaved, she thinks.

The fields and woods flash by on either side. The romance of the open road has disappeared since last Sunday. Now all she can see is people in cars. Whole families of them, going to swimming pools or theme parks, or shopping malls or out of town carpet outlets. They pass supermarkets with car parks that cover acres, football pitches spattered with coloured shirts of all sizes, garden centres, notices pointing to BMX tracks and riding stables. The world, it seems, on a Saturday morning, is in pursuit of leisure, or shopping, or both.

But she must say something. It will be so rude of her, and ungrateful, if she stays quiet for mile after mile.

'How is your family doing?' Because last night this was a subject they did not get round to.

'James is doing fine,' says Keith. 'In fact I went up to see him last month. Very interesting work.'

'Where is he now?' As if she has ever known where he is, since he left school.

'Inner Hebrides,' says Keith. 'And married now, to a lovely girl. Scottish. In fact, in a way he's returned to his roots. My parents were from that part of the world, though on the mainland, not an island. I ought to do some research into my family tree, as so many people seem to do. They must find it rewarding, maybe I will too.'

This strikes Joan as a very sad speech, and she does not dare ask him what has happened to his wife.

'I expect you're too busy to do much in the way of family research,' she says, meaning to be kind. 'I mean you're still involved in things aren't you.'

'This and that,' he says. 'Several organisations have me on their committees – I try to be useful but actually, having been away for a year, I find I've lost touch with a lot of the issues. You come back and find everything has moved on and last year's big problem has been solved, or more likely, been superseded by an even bigger one. Mostly funding of course, which is not something I've ever had to do – raising funds was done by other people wasn't it. I can spend them easily enough. It makes you nostalgic for the old days, when there were funds to spend.'

Joan finds that she is bored with this topic of conversation, but Keith is not. While he expands on the problems of the voluntary sector in the face of government cuts to the council's grant, she wonders again about Viv's message, which Tiff passed on to her this morning before they left. She will wait, she decides, for a suitable moment. While she waits she worries about what has been taken, what has been damaged. How will her insurance deal with her, when she is claiming on so many fronts?

Her expensive, quiet car swishes up the A1, past scenery that goes on for ever behind hedges and fences without her taking any notice of it. She notices though, the bodies of dead crows by the roadside, stiff feathers sticking up at odd, very dead angles, and litter and shreds of lorry tyres, and little numbered posts that mean nothing to her. They stop for coffee at a Little Chef. 'Pretty ghastly,' she comments, looking round.

'Is it?' Keith seems to have no way of noticing what is around him.

'You must,' she tries, 'have seen some interesting things in Africa.' She doesn't even know which country he was in.

'Not that interesting,' he says. 'There were no historic sights near where we were. And the town was very small – not really more than a village.'

'But isn't that interesting? Different customs and things?'

'We were there to work,' he says, and she has a sense of being dismissed, and wonders whether she hurt his feelings by criticising the Little Chef ambience.

All those years of anticipating his wants and needs – in an office sense – of having the right documents on his desk at the right time, of knowing who to allow through on the phone and who not to, of the mutual congratulation when a funding application went well, or a decision was approved at a higher level; all those years count for nothing it seems. The vague feeling she once had, of maybe growing close to him, of maybe getting to be friends one day, the feeling that Viv had divined and teased her about, was dissipated by his social ineptness. He was hard to be with, that was all that could be said. A manifestly good and admirable person, but with no skill at interaction. Cold, even. How could she not have known it?

She waits until Keith is driving along the Parkway into the city before she says, 'I'm sorry, I should have told you – don't take me home, I need to get my door key from Viv. She keeps my spare.'

'I'll wait while you pick it up,' he says. 'Then I can run you home from there.'

'Apparently,' she says,' there's a bit of a problem. It seems someone broke into my flat while I was away. The police have secured the door so I won't be able to get in until I've been in touch with them.'

'Do it now,' he says, offering her his phone.

'I can't,' she says. 'I need the crime number and Viv has got that too.'

'Call her then.'

Joan sits for a while with his phone in her lap, and then puts in a number which she knows will not get through to Viv.

'She's not in,' she says.

'Then there's no point going to her house is there?'

'I'll try again in a few minutes,' says Joan, furious with herself for being so stupid. 'She may just be out in the garden.'

And sure enough, when she tries again Viv unsurprisingly does answer.

'You won't be able to get in,' says Viv, 'Not at this time of night. You'll have to stay here for the night.'

That is something Joan has been resisting for many years, staying over at Viv's, but now it is the solution to her problem. She explains to Keith.

'So if you could take the car,' she says. 'I'll call you when I have managed to access my flat, if you don't mind bringing it back to me. Tomorrow, hopefully.' She does not dare look at him to see if he is relieved, but she thinks he might be.

'So where does this Viv live?'

'Go up to Crookes,' says Joan, 'and turn left at the greengrocer's. Number twenty-two.'

But he does not turn left. He parks on the main road. 'You don't mind getting out here,' he says, in a voice that seems to come from another man, some brusque unknown man.

Joan is pleased that he is not wanting to come and meet Viv with all the questions and explanations that would involve, but faintly offended at his attitude. He does not get out of the car to help her with her bag, but remains sitting, looking straight ahead, not at her or at where she is going.

'Let me know,' he says.

All that is left after that is being welcomed into Viv's house, making phone calls to the police and being told, Tomorrow morning, can't tell you what time, love, as soon as we can fit it in; phoning Keith to tell him, phoning Rachel to tell her she is home, drinking some of Viv's (too strong) tea and eating some of her bread and salad, and going to bed in Viv's spare room. Exhausted.

*

Viv washes up the plate from Joan's meal and tidies the kitchen. She sits down with her tapestry and a glass of water, and turns the TV on quietly. Having Joan sleeping upstairs in her house is not something that has ever happened before. Her presence can be felt all over the house.

Viv and Joan grew up in the same city at the same time, but had never met before their parents' wedding, nor was it likely that they would have. Viv grew up in the north of the city, Parson Cross it was called, which sounds as if it might possibly be a rural village but was – and is – a very large council estate. Viv spent her childhood playing in the street with neighbourhood children while her brother read his books by their Nannan's fire. She had lots of friends. 'We knew everyone,' she says now, which isn't quite true but it definitely feels that way. She went to school with the children she played with, when they were all a bit older they roamed further afield, in the fields by Hartley Brook, and later even further, across Halifax Road on Fox Hill, where there were a different set of children, slightly frightening because unfamiliar. Not that Viv was often frightened. Even if she was confronted by a scary big girl, or a boy with a dog, she would face them down, being too short and fat to run away.

She is sorry for the children of today, Daniel and Callum for example, who never go out without an adult, who only play outside in back gardens if they are lucky, or supervised in the park. It's true that there were sometimes accidents – Viv's best friend

144

jumped off a wall and broke her arm, a boy down the road shot a home-made arrow from a home-made bow into another boy's eye – 'but we learned,' says Viv. 'We could look after ourselves. Even the flashers didn't bother us.'

Joan had a more sheltered childhood, if only because there was more space between her house and the next one. Though the road was not busy with traffic, it was not busy with children either. They played more genteelly in gardens and each other's houses, and went to ballet lessons and Brownies. When Viv left school at fifteen, Joan was just doing her O levels; when Viv was, though under age, going to pubs and clubs, Joan was studying for her A levels and enjoying pleasant and largely chaste romances with boys from the year above her.

The day of their parents' wedding was the first time the two girls met. Afterwards, at seven o'clock sharp Arthur and Vicky were driven away in a white taxi to a hotel in the Peak District for dinner (not that they could possibly need any on top of the spread Vicky had laid on) and two nights in the honeymoon suite. Joan and Viv were left in charge of the house. 'I shall expect it spotless when I come back,' said Vicky. She said it to Viv but Joan knew it was meant for her too and she was offended. It was her house, wasn't it, not Vicky's, and she resented everything about it – the fact that Vicky was now in charge, the notion that she was some kind of skivvy, and that it should be Viv who had been told to tidy up instead of her.

People did not stay late. As soon as the wedding couple were gone the older folk departed in a body, home to take off their shoes and have a nice cup of tea in front of the telly. Colin and Carol went back to her college room; Roland went back to Vicky's council house, where he would be staying for the short time until he went off to university himself.

Joan and Viv sat in the kitchen drinking white wine that was now too warm to sparkle and talking, warily, like two dogs that meet in a park. Viv told

145

Joan about her new boyfriend and Joan told Viv about hers.

'So how did you meet him?'

'Oh, you know, the way you meet anyone, they're just around and gradually you get to know them. Where did you meet yours?'

'Baileys. Ever been there?'

'Of course,' said Joan.

'Are they good clubs where you are?'

'Colchester? No, we don't go there. We have discos and dances on campus.'

'Same people every time then?'

'I suppose so. But why not?'

'So this one, are you serious about him?'

'I think he might be – no, I think he *is* going to be the one,' said Joan.

'What do they call him?'

'Aughton.'

'What, like that village out past Rotherham?'

'I suppose so.' Joan suddenly giggled. 'I think his mother must be a bit peculiar. He's got three sisters and they're all named in alphabetical order, and all weird. Their names I mean.'

'Go on then.'

'A – Aughton; B – Belinda, that's not so weird I suppose; C – Carenza; D – Demelza.'

'They could go for Ermintrude next,' said Viv, and cackled.

Vicky had decided the two girls should share Joan's old bedroom. 'There's no need to air out and bottom another room,' she said. But when Viv went to bed Joan was not there in the room, and though Viv stayed awake for a little while – as long as she could after all the alcohol – Joan never appeared and in the morning her bed had not been slept in.

'Where did you sleep?' asked Viv, when they met over the washing up, and Joan did not answer. Later, when Joan had gone, Viv looked in the other bedrooms and deduced that Joan had slept in her father's big double bed, the one, presumably that he had shared with his first wife and would from now on be sharing with his second. It was untidy and rumpled – Vicky would never have gone out and left it like that.

Viv did not straighten it or do anything to disguise that someone had slept there. Let them think what they like, she thought.

Viv had not had a lot to do with Arthur. He was a nice enough bloke, she thought, if she thought anything. He seemed to make her mother happy, and to indulge her with clothes and jewellery and holidays that she had never been able to have before. But Viv did not see them very often. Why should she? How should she? They were working still, she was working, weekends they had a social life and so did she, and there was little chance of them meeting at the bars and nightclubs Viv went to, nor yet at the country pubs and golf club dinners they went to. She spent Christmases with them, insofar as she ate her Christmas dinner with them. Joan was usually there but Viv could not remember a single proper conversation they ever had, and Joan always made her escape as soon as the trains started running again. Of the boyfriend there was never a sign.

And then poor Arthur died. Just like that. On the seventh tee of the Hallamshire Golf Course, one Saturday morning while his wife was shopping in Rackhams for a new dress to wear at the Ladies' Night at the self-same golf club. Viv remembers how she drove – she had only just passed her test – to Leeds to pick up Joan that night. She was dressed, she recalls – Joan that is – in a cheesecloth smock and a pair of jeans cut off at the knee. Viv thought Joan was stuck up and superior, and she also admired her for being cool and stylish and clever enough to have a degree and work in London. Now, though the night was warm for England, she was hunched and shivering and tearful.

'Thank you,' she whispered to Viv as they parted in the hall at home. Tears were running down her face in increased quantities since she got out of the car.

'It's ok,' said Viv. She would have hugged her but Joan seemed too tall to make it easy. She patted her on the arm instead, and watched Joan climb quietly up to her old bedroom. We'll be friends from now on, she thought to herself, wait and see.

Sunday

This time last week, thinks Joan, I was getting up and getting ready to make a journey. I don't think I will ever want to do that again.

She has woken so early that the world is still quiet. She is lying in the single bed in Viv's spare room. This is not the homecoming she expected.

Some sparrows chip-chip away now in the gutter above the window. Soon she will have to get up and face Viv. Viv will want to know everything. Where has she been, why did she go? Where did she stay, why did she lie? What did Keith say, was it nice to be with him? Joan does not know what she will say in answer to any one of these questions.

In the event, it does not happen quite like that. There is a phone call from the police before Joan is even out of the shower. A policeman comes and takes a statement from Joan – Viv meanwhile potters outside in the garden. Then Joan is taken home and allowed in to her flat. A man comes and puts a new door on. She calls Keith and asks him to bring her car back. She meets him by her garage, and hands him a cheque for every expense he had in coming to get her. She does not ask him into the house, saying that she is tired and needs to rest.

'I hope I'll see you again soon,' he says, stiffly.

'I'm sure you will,' she says.

She goes back inside and closes her new door behind her. That's that, she says out loud.

Monday

Viv spends her Monday morning at the charity shop, serving. In the afternoon she phones Joan to see how she is.

'Fine,' says Joan. 'Everything back to normal.'

Viv does not believe life can be normal. It doesn't feel normal. There is a great weight of information in her, waiting to be told to Joan, and a great press of questions, waiting for answers from Joan, but somehow – how did she do it? – Joan has escaped from the conversation which was there between them, unspoken, all of Saturday evening and night. 'Tomorrow,' she said, but when tomorrow came there were other things, practical things, to do.

'Tomorrow,' she says again, but Viv does not believe she means it.

Viv goes to the choir as usual. She imagines herself telling Sandra or Pamela the story, she imagines Richard overhearing and bursting into great guffaws at the tale of what his friend has done. She imagines the sympathy and concern she will get for her trial and long journey. She imagines the speculation that will follow about Joan (who some of them know a little) and where she went and why.

In the event she misses a bus and arrives at the choir when everyone else is already settled and quiet, listening to Richard.

'So I've taken it all on board,' he is saying, as Viv puts her money in the box and slides into a chair behind Sandra. 'My suggestion is that we hang on to the three we've started – Sunshine, Starshine and the Hamlet one – and fill up the programme with other songs from that era. I've got some ideas, and I'm open to any ideas from any of you.'

Pamela turns to Viv nodding with satisfaction. 'Did you hear that then?'

'Did he say why?'

'People have said things. Which people and what they said, he didn't say.'

'I see Mr Fairlie isn't here.'

'Nor that new man.'

'Bill,' says Viv. 'I believe he's gone back to where he came from.'

OCTOBER

Bill has not seen either of his daughters since their mother's funeral, back in April. Some people might think this is odd, but for Bill it isn't really anything new.

'We've never been the sort of family who live in each other's pockets,' Lydia used to say, maybe defensively, or maybe as a matter of pride. 'We brought them up to be independent, didn't we Bill.'

'They would come if we needed them.' He remembers saying this, to excuse them or to comfort himself, and it's true that when Lydia was ill they visited more often, but since that time, although they have phoned him and no doubt if he ever switched on the old office computer he would be able to send and receive emails, or follow their lives on Facebook or some such abomination, since that time he has not seen them.

It's Emily who comes to see him first. Emily is the daughter who is most like her mother. She is the younger one, the sensible one, with a proper career as a nurse, a proper boyfriend, and almost a proper sense of duty towards her father, and now, this dark October evening, clocks just gone back, she phones to say she will be arriving tomorrow.

She arrives in a hired van.

'What's that for?' says Bill.

'I thought I'd take some stuff off your hands,' she says. 'You know we had that girl sharing with us? Well she's gone so we've got an extra bedroom now.'

'Won't you get someone else in to help with the rent?'

'We might. If we can. But she had her own bed so she's taken it with her of course. I thought I'd take mine from my old room.'

'It's not yours.' Bill wishes he hadn't said this, but it's too late.

'Dad, surely. It's no good to you is it? I thought you were thinking of selling anyway.'

'So won't I need to have the rooms furnished? Isn't that what they say, when you're selling you have to have furniture in all the rooms?'

'You'll have no trouble selling this. Not when you've cleaned it up a bit.' She is barely inside the house and they are arguing already.

'It is clean,' he says.

'It's not,' she says. 'It needs a proper going over. And while you're at it you might as well redecorate. Some of this has been here since I was four years old.'

'Not that long,' says Bill. You lose your children, he thinks to himself. Bad enough to lose your wife, but then you lose your children, and your dignity. 'I'll put the kettle on,' he says. 'Come and sit down and tell me what you've been doing.'

She searches out the coffee from the back of the cupboard. 'Dad. This is solid. How long have you had it?'

'You know I don't drink the stuff,' he says.

She sighs and scrapes away with a spoon until she has enough to make a cup.

'I'll go down the shop tomorrow,' he offers. 'I'll buy a new jar.'

'I'm only here tonight,' she says. 'I need to be off first thing in the morning. It's a long way to Cardiff you know.'

'Why don't I take you out for a meal,' he says. 'My treat.' Really, he's only just thought of it and he hopes it will convince her to be nice to him, and will make a situation where they can sit opposite each other and talk intimately, rather than – what he dreads might happen – sit with the TV on and nothing to say to one another, except for her to criticise his standards of hygiene and for him to feel disappointed that she hasn't noticed his efforts.

'Let's see how much we can get done,' she says.

Get done? We?

'I thought you only came for the bed,' he says.

'I'll have a look round,' she says. 'While I've got this van it would be silly not to fill it. I mean, if there's stuff you want to be rid of.'

'So where did you go?' she says. They are sitting in the pub where only a few weeks ago Joan sat trying to make conversation with Keith Fairlie.

'Just a little trip,' says Bill. 'Up to Sheffield to see someone.'

'Who?'

'Bloke called Rick. You don't know him. Ricky Pyke. Old mate from London days. I played in his band for a bit, but quite honestly, they were too good for me.'

Laura would have asked what sort of music, how good were they, things like that, but Emily has no known interest in music, even less than Lydia had.

'You were away a long time.'

'I know I was. But I wasn't staying with him. I borrowed this campervan off Pete. You know Pete.'

'How is he? Last time I saw him his knees were giving him trouble.'

'Were they? I think he's ok.'

'Honestly Dad, you don't take much notice do you.'

'Pete's fine,' says Bill, wondering why it matters. 'I'd know if he wasn't.'

'Laura's still really annoyed with you,' she says.

'What did I do?'

'You called her Cheesy. In front of her boyfriend, that made it worse.'

'I was overwrought,' says Bill. 'It was your mother's funeral for Christ's sake. I regressed for a minute. She can't hold it against me for ever.'

'You think?' says Emily, who had herself been known, within the family, as Chalky.

'You never minded, did you?'

'Dad, it was just a family joke. I know that. But we left it behind when we were about twelve. No one

154

wants that sort of thing once they get old enough to know better. Besides, Julian –'

'Julian?'

'The boyfriend. You've met him Dad, you should remember his name. Julian thinks it's so funny that he uses it.'

'He can't do that, can he?'

'Who's going to stop him, if Loz can't? Anyway, that's why she's furious with you.'

'Honestly,' says Bill. 'You'd think she'd have bigger and better things to worry about than a baby nickname. What's a name after all?'

'Chalk and cheese,' Lydia, and others, used to say about their daughters, but Bill has never accepted the comparison. Chalk and cheese after all have some similarities, in colour, or texture – some sorts of chalk, some sorts of cheese. The daughters are as different as – winter and summer? But summer has rain and wind, winter has sunny days. As different as – up and down? That makes more sense to him, one being the diametric opposite to the other. Rosy, stubby Emily, who spent her childhood trying to keep her older sister out of trouble. Thin, serious Laura, selfish, clever and shameless.

'What's this?' says Emily. She has Joanie's address book in her hand.

'Nothing,' says Bill.

'It's not yours,' she says. 'It's not Mum's. Where did it come from?'

'I don't know,' he says.

She is leafing through the names. 'You're in here. But not Mum. Whose is it?' She flicks on through. 'A lot of Joneses,' she comments.

'I found it in the van,' he says. 'Pete's van. I cleared it out when I came back and somehow brought this in with my stuff. I'll give it to him when I see him.'

'Doesn't look like a bloke's book,' says Em. 'Very tidy, very organised. A lot of Sheffield addresses.

Fancy Pete knowing all these people in Sheffield. I thought he'd never been out of Essex.'

'He's just been to Brittany,' says Bill, more to deflect her than because it's relevant.

'A lot of women too,' she says. 'I never had Pete down as such a ladies' man.'

'Really?' says Bill. 'I haven't actually looked at it myself.' Which is the biggest lie of all.

*

Joan looks out of her window at the leaves falling and hears herself sigh. She has slept late, after lying awake through what seemed like most of the night. She thought of getting up and having a glass of whisky but didn't. She thought of turning on the computer and doing something but couldn't think what. Now, as the leaves spin down and land on the paths and the grass of the park she searches for the word that describes herself. Unsettled, she thinks, that's what I am.

Has she ever felt like this before? Maybe. Maybe there was once a time. She shuts it out. She decides she will clean her windows. Decides, but does nothing.

How ridiculous, to be named, deliberately, Joan Jones.

'You were called after your grandmother,' her father told her, on many occasions. 'She died just after you were born. She only ever saw you once.'

'Yes but Dad, she wasn't called that from the start, she married a Jones.'

'Ah but,' he would say, 'she were very proud of it. It were unusual you see. I told her we were calling you after her and I could tell she heard me and she were pleased. She understood. It made her happy. And she were a grand woman – you should be proud to be named after her.'

If the old lady was dying, Joan thought on many occasions, they could have made her happy and then called their new baby something more sensible. But she never said it out loud to her father.

How she suffered, through school. A name that was not only ridiculous but old-fashioned. Plain and redolent of old aunties sitting by gas fires, in lisle stockings and slippers that kept their ankles warm.

'Change your name then,' said her friend Madeline. 'You can call yourself what you like you know.'

'My dad would have a fit,' said Joan.

'He doesn't have to know,' said Madeline. 'Wait till you get to university. You can do what you like there.'

Perhaps it would have happened, she might have translated herself into a Joanna, or even a Juanita, if her mother hadn't died. If she thought of it again – and she can't now remember whether or not she did – it would have felt disloyal. Her name was something her mother, as well as her father had given her and she felt obliged to keep it, along with her antique sewing box and her long legs and red hair and her grandmother Edwards' gold and ebony necklace.

Joan would have liked to have given Rachel an exotic name but Martin dissuaded her. 'Nobody wants to stand out of the crowd,' he said. He had very clear ideas, very certain; he always knew what was right. Joan thought of Viv, and agreed to have a daughter called plain and sensible Rachel Jones.

He will never be old, Martin. He will never have to have false teeth or a hearing aid. He will never be on a list for a hip or knee replacement. She wonders if he would be pleased about that – he might, all things considered. At least he will never have to go into a Home, never have a walking frame, a catheter, a bib, a special non-spill cup.

She remembers, just, her Grandmother Edwards, when she must have known she was dying, though Joan was too young then to understand. 'We don't make old bones,' said Grandmother. She stayed in bed most of the time and had a number of fascinating little pill boxes which Joan was forbidden to touch. My mother was an only child, and then my parents had one daughter – me – and when I was a teenager my mother died. Exactly what of, they never told me. Then Dad died, then I married Martin and we had just the one daughter. Then Martin died. Like a repeating pattern.

She can imagine Rachel getting married – maybe even to this Ryan – having one daughter, repeating the pattern – marriage, one daughter, for a third time. Of course, she thinks, the difference is, Rachel still has one parent. She looks at the window which is now only a dark square. I ought to shut the curtains to keep the warmth in. But she continues to stand there, looking at the darkness.

To keep the pattern straight, I ought to die too.

As the thought spools across her mind – like one of those electronic displays – she is tempted. Not dying, that doesn't sound very pleasant – but being dead, I could cope with that.

*

Viv waits to hear from Joan. She holds herself back from being the one to make the first move. She will give Joan some space, knowing as she does that she hates being crowded, especially when she is in need of support. She is like that bloody rose, thinks Viv, it needs tying in to the trellis but you can't get near it for the prickles. At the beginning Joan made excuses – hospital appointments, being busy sorting out her insurance, waiting for a new lock for her door – until their friendship has become a thing of the past; they no longer meet at all.

But Viv still goes every Tuesday morning to the Botanical Gardens for a coffee, hoping that Joan might walk by, like old times. After her lonely Americano and croissant she often, as long as the weather is dry, walks through the park and past Joan's block of flats. If asked, she would say that she is walking off her morning's indulgence, but she is clear to herself that she is looking for some sign that Joan is still there, and all right.

There never is a sign though. Joan's curtains are always open, but no one can be seen looking out. From week to week, nothing changes.

'Give up,' advises Maggie. 'It's not as if you don't have any other friends.'

'She's more like family,' says Viv. 'You don't give up on family.'

'If you say so,' says Maggie.

Coming out of the greengrocer's one day Viv finds herself walking beside her next door neighbour, who has just got off the bus.

'Settled in?' she says.

'Very settled,' says the woman.

'I'm sorry, I don't know your name. I'm Viv.'

'Elaine,' she says.

'I don't know if I ever said a proper thank you,' says Viv, 'for looking after me that evening –'

'– It was nothing –'

'– and for giving me Keith Fairlie's number. It helped my friend no end.'

'It was nothing,' she says again.

'How do you know Mr Fairlie? You didn't work at the Town Hall?'

'Oh no. Library service.'

'So?'

They have reached Viv's back door. They are twelve feet from Elaine's back door. She pauses. She says, so quickly that Viv can hardly believe she heard right, 'I used to be married to him.'

She opens her door and disappears inside.

'Well,' says Viv, once inside her own house. 'Wait till I tell Joan.' And wonders sadly if she will ever get the chance.

DECEMBER

Bill sees a feeble winter sun shining on his extensive back lawn. Not a lawn really, just an expanse of grass, though Lydia used to sometimes mention that they could improve it with a roller, some fertiliser and an application of grass seed. Bill resolves that he will see to it, partly for Lydia's sake and more especially because it will help to sell the house. And he should get rid of that old Wendy house that has been there since Emily was in nursery, that Lyd would not throw away, out of sentimentality and in case it should come in useful when their future grandchildren came to visit. He will take it to the tip. Not today though, because he has a full day of jobs lined up.

He sits at his kitchen table and brings out his collection of lists from under the various piles of brochures, paint colour charts and tradesmen's flyers that cover it. He has a master list, which encourages him to improve his house and garden, be more healthy, and have a better relationship with his daughters. This list is rather like the Commandments, in that it doesn't tell him exactly how he should do these things, so he has another set of lists, headed House, Learn to cook, Em and Loz. These consist of major projects – every room in the house is on House, for example, and on the cooking one, a list of healthy-ish meals that he needs to learn to make for himself.

He finds House, and looks with pleasure at the items already crossed off. Over the autumn he has given the kitchen a thorough clean, painted the woodwork on the ground floor, shampooed the carpets and organised his paperwork. Lyd would be proud of him. He adds 'Lawn' to the list – he will save it until the early spring, before he gets back into the boat. He takes a clean piece of paper and heads it 'Tuesday', then writes his objectives for the day. Back bedroom – empty cupboards. Shop: fish, curry paste, fruit. Phone Emily. If he completes this list he will go to the pub for a pint this evening, if not he will watch TV with a cup of herbal tea.

First he goes to the shops. He is proud of this routine. He could go to Tesco once a fortnight and fill his freezer, but instead he walks down to the village every day, or every other day, and buys what he needs. He speaks to some people, smiles at some others, feels he is continuing his place in this community. This is how Lyd would like him to live.

Then after a cup of tea and a brief strum on the guitar it is time to tackle the back bedroom cupboard. This was the guest bedroom, and its cupboard was the place where things were put when there was no other obvious place for them. Lydia always had an ambition to sort it out but for years was too busy, and then too ill to do the job. Sometimes she started it but it was always too much and she would bundle it all back inside and lean on the door to shut it.

It is like an old-fashioned comedy, opening the door and stepping hurriedly out of the way as an avalanche of random objects comes spilling down. He stands and looks. He cannot get to the shelves to bring out the rest of the stuff, for the pile of stuff now on the floor. But his plan was to clear the whole lot out and not put anything back unless there was a really good reason for doing so. He goes downstairs and outside to fetch an implement – a rake – from the garage. The garage too is on his list for a clear out, when the weather warms up again.

He rakes the pile of stuff out of the way of the cupboard doors. He hears sounds of cracking, but that's ok – anything broken is one thing less to make a decision about. He pulls the rest off the shelves and heaps it with the first lot. He sits on the bed and looks at it. Boxes are spilling photographs from previous generations. There the padded white, silver-embossed photograph album from Lydia's first marriage. So this is where she kept it, he thinks. He extracts it from the pile, opens it and looks. White dress, church door, groom's parents next to her, her parents over next to him. Hats and high heels. A windy day, you can tell from the way her veil is blowing backwards and someone is holding on to their hat with the same hand that clutches their handbag, so it looks as if they are being hit in the face by a square white missile. His wedding, his and Lyd's was a much quieter affair. No one at the time, not her, or him, or her mother, and certainly not her father, had any ambition to go through all that again. It seemed more a case of, Let's do it quietly, so if it doesn't work again we can pretend it never happened. He smoothes the tissue paper over the faces and closes the book. It can go to Laura and Emily. Laura *or* Emily.

Photographs are not all, by no means. Curtains and tablecloths and sheets still in their packaging are slipping over each other. Racquets of every size, age and sport stick up at all angles. Boxes of board games and jigsaws. Knitting needles – Lydia's mother had been a great knitter – and bags of wool. A pile of Haynes car repair manuals for long obsolete models. Bill has heard of the concept of peak stuff; this seems to be it.

He decides he needs a large box to put stuff in. That will be for items that can go to the charity shop. Then he will put by anything that he thinks Emily or Laura (more likely Emily) might want and wait till she (or they) come to visit. And anything that is clearly rubbish will go into black bags and into the dustbin. He will be done by lunchtime.

He goes to the garage, where he knows there is a tea chest. It has been there, untouched, since they moved into this house in 1975; it is another thing that is full of stuff, but he will take it all out and pile it in the garage for another day. He takes off the layers of newspaper that have been carefully tucked in to protect the contents. They carry front page news of a referendum on the EEC, one where Bill chose not to exercise his vote. He takes out a pair of lady's boots – light brown suede, but stiff and mildewed all over.

Not Lydia's, too big for her – and suddenly he knows what this box contains. It is Joanie's belongings, that she left in their flat in Camden and that he promised, in the course of several drunken phone calls, to send on to her. That was when he still thought she might come back, so he never sent them – she would come back when the cold weather started, wouldn't she, to fetch her winter coat and boots, and when she did he would be there and they would be back together because there was no reason for them to be apart. He loved her. She loved him. What else was there?

There are her records too – Judy Collins, the Broadway cast recording of *Hair*, Crosby, Stills and Nash, Steeleye Span –and her books – some sociology text books, and some novels, damp and curling copies of *Gormenghast* and *Voyage to Arcturus*. He never sent them. It occurs to him for the first time that maybe it was a test she had set him, and that he failed it. He could send them now, with her address book, and some flowers by way of apology for breaking her front door down. But he knows he will not, not yet. It isn't on his list. He takes everything into the kitchen, and takes the chest upstairs.

By lunchtime he has two full black bags of broken toys and bent sports goods. He has a plastic box of assorted papers, photographs, documents which need to be gone through. He will put it on his list as a separate item. He is wondering whether clothes – coats, jackets, shoes – are things that Laura would want, or despise. Will she be insulted if he offers them to her, or angry if she finds out he hasn't? He decides to consult Emily about it. Moves on. Children's books. Should he keep them for Emily's – as yet unconceived – baby, or are they too out of date, too chewed and dilapidated? He puts them to one side.

He considers the tea chest, which so far contains only curtains – he is fairly sure that neither of his daughters will want, in the foreseeable future, curtains whose purple swirls so stridently shout 'Seventies.' But he picks them up again, to wonder.

Retro? Is he throwing out some family heirloom? The tea chest is not the ideal sort of box anyway – he can see why people stopped using them, with the protruding sharp edges, and inconvenient depth. All right for tea, presumably.

He goes to make himself a sandwich and listen to something on the radio. Anything will do. Sometimes he talks back to it, more often he talks to himself. Today they are softening people up for Christmas. Radio Four has an item about the number of children set to receive electronic equipment; Radio Two is trailing a programme about Christmas number ones. He turns it off and turns over Joanie's pile of records, shaking his head in a sort of tolerant bemusement at the stabs of regret he is feeling. Not his taste, these, and he hasn't heard them for decades, yet he could sing along to every one.

At the bottom of the pile, a record that is not Joanie's, but his. He hasn't set eyes on it since the day he packed up the tea chest and drove out of London in a van borrowed from Rick, up the A12, trying to go home again. He knows immediately why it's there and not with his own vinyl collection. It was almost worn out with playing – that one track – and he was determined to put it behind him. Not to throw it away – he couldn't bring himself to do that – but to hide it, and pretend it no longer existed. He would not, he promised, ever again, get drunk and remember Corfu, and torture himself with "Tales of Brave Ulysses". Cream. It seemed at the time that those evenings steeped in a misery that was adolescent went on for ever, but it can only have been a few weeks, and even then, only when he had the money for whisky. Whisky seemed to be called for if he was to be properly miserable. He was relieved when he found himself moving on, even if it was in a backwards direction. He turns the record over. 1967 he bought it, with money his Nan gave him for Christmas. Before he even met Joanie. The back of the cover bears a small mark made when a crumb of resin fell off the lump someone was burning, almost as soon as he got it back to university. He remembers how outraged he was when that happened. 'Set fire to your own fucking property,' he remembers shouting, though he can't recall who he was shouting at.

Five years later he struggled back here, to the edge of Essex, at this time of the year, everything dead and dry, most of his friends gone away, some permanently, some just back to their families for Christmas. He would not do that. He hadn't told the family about breaking up with Joanie. It would mean his dad taking him to one side and giving him advice, and his mum making helpful suggestions. He could imagine them now. 'Why don't you phone her?' As if he hadn't. 'Why don't you say sorry?' As if he wasn't. So he stayed away, and missed them, and drank a lot, mostly on his own, and sometimes with another loser called Brian, until the new year came, and he found a job, digging, and put it all, after a fashion, behind him.

Now the first Christmas without Lydia advances towards him. Laura, so she has informed him, is off to Thailand with her boyfriend for the holiday. Emily is going to spend it in Monmouth with her boyfriend's folks. They have kindly invited Bill as well, she tells him, but he replies that he doesn't feel up to it and will just stay at home quietly by himself. She does not press him to change his mind.

'What's Christmas anyway?' he says aloud. 'Crap television and obscene amounts of consumption. I'll be glad to be out of it. Cheques for the girls, half a dozen cards for people I can't ignore, job done. Nice quiet time for me, playing my guitar. Bit of twelve bar blues.'

His guitar stands in the corner of the room, shining as it has never shone before, on its proper stand that Lydia bought him in an attempt to get him to stop leaving it lying on chairs and tables and beds. 'Tell you what Lyd, it's not a bad feeling, being orderly. You'd be proud of me Lyd. And I hope you've noticed the cupboard under the sink, shining like the sun it is, and everything in straight lines. You wouldn't recognise it. And when the weather gets warmer I'm going to sort out the shed, and the boat – there's a few things want doing there. I never knew I had it in me Lyd, I'm tidier than you even. You wouldn't know me.'

He stands for a few long moments, listening to the echo of what he has said, then puts on a record. The Doors. 'You don't mind this Lyd. I know it's not Adele, but it's still power ballads by a different name, listen to it, you'll like it.'

His post comes through the letter box, another pizza delivery flyer and a couple of cards, one from Richard. 'Happy Christmas Oggy Badger,' it says. 'Putting on concert in spring, why not come, bring your van.'

'I might just do that.' says Bill. 'But maybe not. But maybe.'

He puts the cards on his mantelpiece, and notices Viv's earrings, still there, sitting on top of Joan's address book. In a spirit of tidiness and tying up loose ends, he puts it all into a jiffy bag and considers. Why not two packages? But he only has the one jiffy bag, and can't be bothered with the trouble of finding paper and sticky tape for the other item. So send it to Joan or to Viv? To send it to Joan would require an explanation. 'Dear Mrs Jones,' he says aloud, 'here is your address book, which I have had since I broke down your front door. I apologise for the inconvenience.' Would that do?

He seals up the jiffy bag and writes Viv's address on it. No note of explanation, no apology. He will take it with him to the post office next time he goes for his groceries.

*

I have friends, thinks Joan to herself. I do. Her Christmas cards – ordered online from the RSPB –

have arrived and she is gathering the courage to write them.

She switches on her computer and prints off her list, one that she keeps up to date year by year. And just as well, she thinks, since she has not had her address book returned to her, nor has she gone out and bought another one. She arranges her cards in tidy piles in front of her – all tasteful-not-garish, medium-sized neither look-at-me big nor insultingly small, displaying no sparkle. Her list is arranged in alphabetical order. She fixes her eyes on the Andersons, avoiding so much as glancing down to the Bs, and polishes off the Andersons – card, brief message, sticker with her new address, envelope, stamp, done. Ticks them off.

Next is Badger, Aughton and Lydia. She crosses out Lydia – she will amend it on the computer later – and considers. She has heard nothing from him directly since the postcard, the redirected too late postcard, probably dropped down a grating by the teenage muggers and by now pulped to mush by the sea. She has willed herself not to think about him. Rachel has tried to tell her things, but she has stopped her, on two occasions hanging up on her. Viv would no doubt give her a full account, given half an opportunity, if Joan had not avoided seeing her. It hasn't been easy.

She does not want to know. He was here, that much is clear. She suspects he was the breaker-in of her flat, but will not seek to have it confirmed or refuted. She suspects that Viv and Rachel suspect that she went away to meet him, but she will not talk about it. Thumbscrews would not get it out of her. The whole thing was ridiculous, shaming, silly. She does not want to remember it, or share it, or discuss it, or laugh about it. She wants to forget it. She crosses him off her list – she will amend it on the computer later.

She writes Christmas cards to Broadfoots, to Chans, to Carenza (now Carter), to Davises and

Edwardses – lots of Edwardses, they being her mother's family. And reaches Keith Fairlie.

They used to exchange cards – Christmas, not birthday – when they worked together, but that was a workplace thing which has lapsed since they both retired. For one thing, he went away to do that old-age gap-year thing, for another there was the question of how to address such a card, when it was rumoured that he and his wife were no longer together. But having summoned him back into her life she cannot in all conscience leave him ungreeted at Christmas. It would be bad manners, and he would notice. Whatever his festive season holds for him – and it will include church services and carol singing, she knows that about him – whatever, he will notice, he has that eye for detail, that stickling for correctness – he will notice if he does not receive some acknowledgement from her. And she will care if he notices and thinks badly of her. She selects a picture of some sort of seabirds, hoping it will make him think of his son up there on that island, and prepares to write. What to put? She surely can't thank him any more than she has already done, though he travelled all the way to the Essex coast to rescue her. He behaved like a gentleman – mostly – and it is not his fault that he has a chilly heart. If indeed he does.

The last time she saw him she was ungracious. He parked her car in the garage for her while she stood with the cheque in her hand. Standing out in a slight autumn drizzle, he offered to drive her anywhere she needed to go, any time – hospital? Physio? Supermarket? – but she rejected his goodwill. She wasn't ready for company, she told him so, she needed time to herself. She did not invite him into her flat.

When she replayed the scene she realised there was something different about him and it took her nearly an hour before it came to her that he had shaved off his moustache. She thinks of it again now. Why would he do that after most of a lifetime of having one? But it is no business of hers. She signs her name on the card and leaves it at that.

After her last meeting with Keith, all through the autumn she went to her appointments by bus, practically in disguise with dark glasses and an enveloping scarf. She looked out of the bus windows, at people in groups, in families, in couples, alone. She noted especially women's handbags, how vulnerable they looked, how ready to be snatched, something she had never bothered to notice before. And it reminded her how, after Martin's death, she noticed how many couples there were. She was a single person, the only single person in the world and everyone else was a half of a couple. Especially she noticed how many of the men looked older than Martin. They walked beside their wives, carrying shopping bags, they paused beside their wives to look in shop windows, things Martin would have hated doing, unless maybe it was the price of being still alive.

He would have hated this flat too, Martin. She looks around at the bare magnolia walls, the big flat window, trying to imagine him in this space. It almost makes her laugh, the idea is so impossible. Maybe, she thinks, maybe he only married me to get his hands on the house. But she knows it's not true.

Why did I marry him though? What on earth did I think I was doing? Viv would say – she has said it, reasonably politely, in the past – that Joan married Martin only because he was a direct replacement for her father. That was the story she and Colin made up between them, that Joan had that hippy boyfriend who let her down in some way that they never knew about in detail, so she got rid of him and reverted to a nice safe marriage with someone of her own sort. Her own family even. Joan could see the justice of what they believed but she didn't agree. She saw them – Viv and Colin – as behaving like children, conspiratorial children, who made themselves feel better by criticising everyone else's relationships.

Colin was Martin's younger brother but he knew nothing about what he was like. There were Joneses and there were Joneses.

She imagines telling Martin she has sold her new car. Five months old and less than two thousand miles on the clock and now it belongs to someone else. Someone else is getting the benefit of her initial outlay and her careful and parsimonious use. Martin would be furious.

She puts the cards she has written in a pile for posting, Carenza's, by chance, is on the top. She lives in the Midlands now, still working in local government, still boasting about her sons and their sporting achievements in every annual newsletter. 'Unfriend me,' Joan sometimes thinks as she opens the envelope.

It must be a quarter of a century at least since she was sent, along with two young men who were said to know about computers, to a conference on networking. This was when 'networking' meant hooking one or more computers up together and sharing their information – this was before the internet made all things possible. Joan knew nothing about computers; her job on this day was to chaperon the two young men and restrain them from getting too carried away by new and wonderful innovations which would cost the council money.

She failed to recognise Carenza when she stopped in front of her in a coffee queue, but Carenza knew her, and pounced on her, and talked to her for the rest of the day, without stopping, it seemed, and pressed upon Joan the addresses and phone numbers of the entire Badger family. Joan was relieved to get away from her at the end of it, but the meeting had a strange effect on her. She was fidgety. She told Martin about meeting her but he was more interested in the technical news she brought back. Joan lay awake one night and thought how glad she was that Carenza had not become her sister-in-law, and how it just went to show how things worked out for the best, in spite of all the anguish. Then the next day she took advantage of having the office to herself in the late afternoon, and phoned him. So it was that the Christmas cards began.

She looks out of her front window, towards the park. A misty rain has been falling all day and few people are about in the wet and cold. There are no leaves left on the trees and no movement among the branches. Cars swish past with their lights on. Joan watches until the last of the children have walked past on their way home from school. Then she shivers, and closes the curtains, and wonders what to do next.

*

'She doesn't pick up the phone when I call,' says Viv. 'Hardly ever. I text her but she doesn't reply.'

I call her, says Rachel, 'and she says nothing.'

'Nothing at all?'

'Well no, not nothing at all, but nothing sensible. Just, Oh, and, I suppose so. I ask her what she does and she says, Oh, you know, this and that. What does she do?'

'I don't know,' says Viv. 'She says the same to me. She won't come out and see me, she won't let me in to see her. She pretends she's not in, but I can see the light's on. I ring the intercom, she doesn't answer. She can't know it's me at the door, so she must be the same with everyone.'

'What can we do?' says Rachel.

'I know,' says Viv. 'It's hard for you, being so far away. I know you're worried about her, I bet even she's worried about herself. Of course I'll go on keeping an eye on her, as much as I can, but you have to understand, she doesn't welcome it, it's not easy even getting to see her.'

The phone call from Rachel on Sunday evenings has become a settled routine, – well, Viv doesn't mind, it's good to be able to discuss the problem of Joan, and if it helps Rachel, that's good too.

171

'She'll talk to me on the phone,' says Rachel, 'as long as it's about me. If I ask her questions about how she is, she just bats them away. And if I mention that man she hangs up on me.'

'Does she see anyone?' they ask each other, but they are unable to answer the question.

'Surely the hospital would notice if she was really in a state?' but they both know that it is asking a lot of a fracture clinic or a physiotherapist to diagnose a mental disorder in the course of a five minute appointment.

They have gone over and over it, speculating, guessing, until they agree that there is no point and that at Christmas Rachel will come down and see her mother and find out how she really is.

Viv puts the phone down and surveys the week ahead, wondering again how she can entice Joan to do something outside the flat, or even let Viv into the flat for a short visit. Or even answer her phone. She has offered Joan all her activities, first those she thought she would like and later even those she thought she would hate. But Joan will not agree to do anything active, no form of dancing or singing. She does not want to help anyone else so the charity shop and the food bank are out of the picture. And she doesn't want to be sociable. Viv has been considerably more pushy than she used to be in the days when Joan seemed to be reasonably happy and active with her own pursuits. Whatever they might have been. Being pushy doesn't work with Joan. But there is no one else to do it. She seems to have no other friends.

Her arm healed up without any problem, she has told Rachel, as good as new. But will she go out? No she will not. Agoraphobic? Or just awkward? She must get her groceries delivered.

'What do you do all day?' Viv more than once asked her in the days when they could still speak on the phone and Joan said nothing though Viv imagined her waving a hand vaguely at the TV. One of the problems, as Viv sees it, is that she has never had the real conversation about Bill and what he represents.

Or could it be that this is all a lie, and that really Joan is out having a good time with Mr Fairlie. Keith Fairlie who no longer comes to the choir, even though Richard has dropped the questionable songs from *Hair* in favour of things like safe and jolly songs by the Monkees and the Beatles. No one knows what really happened about all that – was it just a wind-up on Richard's part? Or did Keith Fairlie really intervene, and then withdraw, from embarrassment, or pique?

Pamela still isn't happy though. 'Let's go to San Fran bloody Cisco,' she says. 'I don't think so.'

*

Viv receives a package through the post. In it is Joan's address book and her own earrings. About time too, she thinks, but is nevertheless pleased to have them again. She checks inside the battered jiffy bag but there is no message, no card.

Perhaps this is the thing that will enable her to see Joan. She has been surprised by how much she has missed her. She dials the number and Joan, for a change, actually picks up the phone.

'It's Viv,' says Viv. 'How are you?'

'I'm fine,' says Joan. She does not add, What do you want, but Viv can hear it anyway.

'I've got a surprise for you,' says Viv.

'What?'

'I can't tell you, it wouldn't be a surprise if I did. Can I pop round and see you? I won't stay long.'

'I'm busy,' says Joan, and puts the phone down.

Viv feels like crying. She has to blink a bit, and then begins to feel angry. What is the matter with Joan? She has never been known to be rude before. Private, yes, defended, yes, but never before so hostile. What is it that she thinks Viv has done to her? Or has she never even liked Viv from the beginning, but now, in her odd state, can't be bothered to hide the fact? It is weeks since Viv has managed to see her, and now it looks like it will be Christmas before Joan will allow it. If indeed she will allow it.

Viv thinks of the Christmas after Arthur died, only a few months after, when Joan had come back to Sheffield and was living, as unhappy as it was possible to be, with Vicky in the big house, and working down the corridor from Viv, at the Town Hall. It was probably the worst Christmas any of them ever spent in the whole of their lives. Vicky dressed entirely in black the whole time, which Viv felt was a mite self-dramatising.

'I bet even her nightie is black,' she said to Joan, but Joan did not smile.

Clothes were a big issue for her at that time, in a different way. All her winter clothes were still down in London, and in spite of requests, had not been sent on to her. 'I'm not going down to get them,' she said. 'I said I'm not, and I'm not.'

She was still having tearful phone calls with the London ex-boyfriend, and had also started seeing her second cousin Martin. On the rebound, Viv called it. He bought her a pair of boots for Christmas, which was extravagant, Viv thought, when they had only been going out for a matter of weeks.

That Christmas was when Vicky revealed the content of Arthur's topsy-turvy will. Vicky was to get all the money, and Joan was to have the house.

'I don't want it,' she kept saying, though it had been her mother's house and Viv was pretty sure she did want it.

'Sell it,' advised Vicky.

'To you?' said Joan. Maybe her tone of voice was not intended to be rude and abrupt, but it came out that way and Viv could see that her mother was offended, when she was only trying to help.

'I just think the money will be more use to you than a great big old house,' said Vicky.

'If my dad wanted me to have it,' said Joan, 'then I'll have it, and I'll live in it.'

And by the time the next Christmas came around, Joan and Martin had had a quiet little wedding and were established in the house she had grown up in. Vicky had retired on the money she'd been left and moved away to Bridlington – (why would she do that, Viv still wonders, when all her friends and her only daughter were still in Sheffield) – where she stayed until, much later, she followed Roland down to the south-west, to a granny annexe built on to his house. Where she remains to this day, nearly ninety and still stubbornly cooking and cleaning.

That Christmas there was a little party on Boxing Day. People – mostly men from Martin's rugby club, and their wives – stood around nibbling stuffed eggs and Ritz crackers spread with pate, and smoking. Joan's replacement wardrobe was less impressive, Viv thought, than her old, lost one; she wore a plain black long skirt for the party, with a sensible dull sweater. She had cut her long hair and taken up a neat auburn bob which was to last her, latterly with the assistance of the colourist, until now.

Viv was there, with a boyfriend; and Martin's brother Colin and his wife, who brought with them their two year old son and their month old baby. Halfway through the evening, as Viv was going upstairs to the bathroom, she met Colin coming down, from checking on the children, and he grabbed her on the stairs and kissed her very firmly on the mouth.

Halfway up the stairs, thinks Viv nowadays, when she thinks of him at all, neither one thing nor the other. When she got to the top and looked down at him, he was standing at the bottom looking up at her. He winked. Later, when Carol was upstairs feeding the baby, Colin stood next to Viv in the kitchen, fondling her bottom as they leaned against the stripped pine kitchen units, so lately installed by Vicky.

The three years it took for Joan to conceive and carry and give birth to Rachel were employed by Colin and Viv in an extra-marital affair, and by Colin and Carol in unpicking a fairly serviceable marriage, so that he could marry Viv instead.

In the years that Viv was married to Colin, they always saw Joan and Martin at Christmas, sometimes for the whole two days, sometimes for one of them. Sometimes just for a drink, or as a part of a bigger gathering. Sometimes they arranged it so that they took Colin's children, sometimes not. And then, when he and Viv divorced, and he remarried Carol, Viv was dropped from the party list.

'You understand,' Joan said to her, as they ate a lunch in the Egg Box canteen. 'I can see you any time, but Colin is Martin's only relative now.'

'I don't mind,' said Viv, although she did. 'But if you want to ask me, I think I can get through an hour or two without battering Carol to fragments. We get on all right actually.'

'Let's not put it to the test,' said Joan. 'Maybe next year.'

Since Martin died though, Viv has become an indispensable part of Christmas for Joan and for Rachel. She is the one who remembers the old days, can tell the funny stories, will fit in with whatever mood they are in, can get a little sentimental if necessary. As the wife – however ex – of Colin, she qualifies as family again. So usually she goes for Christmas dinner, the three of them cooking together in the kitchen, drinking as they go, and drinking so much that she has to stay overnight. Then on Boxing Day they might have a walk through the park to blow away the cobwebs, before eating and drinking some more.

This year, it has been apparent that Joan will not invite her to come, or even speak long enough to confirm that she is not invited. Still Rachel has made a plan. She will spend Christmas Day with her mother

176

– 'Nice quiet time, you know. Let her get used to me.'
– and Viv will come over on Boxing Day. 'I'm sure
she wants to see you really,' said Rachel. 'If she
doesn't, well, I do.' Which warmed Viv's heart.

So this year Viv spends Christmas day on her own –
that is, she makes a visit to Daniel and Callum, with
presents, declines without any anguish the offer of
staying for dinner and then spends the rest of the day
on her own. Her neighbours have all gone away – the
students home to their families, the couple on the
other side presumably to some part of their family.
Viv doesn't mind – she has nice things to eat and
opens a bottle of white wine which will last her until
she goes to bed. Just another day, and she has an
outing the following day to look forward to.

She gets up and sets out cheerfully to walk to
Joan's flat. She takes presents for Joan and for Rachel,
and flowers, and a bottle. And Joan's address book.
She gains entry to the building for the first time since
the break-in, and goes up to the first floor. Rachel
opens the door.

Viv hugs Rachel and then becomes aware that she
is making a face at her which is some kind of
warning. Her eyes are fiercely wide open and she
puts her finger to her lips until they are in the sitting
room.

'Where's your mum?' Viv whispers it.

'She's in her room, getting dressed. She can't
decide what to wear.'

'Does it matter?' Rachel is wearing leggings and a
baggy jumper, Viv a new sweater and her most
festive earrings.

Rachel sits down suddenly as if she is a puppet
whose strings have been released. 'I'm so glad you're
here Auntie.'

Viv feels a little thrill at being called Auntie – she
is not, most of the time, anything to anybody and it is
years since Rachel has said it. She says, 'Is it hard
going?'

'I'm so worried about her. She's depressed, I'm sure that's what it is, but she won't go to the doctor, and I've got to go home tomorrow, my train's booked. She's gone very peculiar.'

When Joan finally appears Viv feels that to most people, to anyone who didn't know her, she could seem quite normal. But to herself and Rachel it is clear that she is not the Joan they are used to.

Lipstick is the first thing Viv notices. Joan is usually the last word in discreet make-up – foundation, mascara, lipstick of a subtle peachy pink, all carefully applied. The fact that she even owns a scarlet lipstick is a worry. She has made up her eyes as well, as if to deny the fact that they are hers. She is wearing a dress, sleeveless and low-necked, that she probably bought for a golf club dance some time about twenty years ago, a particularly unpleasant shade of green and much too big for her. She has certainly lost some weight over the last few months. The skin on her upper arms hangs as if there is no muscle underneath. Her hair, far from being her trademark short bob, has grown so much that she has tied it back in a clumsy ponytail. She does not seem to realise that while the ponytail is auburn, the hair scraped back over her head is dull and grey. Viv thinks that this is the first time she has ever seen Joan's ears, and has to stop herself commenting on how unusually big they are.

But there is a whole day to get through and Viv chooses to remain cheerful. 'You look lovely,' she says. 'I'm sorry I didn't dress up, I didn't know what to wear.'

'Rachel asked you to come,' says Joan. 'I didn't think there'd be room for us all in this little flat.' She sounds like she always does, straightforward and sober, but it is obvious that this little speech is an excuse that she has been some time making up, and probably rehearsing.

'We can squeeze in,' says Viv, too heartily it sounds to her own ears. 'Did you have a nice day yesterday?'

'No,' says Joan, and Rachel adds, 'We were very quiet, weren't we Mum?'

'I suppose,' says Joan to Viv, 'you've been brought in to liven things up.'

'I always see you at Christmas,' says Viv stoutly. 'Custom and practice you know. It wouldn't be Christmas if I didn't come to yours.' She thinks to herself that Joan is not depressed, but sulking. She's working very hard, thinks Viv, to keep her face straight, she's like a little kid who won't give up her bad mood even when it would be to her advantage. But what do I know? she has to add to herself.

Viv gives scarves for Christmas. Beautiful ones, even though they came from the charity shop – as she always does, she has been looking out all year for something with distinction and a designer label. She has sewn little fabric bags to serve as packaging, and wrapped them in paper tied with an intricate bow. She is good at this sort of thing. Rachel is delighted with hers. Joan puts hers aside, murmuring something.

Rude, thinks Viv. She hands over Joan's address book, unwrapped. She planned to make a joke out of it, a game ('Guess what I've got here.') But she can see there is no point. Joan looks at it, and puts it to one side, without looking inside, on top of the scarf.

She's dying to ask, thinks Viv, but she won't let herself.

Rachel, who also has practical talents, has cooked an elegant lunch of salmon en croute. They have polished off the remains of yesterday's two desserts and are on their second bottle of wine ('Go for it,' Viv said, 'I can get a taxi.') when they move from the table. Nuts and oranges and chocolates are on the coffee table. Viv and Rachel sit together on the sofa, Joan leans back in her armchair and closes her eyes.

'I'm going to ask you something,' says Viv. She has been trying to think of an indirect way to get Joan to talk. 'Did you ever go to a music festival? Like the Isle of Wight.'

Joan does not open her eyes. 'Hated every minute,' she says, and it is clear that she will say no more.

Viv knows when to give up. 'So Rachel, are you still with Ryan? He seemed a nice young man. Has your mother met him yet?'

Viv says this with her eyes on Joan, but she makes no move to show whether or not she's interested.

Rachel makes a face. 'He's still around,' she says. 'He is nice, but so young. Not thirty yet, so I don't know if it will come to anything. I'm ready to settle down, me, but I'm not sure if he is.'

'Job going OK?'

'I love it,' says Rachel. 'Conservation buildings are definitely my thing. Much more interesting than new-builds and kitchen extensions.'

'I thought I'd see you in your hard hat when we came, and there you were dressed up to the nines.'

'I was in a meeting, luckily for you, or you wouldn't have got hold of me at all.' She smiles, all dimples. 'It's quite good fun, showing up in a skirt and heels, when they've only seen me in site clothes.'

'But you're beautiful Miss Jones,' says Viv. They are quiet for a little while. Joan does not move, except for her exposed collar bones rising and falling as she breathes.

'That was so bizarre,' says Rachel. 'When you turned up at mine. Ryan was so totally confused – he was on nights you see and he'd just got to bed.'

Viv shakes her head. They have referred to the incident before of course, during their phone calls, but never after three quarters of a bottle of wine each, and this is a new detail.

'I was confused myself,' she says. 'It was a weird thing to get involved in.'

'And you looked so funny,' says Rachel. 'Honestly, your hair was all over the place and your face was all smudged.'

'I probably smelled rank. I'd been sleeping in my clothes. Well, you saw that van – it didn't have modern conveniences like some do.'

'It was a heap of rust,' says Rachel. 'Ryan said you'd never make it over the border.'

'Well, he was right,' says Viv. She looks at Joan, who has not moved. 'I've never told you this bit – it's quite embarrassing really – but me and Bill fell out after we left you, and I ended up hitching a lift home.' Put like that, it doesn't sound too traumatic, she thinks, but Rachel chokes on her chocolate caramel.

'You didn't.'

'I did.'

'Go on then. Tell me about it.'

Viv hesitates. Joan might be listening. But then what the hell, she would have told her back in September if there had been a chance to, why should she not be told now?

'He was a funny bloke, Bill.' She tells Rachel the funny version of the story, camping up the accents of the Dutch lorry driver and the old Scotsman. She gets up off the sofa to act out the last mile's uphill walking, and Rachel laughs as she is meant to do. Joan moves a little, as if Viv's voice has disturbed her sleep.

'I'll put the kettle on,' says Rachel.

'Let me help you wash up.'

'I can't believe,' says Rachel, getting to her feet, 'what's really strange is the coincidence. Don't you think? You and Mum, on the same day, both losing your belongings, at opposite ends of the country. You couldn't make it up. No, don't get up, it will all go in the dishwasher, sit there, I'll bring you a cup of tea. And a piece of Christmas cake?'

'Well, why not. It's only once a year.' Though Viv has one of her own at home, which she will be eating on her own for the foreseeable future.

Rachel is going home to Paisley. Joan has closed the door on her and watched out of the window as she has climbed into a taxi and looked up and waved. Joan lifts her hand in reply, then lets it drop. Waving is too much effort.

Bill? Who in the world is Bill?

She goes into the guest bedroom, intending to strip Rachel's bed, but sits on it instead, looking at the wall. This has been her first Christmas in this new home. Inauspicious. Downright depressing. Maybe I should move house, she thinks, but even the fleeting idea brings on panic, and she knows at that moment that she is here for good. Until they carry me out feet first.

She thinks with longing of her proper home. That big solid house, detached and surrounded by garden, screened from the big solid houses on either side by laurel and holly and viburnum. Christmas there was exactly as it should be. Central heating on full tilt, neighbours invited in for drinks and canapés, carol singers outside, knocking respectfully on the door and being offered hot mince pies. Her father broad and rosy in his suit, telling jokes and drinking too much. The tree so tall it had to stand in the hall, the holly wreath on the door, the smell of cooking, the big deep armchairs. How she had loved it as a child. She used to turn off the hall lights and sit on the stairs just looking at the tree. Coloured lights and baubles, tin and glass and tinsel. Maybe there was less colour in the world in those days. Maybe there was less shininess. Or maybe it was just being a little girl that made her chest feel tight and breathless with the beauty of it.

Later on, of course, she despised it. When she met people who mocked and derided the way she and her parents lived, when she learned the word bourgeois, when she had to keep Aughton away from her home because he would sneer at it for being too comfortable, and her parents for being too prosperous.

'We're not posh,' she had to protest. 'My dad worked his way up through being a draughtsman, he never went to Oxford or anything. We're not even rich.' Because she had been told by both her parents, consistently, that they were not rich, and that she was not going to be spoiled by getting everything she wanted. She could have riding lessons, but not a horse. Only rich girls had horses. They would pay for her to go on a trip with the school, skiing, but it was out of the question for them all to go as a family – only rich families would do that. Joan went to High Storrs, which was a grammar school, and a good one, they said, but rich girls went to the Girls' High, which was private.

Her parents were Sheffield people, with Sheffield accents. Her mother bought her clothes at Cole Brothers, but was not above going to the market for fish or vegetables. She employed a woman called Mrs Twigg to help with the cleaning, but only two mornings a week, not every day. They were churchgoers, but United Reform, not C of E. There was enough money coming in for her mother not to work outside the home after Joan was born. She did hospital visiting and belonged to the Mothers' Union and the Townswomen's Guild. Their house was substantial, and by the time Joan was a teenager, paid for.

'We could get twelve thousand for this property,' said her father with immense satisfaction, at about the time Joan went off to university. But they did not feel rich, and Joan found that Essex University contained people substantially better off than she was, girls with sports cars, girls who went home to other countries in the summer and returned with complete new wardrobes of fashions which a trip to Cole Brothers, or even Oxford Street, would not have been able to supply. On the other hand, there were people who lived entirely upon their grants, some of them making a big thing of it, boys walking round in donkey jackets revving up their cockney accents.

She had no more money than other people, it was just that hers came from her father, not from the local council. And because he kept to the letter of what the poorer students received, he did not include, as some councils did, fares home every term, or bus fares to and from the university every day. Years later, when Rachel went to Liverpool she did not qualify for a grant because of what Martin and Joan earned between them. But she took out a loan, because she could, and spent it – Joan paid it off for her later. Nowadays, so Joan gathers, they would have been stumping up nine thousand a year, on top.

She goes over, again and again, in her mind, like a tune she can't get rid of, the years since she last saw Aughton. They were in love, there is no doubt about that. Just because he was more musical than she was, more idealistic, more carefree, just because she was more cautious, better at spelling, more sensitive to what other people might think – the differences made no difference. How they felt was how they felt, and what they felt was love. They felt no doubt.

For four and a half months after she left him standing in the dark, for all those months, she had the choice to go back to him. He wrote her letters, he made phone calls to her house, often late at night, phone calls where she could almost smell the whisky, where they both cried down the phone. He said sorry, he promised never to do it again – well though, how could he? She didn't have another father to die.

She said sorry, she wished things were different, she couldn't even meet him, she couldn't even see him as a friend, she couldn't leave Sheffield, maybe not ever and no, he couldn't come up and see her, no, it wouldn't work, it would make things worse. No, she kept on saying, and he kept on saying, Why.

Several times a week she saw her cousin Martin. He was not such a close relative, her father's cousin's son, only a pair of great grandparents in common, someone she had met a few times as a child, at weddings and such occasions. Older than Aughton by several years, professionally qualified and gainfully employed in manful and useful work. Sometimes they went to the cinema, sometimes they went for a drink at the rugby club, bleak and comfortless though it was there in the clubhouse on a week night. They did not have much in common to talk about and she found it quite restful.

Just before Christmas, after the Rugby Cub dinner dance, walking home under a black sky sprinkled with frosty stars, Martin suggested that they could be married.

No, she said, she didn't want to marry anyone. Then at Christmas he came to the house with a large box wrapped in paper decorated with silver bells, and inside the box was a pair of brown suede boots, slightly darker in colour than the ones she had left in London, but otherwise identical.

'How did you know,' she said, and he said, 'What do you mean? Know what?'

'How much I missed my boots.'

And the next time he proposed that they should be married, which happened on New Year's Day in the afternoon, she said yes. They were walking through Endcliffe Park. She was wearing her new boots. Without any discussion she went with him, for the first time, to his little flat and for the first time since Corfu she made love with someone. Or rather, she allowed someone to make love to her. The next time Aughton phoned – from a call box in Brightlingsea, he informed her – she was able to tell him she was planning to marry in the spring.

JANUARY

Bill picks up the phone.

'Hi Dad.'

'Em,' he says, pleased. 'Happy New Year.'

'Yes well,' she says. 'It's not really happy is it? For any of us I mean.'

'I suppose not,' he says. This may be the first time that he considers that Emily and Laura could have been feeling as bad as he does.

'What have you been doing?'

'Not a lot,' he says. 'Just getting through the days, to be truthful. What about you? How was Christmas?'

'All right I suppose. No, actually, they are nice people. We managed.'

It's not as if, thinks Bill, we ever had some big family thing here; it must be a decade since we saw the girls at Christmas. 'So,' he says. 'Did you go out last night? You don't sound like a person with a hangover.'

'Stayed in,' she says. 'Matt's on early shift this morning. You?'

'Stayed in too. I'm not very good in company at the moment.'

'Not been away anywhere then? No trips to Sheffield?'

'Em,' he says. 'I don't know what you're thinking, but you're wrong. There's no one in Sheffield, or anywhere else. Only Ricky Pyke and he doesn't count for much.'

'I'm sorry,' she says, and then is quiet for so long that he thinks he might have to end the call out of consideration for her.

'Have you heard from Loz?' she says at last.

'No. Have you?'

'She messaged me,' she says. 'She's on her way back. She says she might come and see you.'

'When?'

'This week I guess. Before she goes back to work.'

After he has said goodbye to Emily, Bill wonders whether Laura will really come. She has just spent ten days in Thailand, she will be going home to Somerset, where she is a teaching assistant in a primary school. She surely won't have time to be trekking up to Essex before term starts next week.

But she phones the next day.

'Dad.'

He does not at first recognise her voice, clogged as it is with tears and tiredness.

'Dad. Can you come and get me?'

'Loz? Is that you? Where are you?'

'At the station Dad. There's no buses and I've no money, and there's no taxis anyway. Come and get me.' She sounds whiney, and he doesn't believe there are no taxis, but he decides, in the absence of a good excuse and because she is, after all, his daughter, he will go anyway.

When he pulls up outside the station he sees her straight away, there being no one else around by now. She is hugging herself with cold, wearing only jeans and a thin jacket over a t-shirt. She does not manage to smile at him, just throws her rucksack on the back seat and herself in the front, and reaches immediately to turn up the heater. It dawns on Bill that she has come straight from the airport, still in her holiday clothes.

'What's up Loz?' he says. 'I thought you would be going home.'

'What home?' she says.

'Flat in Taunton?' he says, diffidently. 'That you share with –'

'Julian,' she supplies, bitterly. 'I'll tell you later Dad, right now I just want to sleep. When I've had something to eat.'

He can't ask her, the signs being what they are, if she had a good holiday, so he says nothing as he drives her through the dusk of the midwinter afternoon.

When she's had a bowl of cereal with hot milk and a plate of toast and honey – she always did have a nursery taste in food – she goes to what used to be her room. He hears her shout.

'Dad.'

'What?'

'What's happened to my bedroom?'

He goes to the bottom of the stairs. 'What's the matter?'

'It's all wrong,' she says, and he goes up to find her sitting on the bed, with mascara running down her cheeks.

'This isn't my bed,' she says. 'What happened to my bed?'

'Beds don't last for ever,' he says. You'd had it since you were twelve. This is the one from the spare bedroom – it hasn't had so much wear. And it's a double. I thought it would be better.'

'Did you throw Em's bed away too?'

'She took it. I don't think it was worth coming all the way from Cardiff for it, but she wanted it.'

'I wanted mine.'

What would Lydia do, thinks Bill. What would she say? 'I'm sorry,' he says. 'Look why don't you have a nice hot bath and an early night. You must be jet-lagged. You must be exhausted.' Does he sound caring, or just irritable?

She says nothing else, just sits there, sniffing and occasionally shivering. The words Drama Queen come into his head. She is a grown-up, isn't she? So why does she have to be such a pain, she must know how she looks and sounds. Then he knows that she can't help it, any more than he could help being rude to that Viv, or idiotic about Joan. He would like to put his arm round her – both arms even – and let her have a good cry, the way he must have done when she was little, but he does not dare. What would Lydia do?

'Leave me alone Dad,' she says finally, flatly. 'I'm going to have a little sleep. Jet-lag, that's all.'

As he closes the door he finds that his chest is painful with the by-now-familiar feeling of grief and helplessness. He wishes, beyond anything, that he could make it right for her.

Next day she is more composed, though in a grim sort of way. She is up early and he hears parcel tape being ripped off a cardboard box, and the crackle of plastic bags. It is the sound of her rootling through the remaining stuff in the spare bedroom.

After she has eaten breakfast – does she eat nothing but cereal? – she gets out Lydia's sewing box and sets to ripping the sleeves out of a jacket.

'Tea?' says Bill.

'Got any decaf? I'm going to need to sleep in a bit.'

'Fraid not. But I've got camomile.'

She looks up and smiles for the first time, gratefully. 'Yes please.'

She doesn't tell him much, over the next few days. Just that it was an awful holiday, she and Julian bickered and carped from start to finish. –'He just moans all the time, Dad.'– and ended by having a major row on the plane back. 'And none of the places were what we thought they'd be like, it was so busy and horrible and full of tourists.'

'What did you expect?' says Bill.

'I don't know,' she says miserably.

'Who's idea was it, anyway?'

'Mine,' she says. 'I thought it would be – oh I don't know. I haven't even paid for it yet.'

Bill wonders if he should offer her the money, just to cheer her up, but hesitates. Might she be insulted at being treated like a child? And how much money are they talking about anyway? And then to be fair to Em he would have to give her the same amount. It's too difficult and he puts the thought aside for later.

'There must have been some nice bits,' he says carefully. 'I mean, in ten days, or – '

'No,' she says. 'There weren't any.'

'So you and Julian –?'

189

She shrugs and he doesn't dare to ask any more.

At the weekend she goes home. Bill pays for her train ticket, which is about as eye-watering as a flight to Bangkok, and he squares it as far as Emily is concerned by remembering that she had all sorts of bits from the house.

He misses Laura now that she's gone, even though she never cheered up, never washed up, drank his cans of beer when she couldn't sleep, made him watch crap on TV and spent hours fiddling with her phone. The house now seems to echo all over again and he doesn't see how it will ever stop.

*

'Happy New Year Roly,' says Viv.

Her brother's voice comes back to her on the phone, sounding as if he was just about to go out and her call has distracted him.

'Oh. Hi Viv. Yes, Happy New Year to you too.'

'How's everything?' By which she means, How is their mother.

'Good. Yes, everything's good.'

She hears other voices in the room at his end, a child shouting, someone shushing it.

'You've got visitors. I'll call you another day.'

'Sorry Sis. Whole family's just turned up. I won't be able to hear a word you say.'

'Tell Mum I called.'

'Sure.'

'Speak to you soon. Love to everyone.'

She puts the phone down. 'Whole family' she thinks. What about me? But then, how different Roland's life is from hers. Three grown children with partners and children of their own, that big house with its sweep of gravel drive, the rituals, the friends, the cruises. How did he learn all that, she wonders again, when he was just a boy from Parson Cross, a clever boy, it's true, and a lucky one – lucky in his marriage and his profession, lucky, or clever, in his money affairs. But, thinks Viv, What happened to my share of the luck? She shakes herself. Roland would help her out if she needed it, but she never has needed it. She has enough, sufficient, she thinks – I have sufficient, I am self-sufficient. I don't want for anything. I don't want his life, I have my own. She has told herself this on other occasions and it has always done the trick.

*

Joan finds all the Christmas cards she received rammed into a drawer in her spare bedroom. She knows – though she had forgotten – that she put them there before Rachel came so that she didn't have to answer questions about where to display them, and wouldn't therefore have to spend at least a week looking at them, winking and leering from the sideboard.

It has always been her practice, as her mother did before her, to take the cards and decorations down on twelfth night, and read them once again, to enjoy them, and make a note of any that need a reply, a letter of condolence or congratulation; or sometimes, though rarely, a phone call to some distant aunt or cousin.

Thinking this, she shuts the drawer again, as if that will make them go away.

Still, they haunt her and at last she takes them out, intending to put them straight in the bin. But the habit is too strong and she sits down with them at the computer, ready to edit any details she has been informed of, and make a note of anyone she should really, definitely, undeniably contact.

There isn't anyone though. In all the cards, there are very few with any message at all beyond a stale and predictable greeting. Some people wish her joy of her new home, some hope vaguely they might see her soon, a few promise to stay in touch. There is no one, though, who needs her, Joan, to do anything – no condolences or congratulations for any event, any deaths, births and marriages are not considered to be of interest to her. Carenza sends her the news that Aughton's wife died, back in the spring, which is, if Carenza only knew it, not news to her at all.

Joan checks her emails. There is one from her bank informing her of new terms and conditions which she may wish to see by going to the website. That's all. She switches the computer off and tips the pile of cards into the recycling bin. She wonders what to do next.

FEBRUARY

Bill's phone rings one Sunday evening.

'How's it going?' says a voice which he fails at first to identify as Rick's.

'How's the choir going?' says Bill, when they have got over the confusion. It's really all he can think of to talk about – there never was much between him and Rick except music and beer, and music and marijuana.

'Are you going to come?' says Rick. 'I always get anxious about whether we'll fill the room.'

'I might,' says Bill. 'But how are the songs coming on? How's *Hair*?'

'I thought you would know,' says Richard. 'We abandoned that. I would have had a full-on rebellion if I'd tried to do it. Some of the women got a bit antsy about it all and yer man Fairlie, he spoke to me on the quiet and said he didn't think it was a goer, so we pulled the plug. And what do you know, then he went and left anyway, so I've only got five basses to work with now.'

'It was only a wind-up in the first place,' says Bill. It was only a joke, at first, that came out of one of their rare phone calls, a combination of a reminiscence about how they had met, and a question in Richard's head about what to do next with his choir. 'It was never going to happen. I thought you knew that.'

'I know, says Richard, 'I do know that, but I got quite attached to the idea. We've kept "What a Piece of Work is Man", but I'm not happy with it. It's kind of dead, it needs perking up somehow. Anyway, are you going to come, shall I keep a ticket for you? On the house so to speak, as you'll be coming so far.'

'I might,' says Bill again.

There seems not much else to say, but later, when there is nothing on TV and it is too early to go to bed – though not too early to fall asleep in the chair, which sometimes happens – Bill gets out Joanie's old album of *Hair* and puts it on. He's not a vinyl snob, not at all, but there is something warming about carrying out a sequence that requires some practice – dusting the record, blowing the dust off the needle, lifting the arm, putting it down in the right place at the right speed. His daughter Laura would never take the trouble to do this; her music comes at the touch of a screen, into her ear, not into the room. He listens critically this time, not nostalgically. And gets back on the phone to Richard.

'So, do you move on into the next song? That one about walking in space?'

'I'm not going there,' says Richard. 'It'll start the drugs issue all over again. I could be left with no choir at all.'

'Worse things happen,' says Bill. He means to be helpful.

'I've paid for the hall already,' says Richard. 'Anyway, even if I hadn't, I want it to go ahead. And I want them in a good mood too.'

'Well,' says Bill, 'is there another song they could segue into? What about "Let the Sunshine In"?'

'Different key,' says Richard, 'but you might be right. It could be done. Oggy, you may be a genius.'

*

It is a long winter. Viv, from her back door, sees snowdrops and primulas in bloom in the shelter of the wall, but her heart fails to lift as it should. The sun is noticeably higher in the sky, the evenings do not close in quite so early, so where is the springtime optimism, where is the rush of energy? Normally at this time, or even earlier, at the very first, tiniest snowdrop bud, she is full of plans and projects, full of hope and enterprise, but now, though she feels restless, it is a dissatisfied, irritable, grumpy feeling.

Nothing appeals to her any more, the world is flat and dull. She goes to bed at night at her usual time, and sleeps well at first, but wakes early, often before it is light, well before she likes to get up. She goes to her groups and activities as usual though, and people would probably not notice that she is not herself.

But Viv notices.

She closes the back door on the flowers, noticing that last year, and every other year, she would have been outside, in her slippers, lifting the snowdrops' heads to see the neat green markings inside, and then walking around the garden to see if there is anything new since yesterday. Is she getting old?

She catches sight of the man next door going past her window. She has had no further contact with either of them through the winter, doesn't know more than their names, and that she was once Mrs Fairlie. They will be thinking she likes to keep herself to herself, and it's not true, she doesn't, except that it is what she has been doing, ever since – well, ever since something, she's not sure what.

Today, for instance, a Tuesday, she would once have been meeting Joan for coffee, and although it hasn't happened for months she still misses her more on a Tuesday than any other day of the week. The Boxing Day visit did not thaw Joan by so much as a degree, may have even made things worse.

She is still worried about her. She still has long conversations with Rachel on the phone, wondering what happened, and what is still happening. Rachel is worried about Joan too. She and Viv compare the scraps of information they have but it hasn't helped them understand. She went to Essex, Bill came from Essex – surely more than a coincidence. But she claims to know no one called Bill; she claims she just went to have a look at her old university, and that's all she did. So why did she lie and tell Viv she was going to Paisley?

She lied to me, says Viv out loud. She turns on the tap and puts enough water in the kettle for just one cup of coffee, and resolves that she will not talk out loud. She will not become one of those mumbling old ladies who talk to their televisions and their cutlery and the coins in their purses. She continues, silently this time. It was undignified, how much she always wanted to be friends with Joan, ever since she first met her, even though she knew that Joan – better-educated, better-looking – was out of her league. Viv always looked forward to the next time Joan might be home, she always scampered round to Stumperlowe in the hope of seeing her, and she was always left feeling as if Joan did not notice her being there at all. Joan came home to see her father, because she loved him, and she went away again, often very suddenly, because it was hard for her to see him with his new wife instead of with her own mother. Viv worked that out. It was nothing to do with her. Joan was nothing to do with her. She had other friends in Sheffield – well, so did Viv, but they were not likely to overlap.

Only, finally, when Viv married Colin, did Joan take notice that she existed. Viv had joined the club of Joneses and had to be included. And then Joan came back, after Rachel started school, to the Town Hall to work, and she and Viv were colleagues. That was good, thinks Viv now, we had some laughs in those days.

She sits down and sips her coffee, resists the impulse to turn on the TV (she will *not* be one of those old ladies who watch daytime TV) and reaches an awful conclusion. It is not that Joan has changed towards Viv, it is that she has never felt towards her anything more than tolerant neutrality, and now she doesn't even bother to pretend that there is anything more.

She lied to me, thinks Viv again. It seems like a long time ago. She wonders how she can fill a Tuesday until it's time to go to line dancing, and decides to go into town for a look around the shops. On her way she posts her bowel cancer screening test, feeling sorry for whoever will have to open and deal with it, and feeling wonderfully grateful for the way it is done without her GP or anyone else having to poke things up her bum.

As she waits at the bus stop her neighbour Elaine – not such a new neighbour these days – approaches and stands next to her. Viv has had the certain knowledge, since she found out that Elaine was Fairlie's wife, that Elaine has avoided her. But maybe time has done its work on her. They smile, carefully.

'Everything OK?' says Elaine.

Viv gets a distinct impression that she is seen as a bit crazy, a bit chaotic, and it puts her on her dignity. 'Fine,' she says. 'And you?'

'Fine,' she says.

They both look along the road in case the bus is in sight.

'Finished decorating?' offers Viv.

'Nearly. Only the attic to do, and that can wait till next winter. Time to concentrate on the garden now.'

'You like gardening then?' Things seem to be going better.

'Very much,' she says, a little sadly perhaps.

'Did you have a garden where you were before? Big garden?'

'Pretty big. But I was working then and didn't have much time to do it. Now I've got time but only a small garden.'

'You've downsized,' says Viv.

'I suppose I have.'

I, Viv notices, not we.

They sit together on the bus, commenting on the weather, the roadworks, the new community libraries – negotiating their way, Viv feels, through safe neutral subjects towards a possible friendship. They have after all, the prospect of ten or twenty years of living next door to each other.

'You go out a lot,' observes Elaine.

'Keeping busy,' says Viv. 'No good sitting in watching the telly. You have to keep on doing something.'

'What do you do?'

'All sorts. Tonight I'll go to my choir.'

'I'd like to join a choir.'

'Tell you what – come to our concert – it's in May, and if you like it, you could join.'

'I will. We'll both come.'

'I'll be splitting some of my plants soon,' says Viv. 'Would you like some?'

Thank you very much,' says Elaine. 'That will help to fill the garden.'

'Old Marjorie couldn't really get a lot done out there,' says Viv. 'Not that she was very interested in gardening at the best of times.'

Elaine gets up to get off the bus. 'You'll have to come and have a cup of tea with me one day,' she says.

Take that Joan, says Viv to herself, and immediately feels sad again.

*

The window cleaners are here. Joan does not want them, she does not want her windows cleaned, she does not want men on ladders suddenly appearing in view and looking at her as she stands or sits, or walks about. What are you supposed to do when there are young men looking at you? She would like to lie on her bed and look at the ceiling, or stand close to the window and look down at the garages, or sit on the floor and look into space. She does not want to look busy, but she feels she must.

She pulls a cookery book at random from the cupboard and sits at the kitchen table with it open. She was never an ambitious cook. Martin was never an ambitious eater. He liked meat and plenty of it, grilled, roasted or fried, with gravy and vegetables. Pies and stews, they went down all right, but anything with rice or pasta brought out the suspicion in him, though he never turned anything down. You could say, really, that he was easy to cater for. She wonders why she has not already thrown this particular book away – it is glossy and almost unused and should have gone to the charity shop along with the other unwanted ones that she managed to acquire in the course of her life.

The young man's ladder bangs against the window sill and his head appears, and his arm and his squeegee. She bends her head over the book as if she's too busy to notice him. It is, she recalls, a book that Martin's great aunt gave them for a wedding present; it is a lavishly illustrated book for the kind of life that she never wanted to live – detailed instructions for functions of all kinds, family picnics, engagement parties, after-theatre dinners, ideas for Hallowe'en and Easter and Christmas, party food for toddlers and teenagers. There are pictures of tables spread with untouched arrays of luxury dishes, displayed on the sort of heavy peasant crockery that was popular in the 1970s. And there are, on some of the pages, small groups of delighted people eating asparagus rolls and spicy cheese sables (whatever *they* were), women dressed like peasants to go with the crockery, men in suits, smoking as they eat, all pretending to live a life that Joan feels she never lived, a life of social competence and participation.

This was the very book, she knows, that she used for their very first foray into 'entertaining.' It was soon after they married; it was the thing to do, they believed, to invite some people round for a party at Christmas. She remembers worrying for a fortnight about the catering; she remembers the exhaustive instructions from this very book. She had to source the capers and the canned chestnuts from a delicatessen – try finding one of those in Sheffield in 1974; she had to follow a timetable that began 'One month ahead' and went on until the actual day of the party was laid down for her in half-hourly doses. She remembers trying to make 'fans' out of gherkins that resembled even remotely the ones in the book. And then not everyone who had been invited actually turned up. Maybe they had had enough of Christmas by then, maybe they had run out of energy or goodwill. Viv was there, and Colin and Carol, and some neighbours who were compulsory because her father had always asked them in over Christmas, and some people from the rugby club, and a couple of old school friends of hers. Joan was miserable throughout.

The window cleaner now rings the doorbell for his money. Joan closes the book and goes to pay him. When she comes back into the room she decides, wedding present or no, it's going to follow all of the other clutter that she does not have space for in her life. But it is too big to fit in the kitchen bin and she puts it, defeated, back in the cupboard and wonders what she should eat.

MARCH

Six months have made a difference to Lydia's house. Bill's house. True, the garage is jam-packed with stuff – furniture, boxes, bags, electrical items, objects of sentimental significance – but the house is a showpiece. Every room is clean. Every curled up bit of wallpaper is stuck down, all the woodwork freshly painted. All the cupboards are shipshape. Every light fitting contains a light bulb, every remote control contains a live battery. Letters are in the letter rack, magazines are in the magazine rack, vegetables are in the vegetable rack. Regrets in the regret rack.

He should now be ready to put it on the market. He should phone some estate agents and get some valuations, and he should do it soon before his housewifely tidiness begins to slip. But days go by, and his list, that begins, 'Estate agent re house' has been tidied away with all the other papers, and he has not looked at it. Not that he has forgotten it; he knows well enough what his next step is. He has discussed it with Laura and Emily, and promised that when he has sold it and bought something smaller, he will give them some money so that they too can get on the property ladder and start climbing it.

He never thought, when he first came back here, and began digging for a living, that he would be the owner of a house. Rented squalor was the way of life that he chose then, or, to put it another way, freedom from bourgeois values and freedom from the tyranny of bank managers was what he chose. Buying a house was all to do with Lydia. She could let her errant ex-husband buy her out of their newly-built newly-weds' house in Tabor Close, and use the money as a deposit on this one. Bill had shrugged his shoulders and gone along with it. It was a roof, and more than that, it was a project, to refurbish and renovate what was, actually, a pretty run down piece of property into a family home. Lyd wanted a family home, and Bill found gradually that he was happy with the idea too. So, under the influence of DIY, the counter-culture began to fade away.

He looks around now at the house and remembers all the work they did. Not much remains of the original building except the walls. Central heating in 1976 was their first big innovation, with the oil tank outside the back door to run it – a mistake, as the oil price carried on increasing and they had to make a costly decision to convert to gas. The cork tile floor that they laid in the kitchen, the shelves in the alcoves, the homemade kitchen units – they have all been superseded by later fashions. The 1980s came in with a rush and brought a new roof and new windows, made to order to look as much like the originals as it was possible for double glazing to do. In the 1990s most of the walls needed replastering, simply because of their age, and the outside needed to be repainted, going from pink to white.

There was a constant demand for redecorating, as the girls grew up and needed beds instead of cots, wardrobes instead of toy boxes, teenage wallpaper instead of My Little Pony. Lydia was a homemaker, no doubt about it, and Bill was happy for it to be so. Lydia said it should happen, Lydia looked at magazines and catalogues, Lydia shopped and bought and ordered, and she and Bill worked together, measuring cutting, pasting. Washing down, sanding down, painting. Hanging curtains, laying carpets.

It is not until Bill finds himself asking Pete whether or not it would be all right to borrow the van again that he realises he has been taking Rick's invitation seriously.

'Not a problem,' says Pete. 'As long I can use the boat.'

'Sure,' says Bill.

He has no idea what he hopes to achieve. Getting together with Joanie? – not a chance, he knows, and is not even sure if he would want it. Making his peace with Viv? – even more unlikely. Just coming clean? – probably that's the most he can hope for. Because he has heard nothing. They will have discussed him and his stupidity for months. They will still be laughing at his presumption and his incompetence. He would like to hear what they have to say, these women.

It is too late. It is forty years too late. He could have made a protest at the news that she was marrying that man. He knew she was not in love with her cousin. He could hear it in her voice as she told him she was. He could have got on a train and gone up and made her run away with him. Made her. But it was something about the word. Married. I'm getting married, she said. Not, I've got a new boyfriend. He would have done something about that. No – 'married' was just too grown up for him. He couldn't, then, compete with the cut and dried respectability of 'married.'

*

The dog looks miserably at the door and Joan looks miserably at the dog. If she was herself, she knows, she would be more than miserable, she would be furious with Rachel, unspeakably angry at such an intrusion. Who would have believed anyway that you can order a dog on the internet? That someone will choose it for you, and deliver it to your door, along with a bag of food, and a lead and a bowl and a bed, without enquiring at all – at all! – whether you agree to it. She was so taken aback that she accepted it, bewildered, on the back foot, and the smiling young man went away, presumably feeling that he had done a good job. Another dog rescued, another happy customer.

'Come back,' she called to him, but her voice came out as a whisper and she was left looking at the paper he had given her. This tells her that she is in possession of Minnie, a female whippet, age more than six months and less than one year, fully vaccinated and house-trained, ordered and paid for in full by Ms Rachel Jones.

'How dare she,' thinks Joan, but even the voice in her head is a whisper. She wonders if there is anyone she can pass the dog on to, but it is so long since she has spoken to anyone, even Viv, that she would not have the nerve to approach them.

The dog puts its head down on the floor. Miserable, scrawny looking thing, thinks Joan. She is not unused to dogs. Probably that was in Rachel's mind when she did this thing. She will have remembered the bumbling old retriever of her childhood and how Joan was always the one to take him out, except when Martin was on holiday from work – that is, rarely. And it was true that it was Joan then who had the idea that a family should have a dog, and that was because she had a memory of the dogs of her childhood – fox terriers mostly – and remembered taking them for walks along the Porter Valley. It was a good excuse if you wanted to meet some boy or other – her parents would never have thought to prevent her taking the dog for an innocent walk.

She approaches it with its lead and it submits to being tethered to her hand. She will take it into the park. Dogs have to pee after all, she knows that. And shit, and nowadays you have to pick up the shit in little bags that are sold for the purpose, and then you have to carry it about until you find one of those red bins. Joan has never lifted the lid of one of those and has always believed – without having to think about it – that she would never find that she had to.

It's blustery and cold in the park, trees heaving, broken branches on the ground. Insistent brown water torrents down the river. The dog trots beside her as docile as if it really does belong to her, but she feels like a thief. This is not her dog. Or if not a thief, then a fraud. She reaches the far end of the park, decides that's enough, turns.

The dog crouches and quivers and produces some steaming brown turds.

'Finished?' This is the first word Joan has spoken to it.

She reaches into her pocket for the plastic bag – not a proper biodegradable one, but a see-through one from the greengrocers – but it is whipped away by the wind and lands in the river. Joan looks in dismay at the pile of crap in the middle of the path, where joggers and small children are sure to tread in it.

'Lost your bag?' It's a large man, with a beard like a swarm of bees, accompanied by two leaping Weimaraners, who sniff round poor Minnie, one at each end. He hands her a bag from his pocket, and she accepts gratefully, and scoops the unpleasantly soft and warm poo, while hoping fervently she never has to meet him again.

'Thank you,' she says.

'Have another one,' he says. 'Not often they stop at one, I find.'

'Thank you,' she says again.

'There's something wrong with that dog's tail,' says Weimaraner man. 'It ought to turn up at the end.'

'I've only just got it.' says Joan. 'That's how it was.' What does he think? That she has been ill-treating her animal?

'It looks as though it was broken somehow. Did you get it cheap?' He laughs, showing some yellowish teeth.

'It was a rescue dog,' says Joan. 'My daughter found her for me.'

'That'll be it then,' he says. 'Not good enough to sell. Substandard dog, that.' He walks off.

'I don't care,' says Joan, aloud, as if he's still listening. 'Why should I care about her tail. She's not exactly a waggy sort of dog.' Why am I defending this animal, she wonders. I don't even like her myself.

In the evening Rachel phones, but Joan does not answer. It reminds her though, that she has to take

Minnie out again before she is able to go to bed. Rain is falling from the sky as if it will never stop, and she goes only as far as her own empty lock-up garage, hidden from the windows of other residents, so they won't see her dog polluting the ground.

Joan finds that she misses Martin more as time goes on. It should be less, she thinks. Four years – nearly four – many people would say she should have made some sort of progress by now. When they were married, when he was alive, she would not even have said that theirs was a particularly happy marriage, but she sees herself now as a half-demolished building. Just the façade is left standing, shored up with timbers, waiting for someone to put it to some new use, or knock it down completely.

Like her own father, he had liked all the accoutrements of maleness, the hammers and power tools, the technology, the nice big smooth cars. 'I'm a man's man,' he said. 'No good trying to make me into something I'm not meant to be.'

He meant that he did a man's job, striding around half-built motorway interchanges in a hard hat, and in his spare time followed rugby (Union, not League) in the winter and spent his summer turning out for the cricket team, or in the garden, pruning, planting, cutting grass and hedge. He meant that television was for sport, or maybe an old James Bond film on a wet Bank Holiday, and that it was inevitable that he, as a man, would fail to grasp Joan's lasting affection for Coronation Street. He meant that he was not to be expected to have any opinion about soft furnishings until after they were bought and in place, at which time he could tell Joan that she should have known he wouldn't like them.

He meant all those things, and they were all true of him, but – and – he was kind, very, often. If Joan was tired, or ill – and she often struggled, winters, with chest infections – he could not have been more solicitous. He could have been better at it, but being a man's man he didn't really know how. But he brought her trays of soup – never quite hot enough – or boiled eggs with slightly burnt toast, and always offered to sleep in the spare room so that she could have a night without worrying about keeping him awake.

He was proud of Joan's career, and told his friends that whole departments at the Town Hall would fall apart if it weren't for his wife keeping things together. 'Say what you like about the Council,' he said, 'but it would be a whole lot worse without my wife there to keep things on the rails.'

He was nice with Rachel too, when she was little, and even when she became a standard-issue teenager. He took her places and showed her things, and explained things to her that he would have explained to a boy, so that she grew up knowing all about earth-moving equipment and the design of drainage systems. He accepted her dislike of sport, though he couldn't understand it, and he paid for her piano lessons even after she began to play keyboards in a band that she would not let her parents go and watch, and whose lyrics she went to some lengths to hide from them.

He's been dead for years, thinks Joan, and I haven't had any sex ever since he died. What if I'd let Keith Fairlie kiss me, would that have led to something. She shudders. Sex with anyone but Martin seems to be out of the question. Not that it was a major part of their life together – mild occasional sex that allowed her to carry on thinking about whether Rachel was happy, or whether she should put a load of washing in the machine before going to work tomorrow. Affection, though, she misses that. Martin was the affectionate one, not her, but she misses, still, the way he would pat her head or her bottom as he walked past her to the back door, say, or the way he touched her gently on a shoulder to wake her in the mornings. Kisses, small, childish kisses – she never thought much about them, but she misses them.

Rachel will give her a hug, when she sees her, but is not a kissing sort of person. Anyway, it would not be the same.

Next month, thinks Joan, it will be four years that I have been without him.

When he was found dead in the garden, after the confusion of ambulances and police, Rachel came home – she'd been working in Hull at that time – and stayed for two weeks. I remember, thinks Joan, being terrified at how I would manage when she went away, and also wishing she would go. You'd think we could have cried together, that's what relatives are supposed to be for, but mostly we each tried to cheer the other one and pretended that each of us was just fine, really.

Rachel went back to work, and Joan thought, Well if she can, I can, and three weeks and a day after the fatal Sunday afternoon she was back in the outer office of Keith Fairlie's department, rearranging into order the mess that people had made during her absence. It took her mind off it, to an extent.

And she did that for two years, never at ease – when she was at work she yearned to be at home; when she was at home she wanted to be somewhere else. Weekends were the worst times. She used to expect him to be coming and going, in and out of the house. Going to buy a newspaper on Sunday morning, coming back in. Going to watch a rugby match, or a cricket match, coming back in. Setting off in the car to buy wood, or nails, going round the house fixing a gutter, or a bit of fence, or pruning the big bush that always grew to block the garage door, and coming back in.

He would come in to warm up when it was cold, to drink coffee when he was thirsty, to sit down for half an hour when he had been hard at work, to phone someone about something. Then he would be up and off and out again into the garden, he was not a man who stopped for long.

In her father's day there was a gardener who came once a week, to cut the grass and the hedges, and barrow rubbish to the compost heap and leave Joan's mother free to keep the borders tidy and flowering. In fact, the same gardener, Mr Creasey, continued for a good many years, until Martin, on giving up actually playing first rugby and then cricket, transferred his enthusiasm to the garden as his main activity outside work.

After Martin's death, the garden grew uncontrollably for the rest of the summer. The hanging baskets which had been one of his last embellishments, contained only dry dead stalks. The rest of the vegetation seemed to know that having contributed to his death, it was free to surge and frisk and twine and harden until – Viv said, visiting uninvited one day – it was like some fairy tale enchanted wood. What she actually said was, 'It's like bloody Sleeping Beauty out there. You'll need to get someone in.'

Joan did her best. A young man – not Mr Creasey, who was by now really too old – came with a battery of power tools and reduced the hedges and shrubs to stumps. Viv's offers of help were rejected by means of appearing not to hear them and Joan stumbled, weeping, amongst the herbaceous perennials, cutting down and tying up, digging out dandelions which snapped off at the root and regrew, getting stung by nettles and failing to notice until it was too late that the bindweed – hacked off by the young man – was sending new strong shoots up though the newly sprouting hedges and roses.

She was grateful when it died down in the winter. In the spring bulbs pushed through out of the dead land and it began to look as if it might be possible to take back control. Viv came round again one weekend and, unasked, produced her gardening gloves and an assortment of small tools and deftly cleared a small bed near the back door. 'That's chickweed, that's speedwell, get em out because they'll strangle everything.'

'It looks empty,' said Joan.

'There's plenty coming through. Look, there's a geranium coming, it will fill all that space, that looks like some sort of daisy. Just keep it weeded, it'll be fine.'

Joan looked out at the rest of the garden – a third of an acre – and back at the eight foot square that Viv had tamed. 'Thank you,' she said.

While she laboured in the back garden – which at least made her tired enough that she sometimes slept well – the front garden turned itself into a small prairie of groundsel and willow herb, and dandelions – more dandelions – and thistles began to grow in the borders and grass grew like whiskers in the cracks between the block paving. The climbing rose beside the front door threatened to garrotte anyone going in or out. Kind neighbours began to stop her in the street and recommend this or that man who would be able to sort it out for her.

When at last – and she was like a person who has been standing on the cliff edge, gathering the courage – Joan decided to make some changes, giving up the garden was the least of it. Giving up work, giving up her house, that had been left to her by her father – they were the big things. Giving up all reminders of Martin, going through cupboards, drawers, desks, sheds, the loft, finding everywhere clothes he had worn, notes he had written, gadgets he had bought, broken items he had been intending to fix, shoes, suits, glasses, magazines, cricket whites, rugby boots, tins of dubbin. Things in pockets – small coins, shopping lists (bonemeal, string, secateur blades), handkerchief – he was one of the few people who still used fabric handkerchiefs – an odd glove, a packet of Polos, unopened, an empty crisp packet.

So she cleared her house of Martin, even his old gardening coat that she had taken to wearing herself when she went outside, even his old dressing gown that still smelled of him, cleared it of much of her own obsolete stuff as well, had the garden superficially tidied by a professional, sold without any trouble and moved to her flat. Her garden – whatever Viv might say – she misses about as much as she might miss infected tonsils or an intermittently aching tooth. If she wants fresh air, she has her balcony.

*

There is a perceptible lightening in the evenings now, a mere shivering of green on the trees. Viv takes the bus into town for a choir rehearsal. Pamela is telling Sandra about the failure of a central heating boiler.

'I have a new plan,' says Richard. He is looking more than usually rumpled tonight, but animated with it, looking around at everyone as if there is exciting news. 'It will mean going back to the drawing board –'

There are groans, some real, some ironic. Viv does not look at Pamela but knows that she will be jerking her head in disapproval.

'What a piece of work is man' he says. 'We're going to add to it. It gets a bit complex, but I think we can do it.'

'Four more rehearsals,' says Pamela. 'You expect us to be ready? With everything else as well.'

He looks deflated, hurt. Viv would like to stand up for him somehow but doesn't want him to feel patronised.

'Well,' says Terry, 'why don't you tell us what it is?'

'Let's give it a go,' says Viv.

APRIL

Bill collects the campervan from Pete's back yard. He is somewhat surprised at himself for putting himself through all this again. The journey in this old wreck, which, if he were stopped by the police, would surely fail any roadside check. The prospect of watching Richard – Rick, as he still thinks of him – lording it over his choir in that smarmy manner. The prospect of seeing that harridan Viv and having her spit hatred at him. The prospect of yet another failure to meet Joanie, or if they meet, a failure to connect with her. Suppose she is less appealing even than Viv? Suppose she is more haggard and worn that he has been imagining her? Suppose she will not speak to him, having heard all about what he did the last time he was there?

There are so many reasons for him to stay at home, safely, showing prospective buyers round his neat and clean house, and wandering round the village looking for somewhere small to buy.

Yet he is still packing and organising himself for the journey and the stay. He has booked the campsite. He has bought sensible provisions so that he doesn't have to eat exclusively in expensive cafes and pubs. He has kitted out the van with a pillow and an extra blanket as well as his old sleeping bag, and put in a couple of books for the evenings.

He deliberately dampens his expectations of a meeting with Joanie. Why should she be there, at the concert? Why should she even be at home? She might be one of those women who go on cruises – if she is he probably doesn't want to know her at all. She might be one of those women who are devoted to the memory of a late husband – but against that there is the fact that it was she who reopened contact with him.

It was years ago. Must be nearly twenty years. More than that even. Out of the blue, out of the past, there she was, at the end of a telephone cable, speaking, sounding business-like and official.

'Am I speaking to Mr Badger?' she said. Why not, Aughton is that you? he often wondered.

He has never remembered what they talked about, but they talked for half an hour, exchanged addresses. There were pauses, and then they would both start speaking together. It was not an easy conversation. They condensed decades of experience into exchanging the names and ages of their daughters, and even, at one point, talked about the weather.

Only when she said it was time to end the call, did it come to life.

'Don't go,' he said. 'We need a plan.'

'What for?' she said.

'The future,' he said.'

'Aughton,' she said, quite sharply, 'we don't have any future, if you mean what I think you mean. I just rang to see how you were.'

'I don't believe you,' he said. 'You rang because there's something missing in your life.'

'Not at all,' she said.

'Well, he said, 'I've missed you. I'd love to see you again.'

'No,' she said. 'Not unless –'

'Unless they die. You were going to say that, weren't you.'

'I wasn't at all,' she said. 'But that's ok as a plan. If we are both on our own, both of us, remember, then we'll meet.'

'Send me a Christmas card, and I'll send you one, every year, then we'll know we're still here. And if –'

'If we're ever both on our own –'

'We'll meet up.'

It turned out that by some unexpected chance his sister and Joan had met, at a local government conference and Carenza, who as a little girl had been fond of Joan, had taken her address and told her how Aughton was happily married.

He thought on that phone call, occasionally, and felt virtuous because not for one moment did he contemplate leaving Lydia, or cheating on her. If anything he felt more fond of her than he had done in years, softer, more yearning towards her. He had no expectation that she would die before him. Why should she? But if she did, the one per cent of his brain said, very quietly, if she did there was a Plan B.

*

As she opens her balcony door on this fine April morning to check the outside temperature Joan is thinking idly about Viv. She is thinking how Viv never wears quite enough clothes, how there is always a bare neck or a bare pair of legs or arms, and how she always laughs it off and pretends she's fine.

Joan looks out towards the park where the new green leaves shine and shiver in the sun and wind. Today is one of those days when if you are in the sun and out of the wind, then you will be warm. Otherwise not.

A blackbird starts up from the trees across the road. Joan thinks about Viv tediously repeating how much she loves a blackbird's song. Diddley dee, goes the bird, diddley dee.

Just because Viv likes it, says Joan aloud, doesn't mean I have to. Figaro Figaro, sings the bird. She shuts the door on the sound and leans against it, wondering why there are tears running down her cheeks. What is the matter with me? Think of something else, think of something big.

The Department. She and Keith Fairlie steered the department through the first wave of funding cuts, evaluating agencies as never before, managing their closure where necessary, consolidating provision of services, dealing with their appeals and protests, helping them dispose of assets and premises. She was numb. She never shed a tear over the loss of expertise and local knowledge that was dying with all these little support groups and cultural associations.

Mother and baby clubs, support for relatives of substance misusers, anorexics, parents of troublesome teenagers, refugee helplines, housing advice centres, lunch clubs and community visitors for lonely old people.

She was numb. Martin was gone and it did not matter to her what else might go. Keith rushed around from one meeting to the next, agonising and trying to offer hope – but hope was nothing without money. Joan stayed professional. She stayed polite on the phone to people – part-time coordinators asking if there were not some other fund they could apply to. She told them the truth, that, no, there wasn't; or she lied and said that yes, Mr Fairlie had said he would look into the options, but (this was a bit of a lie) he had looked carefully and (this was the honest truth) there really was no other option for them but to close.

And after two years, leaving behind a leaner and maybe, with the right amount of spin, more efficient set of services, she and Keith Fairlie both retired, and he went off to Africa to help himself through his loss, and she set a project for herself: clear her house, that she had lived in all her life except for her five years away down south, clear it and sell it and move to a flat where her life would begin again.

She scanned all her parents' photographs, and her own, into the computer, classified by date and subject, and they now float in some cloud or other, consuming electric energy, and she can view them at the click of a mouse. It's not the same though, as going through a pile in a shoe box, making discoveries and being able to handle the tatty pieces of soft card. It's not the same as knowing that it was her father and mother whose own fingers first took this photo out of its yellow envelope when it came back from the chemist, and whose own voice remarked on the fuzziness or wonkiness of the image and blamed the person behind the camera, or else the one in front of it.

This is not how she meant it to be. She misses Martin, she misses her parents. Moving house was supposed to help with that. Clearing out the past was supposed to help her move on, and it's true she feels less cluttered by redundant and bothersome objects but it's not a de-cluttering that brings any peace, rather a feeling of being deserted by her old possessions.

Joan knows that Rachel sent the dog to give her the courage to go out. Rachel might have guessed, possibly, that since she was mugged she has found it harder and harder to be outside, alone or with someone else. She has that feeling of needing to stand with her back against a wall, as if people only ever get attacked from behind.

Minnie whines softly and scratches at the doormat. She is a good dog, but if Joan doesn't take her out she will wee on the carpet, or worse. Joan opens the door and closes it again. I used to run that office. I managed staff. *I* ran it. I *ran* it. Surely I can take one little dog for a walk. She closes her eyes and the darkness is comforting. She keeps them closed as she takes the lead from its hook, but has to open them to fasten it to Minnie's collar. The dog looks at her imploringly.

'We're going, we're going,' says Joan impatiently.

As she opens the door the sunlight floods in and she sees all the colours of Minnie's coat. The pale fawn along her back, the dark grey streaks around her soft ears, her muzzle cream, her little feet almost black. Joan rubs her head – Minnie's head – with affection for the first time, and speaks to her. 'You're a work of art,' she says. 'A canine work of art.'

*

Viv is finding that dark glasses do not make it easy to use binoculars. She sits on her seat in the park with the binoculars trained on Joan's window.

This is all because the evening before, she had a conversation with Rachel.

'Have you seen her dog yet?' said Rachel.

'Dog? She's got a dog?'

'I sent it to her, said Rachel. 'She won't speak to me now. I phone her and she lifts the phone and puts it straight down. She's that mad with me. I'm worried she might not be able to look after it. I thought it was a good idea at the time.'

'I'll see what I can find out,' said Viv.

So here she is in her new role as stalker. She planned it while doing her stint at the charity shop that morning, fired up by the fact that there was a pair of binoculars in the bag she was sorting. They are yellow plastic, and have been in someone's loft long enough that they have a transfer of Tweetie-Pie on each barrel, but they seem to magnify when she looks through them. She looks up at Joan's first floor window and wonders whether to accost Joan when she comes out, or whether to lurk behind the shelter and then follow her at a distance.

She checks the time on her phone and discovers that she has been sitting there less than half and hour, and it feels like many times more than that. There is no sign of any movement inside Joan's flat, from Joan or the dog. She looks up at the sky, hoping it might rain, and let her go home. Other people walk past with their dogs and their children. A small and cheery walking group call greetings to her as they make their back towards the city centre. A man in black Lycra flashes past on a bike. Richard from the choir walks briskly along from the opposite direction. He appears not to notice Viv – maybe because of the sunglasses – and she does not speak to him, though it's hard for her to explain to herself why that is. His dogs follow him, running free.

Viv decides to give up for today. She will try again on Thursday, later in the afternoon, after Tai chi.

The next time Viv attempts to encounter Joan, the sun is shining and the air, for the first time, is warm. The new leaves on the hawthorns are a brilliant green. She has had a letter from the cancer screening people, telling her that her results have been sent to her GP and that she must make an appointment to see her. She has received a text from her GP asking her to make an appointment. There is a message on her answering machine too, from this morning, that she strongly suspects is also from the surgery but she has not yet had the courage to listen to it. I'm going to die, she thinks.

'Like a spring day,' says a woman going in the opposite direction.'

'Lovely,' agrees Viv, thinking, That's because it *is* a spring day, stupid. Then she repents of her thought. Sure, you can reasonably expect spring-like weather in spring, but it still feels like a gift, and an unmerited one at that.

All this, thinks Viv, the smells, the gold-green of the leaves, the promise, the new warmth of the sun. All this, the feeling of being in one piece, everything all right, in working order. How can there be something wrong? How can there be a nasty filthy thing growing inside me? It doesn't feel true, or even possible, at times, and then, at others, it feels absolutely incontrovertibly certain. I'm going to die, she thinks again. Will I see next spring? Is this the last springtime for me? Will I even see these leaves fall? Will it hurt? Will I have to have a bag to poo in? Would I rather die?

She hasn't told anyone. There is no one she feels able to tell – which must say something, she thinks, about the quality of her friends, or her friendships. Sooner or later of course, they will find out; they will come to her funeral. Maybe even Joan will come. I could tell Joan, she thinks. If I told Maggie she would cry, she cries at anything, that woman; if I told Liz it would make her think of losing her mother so recently; and Judy has herself survived breast cancer and would be full of sensible and helpful advice and encouragement. I couldn't stand it, thinks Viv. But I could tell Joan.

She strolls through the park from one end to the other, and back again, and as she approaches the gate Joan is coming through it, with the dog on a lead beside her. If nothing else, thinks Viv, I can let Rachel know that she hasn't got rid of it.

'Hello Joan,' she says, trying to speak calmly, as if she has not spent the last few months worrying about her.

'Viv,' says Joan.

'And the dog,' says Viv. 'Rachel told me you had a dog.' She is not going to make a secret of the fact that she and Rachel keep in touch.

'Minnie,' says Joan. 'She's called Minnie. What are you doing here?'

'Me? I just came out for a walk, it's such a nice day. Maybe I should get a dog too.'

'I wouldn't,' says Joan, but Viv notices that she doesn't offer to hand Minnie over to her. Surely a good sign?

'How are you?' says Viv. 'I haven't seen you for ages. I've missed you.'

'Yes,' says Joan, which is not an answer to anything, thinks Viv.

'We could sit on that bench,' says Viv.

'I have to walk,' says Joan. 'Minnie needs her exercise.'

'Why don't you let her off the lead? She could run about on her own.'

'I'm not sure. She might run away.'

'You can't keep her on a lead all her life. Can you? You'll have to let her off some time.'

'I suppose so.' Joan bends down and unclips the lead. Minnie goes to a tree and pees on its roots, then mooches about, sniffing.

They are sitting side by side on the bench, and there is nothing to say.

'Well,' says Viv, 'I must say, at least, you're looking more like yourself than the last time I saw you.' Joan does not respond.

'No really,' says Viv. 'You didn't look well at Christmas. Depressed, maybe? But now –?'

'I'm all right,' says Joan.

'What have you been doing?'

'Nothing much. Walking the dog.'

'Not been out anywhere? Seen anyone?'

'No.'

'Rachel's coming down at May Day isn't she? Tell you what, why don't you bring her to the concert? I'll get a couple of tickets for you.'

'What concert?'

'Our choir. I told you, way back. Remember?'

'I don't think so,' says Joan.

'Well, even if you don't remember, I've told you now. You'll like it, I promise.'

Joan says nothing. Stubborn old cow, thinks Viv.

'Another thing,' she says. 'You have to talk to Rachel.'

'What about?'

Anything,' says Viv. 'Don't hang up on her. She's doing her best you know.'

Joan makes a dismissive noise like small horse blowing down its nose.

'I mean it,' says Viv. 'If you don't talk to her yourself she'll only ask me, and you won't know what I'm telling her.'

Joan scowls suspiciously and says nothing for several minutes, while Viv avoids looking at her to observe the effect of her manipulation.

'Well,' says Joan at last. 'Which way are you walking?'

'Either,' says Viv. 'Where's the dog got to?'

Joan stands up. She shakes the lead as if it will make a noise the dog could hear. 'Minnie. Minnie.' She looks straight at Viv for the first time. 'You said she'd be all right off the lead.'

'Don't panic,' says Viv. 'I'll help you look for her.'

But they stand still, wondering which way to look, until Minnie comes tearing out of the trees, pursued by one of the Weimaraners. She hides behind Joan, shaking. The other Weimaraner trots up, and a short way off their owner appears, walking towards them.

'Oh it's Richard,' cries Viv.

Joan has clipped the dog's lead back on, and begins to walk away, passing Richard without looking at him.

I wanted to tell her, thinks Viv, and I may not get another chance. She thinks about waiting in front of Joan's flat until she comes back, but puts it off. Another day.

'All right Richard,' says Viv, watching Joan's departing back.

'Do I know you?' he says.

'You ought to know me,' says Viv. 'I've been in that choir of yours since it started. And I sit on the front row.'

'I'm sorry,' he says. 'I'm not very good with faces.'

His choir manner has gone – that assured, jolly, jokey, in-charge-of-the-situation manner – and he is fidgety, like a boy who knows he has done something wrong. He whistles and his dogs come running.

'Wait a minute, says Viv, on impulse. 'I want to ask you something.'

He looks surprised, then shifty.

'Have you heard from Bill lately?' She doesn't know what she is going to follow up with, she'll just wing it.

'Bill?'

'Don't tell me you don't know who he is either. Bill. He came to the choir before Christmas. Camper van. Friend of yours.'

'Oh. Oggy. Why do you want to know?'

'Oggy?'

'That's how I've always known him. Can't be his proper name, but that what we always called him.'

'Well, he told me he was Bill.'

Richard looks uncertain, as well he might. He fidgets with his dog leads, and starts to walk on, as if hoping Viv will go away. She walks beside him. 'Tell me about him,' she says.

'I don't know,' he says, exasperated. 'I don't know anything about him these days. I was his best man, and he was mine. Long time ago.'

'I didn't know you had a wife,' says Viv.

'Not any more,' he says vaguely, as if he'd mislaid her and couldn't remember where.

'Do you know why Bill came up to Sheffield?'

'Never asked him. Haven't seen him since that wedding day. Odd phone call now and again. Then he said he was coming up this way. Thought he was just having a little trip. I mean a little jaunt, obviously, not that sort of trip, not these days. After his wife died, you know. Get away from things, that sort of thing.'

'So he never told you what he was looking for?'

'He just phoned me out of the blue. I think he might have wanted to stay at my place, but I told him before he got round to asking – I've got this mother you see, that I live with, and it wouldn't have been –'

'No I can see that,' says Viv.

'Was he looking for something?'

'Someone,' says Viv. 'Old girlfriend. In fact –' she pauses to enjoy the moment '– that woman who were here just now, with that little greyhoundy sort of dog.'

'Whippet,' he says.

'Don't you know her? Joan Jones?'

He stares vaguely at two joggers running past. 'Might have heard the name. Can't say I remember meeting her. Does she remember him?'

'That's a silly question,' says Viv. 'Of course people remember old boyfriends.'

'Do they?'

'Well,' says Viv, 'if you talk to Bill, or whatever you call him, you can tell him that she doesn't want anything to do with him.'

'Fair enough,' says Richard. And they part at the gates of the park.

Viv goes back home, slowly, wondering what made her say that.

MAY

Viv, being short, is on the front row of the choir. Pamela is behind her and can be heard complaining about the feeble efforts some people have made with the dress code.

'We agreed blue,' she is saying to Sandra. 'What's the point I ask you. Graham's shirt is white, there's no other word for it, and some of those sopranos might as well have voted for purple if they're going to wear it.'

Richard has booked their usual venue for the concert, a windowless room at the side of a pub. He has made them have extra rehearsals. He takes it all quite seriously, which Viv approves of.

'Good grief,' Pamela has said on more than one occasion. 'It's only a little concert. It's not the Albert Hall is it?'

'Might as well do it properly,' said Sandra, and Viv said, 'You know Pamela, you don't have to sing if you don't want to. If it's too much for you.'

'I never said that,' said Pamela and Viv laughed at her.

Richard's very old mother has a place in the front row of the audience, as usual. Richard is wearing a suit and his mother beckons him over as the choir is taking their places, and makes him kneel down in front of her so that she can straighten his tie.

What would she have said, wonders Viv, watching him struggle painfully to his feet, if he had continued with the hair-brained project to do all the songs from *Hair*? Richard would surely have had a parental telling off. This makes her even more sure that it was only a joke. Not even a funny one, unless you think that winding up Pamela and Fairlie is funny. Which it is.

Viv sees Keith Fairlie walking down between the two banks of chairs, looking for a seat. She sees him stop at the end of the row that contains Viv's next door neighbours. They haven't seen him but he must have seen them, and the sight clearly does something to him. He turns on his heel to go to the back of the room. Rachel and Joan are coming through the double doors. Something swells inside Viv's head – can it be that Joan is back in the world? Though she sent Rachel the tickets she has not dared to hope that Joan would come. Keith Fairlie is walking swiftly down the aisle – maybe on his way out – and comes together with Joan and Rachel, on their way in.

He turns again. His face is pinker than ever and Viv notices that he no longer has his moustache. What will Joan do, wonders Viv. She can't see her expression, but she sees her put out her hand, she must have said something to make him turn and they produce a civilised handshake, then find seats and Joan is between Rachel and Keith Fairlie. She has had her hair cut, Viv sees, but not coloured. She is an ordinary woman with well-cut grey hair.

Viv has not spoken to Joan since the day in the park. She has eventually seen her GP and has an appointment booked for a colonoscopy, but she has not told anyone. She rang Joan once but found herself unable to speak and put the phone down without saying what she wanted to say. Joan will have seen her number on the display and thought that she was being mischievous, or malicious. She has been sleeping badly, and still waking early, running her hand over her stomach which feels the same as usual – smooth and warm and plump – and then snatching her hand away, as if she might make something worse. She can see herself in a hospital bed, pale and pathetic, looking at the doors for visitors to come and see her, and no one will come. She will have to be brave and there will be no one to notice how brave she is being. She will die with only a nurse by her side. If she is lucky.

These thoughts are with her and for all her trying they will not go away. They are there as she tries to get them out of her head so that she can sleep at night; when she wakes in the morning there is a blessed second of peace before she remembers and they pile back into her head. They accompany her as she persists in her normal pursuits. But this evening she hopes – no, she expects – she will put them out of her mind.

Joan, coming into the dim room with Rachel by her side, cannot believe she is doing this. Worse, (worse?) she is looking forward to it. There is a buzz of people talking, there is a hum of expectation. Like bees, people move here and there on missions that are mysterious to her, carrying things – a large metal teapot, a small collection of cardigans, an empty guitar case. A man pushes a wheelchair to the front, then to the back to pick up a youngish man with his leg in plaster and stuck straight out in front of him.

Joan is suddenly confronted by Keith Fairlie, apparently on his way out of the hall. He stops, awkwardly, and shakes her hand.

'This is my daughter Rachel,' she says. 'Keith and I worked together at the Council,' she explains.

'I know,' says Rachel, and shakes Keith's hand, saying, 'I've heard a lot about you, as you can imagine.'

He blushes, and Joan feels as if she is too. She is glad she went to the hairdressers. 'Are you with anybody?' she asks, and then wonders if that was the wrong thing to say. Might he think she was asking about his private life? 'I mean, are you sitting with anybody?' And the upshot is that she finds herself sitting between Rachel and Keith, not far from the front, with a good view of Viv.

Just as Richard is taking his place in front – the choir is already standing, quiet, poised, scared – Viv sees what she thinks might be Bill, squeezing in through the door that is just being closed. She's not sure – Richard is blocking her view – and when she looks again she can't see him. Joan, sitting well towards the front, won't be able to see him, if indeed she does know him. *That* has never been sorted out, not to Viv's satisfaction.

Richard turns and looks at his audience. They go quiet.

'Thank you for coming,' he says. 'I haven't given out a programme for this evening, though one will be available at the end for those that would like one to remember us by. The reason is that I want to surprise you and bring back memories for those of you old enough to remember, and for those of you – those few of you – too young to remember, a little musical education.'

He is at his best when telling an audience something he knows about music. They know – everyone can feel – that he knows more than he is saying, he is making it easy for them, but at he same time he has so much fervent feeling for these songs that they are sympathetic to him, as the choir is too, even while they complain.

'The Summer of Love was the summer of 1967, and nearly all our music tonight comes from that year. You might think that it was all Californian, drug-induced, psychedelia, but – let's be honest – I'm not sure my choir would sing a whole evening's worth of that sort of thing. I'm not going to bore you with my memories – I'm not even sure that I have any – so we will let the music do the work for us.'

Viv, and the rest of the choir, are inured to nostalgia by now, having worked on these songs for half a year. The words and the tunes have become something both more and less than what they once were; they are patterns now, or maps, showing where are the tricky notes, where are the gaps they must leave, where are the breaths they must take. And Richard is no longer just the bloke who runs them through the songs every week, but their support and guide; they lean on him, watching his movements, his arms, his hands, his face. He has told them not to look down at their music – he is their music. Dull, scruffy old Richard.

'First up,' he says, 'a Beatles number. *Sergeant Pepper's Lonely Hearts Club Band* was surely the biggest thing that happened that summer so we had to have something from it. I chose "With a Little Help from my Friends" – because that's what a choir is all about – not just one voice but many voices, working together.'

He accompanies them on guitar. Viv finds her voice straight away. She loves these evenings. Loves being part of something, loves being on stage, loves the sound of the choir – always better in performance than in rehearsal, more power, more conviction, more joy. There is no room in her mind for anything else, no, not tonight.

'Next,' says Richard, 'a big hit. This was written by John Phillips of the Mamas and the Papas – of whom more later – for his friend Scott McKenzie. We think of it as a bit cheesy these days, a bit naïve, but it brings back that summer just perfectly. "San Francisco".'

Viv hasn't liked this one during the practices and in truth it's under-rehearsed. And they sing it too straight, she thinks, not interesting enough, not one of Richard's best arrangements.

'Now,' says Richard, 'a little Simon and Garfunkel. This was actually recorded and released in 1966 but it is another song that seems to me to capture the exuberance and optimism of the times. "59th Street Bridge Song" – or "Feelin Groovy".'

In the audience Joan has a vague memory of driving along with this playing. Where was she on her way to? Then she remembers, and shuts the memory out, along with all the others.

'I said there would be more about the Mamas and the Papas,' says Richard. 'There are many of their songs that lend themselves to choral singing, but this is one from 1967, although it was actually written back in the 1950s. "Dedicated to the One I Love".'

Bill, sitting at the back of the room, feels a wave of dislike for Richard, and his choice of music and his rotten middle-class choir. These are not the songs he wanted to hear, there is nothing here to recall the end of his first year at Essex, nothing that reminds him of himself, then. What about proper, alternative music? What about Cream and Jimi Hendrix? What about Jefferson Airplane and the Grateful Dead?

That summer he bought *Piper at the Gates of Dawn* with his birthday money from his Nan, wished he hadn't and subsequently sold it to someone else. Most of his summer was musicless anyway. It was spent hitch-hiking round Yugoslavia with a bloke called Denzil, living on beer and bread and wondering if his end of term fling with Rosemary was going to lead to anything. He bought a postcard for her in Dubrovnik but never sent it because he had lost her address.

'Now a bit of country,' says Richard, 'for those that like it – and I think most people would appreciate that this is a fine song. We know it mainly as a solo song, sung by Glenn Campbell, but there have been a number of soul versions, and I've borrowed some of their ideas, just to give all of the choir some work to do. "Wichita Lineman".'

Joan thinks that it is years since she heard this. So lonely, such a lonely tune, though she doesn't understand the words, or even know most of them. She feels the loneliness and then is ashamed of herself, because hasn't she got Rachel, and couldn't she have other friends if she – if she what? Wanted? Made the effort? Could bear it? I can't let myself speak, thinks Joan. If I did – if I did – what? It would be all over? What would? I would be all over the place? So what?

The next song is "Up Up and Away". This has caused the choir some trouble as it turned out to be pitched too high for the sopranos and had to be adjusted to fit the available voices.

'This,' says Richard, 'was chosen for its harmonies, but actually, it's a fine song, commercially speaking, combining the optimism of the times with the undemanding safety that older people wanted.'

Bill looks longingly at the door. His mother liked this one, he remembers, and his little sisters. They liked the next one too – "Brown-Eyed Girl" – his mother finding herself a bit daring, his sisters on the edge of wishing to be the object of someone's lust.

'Now, leading up to the interval we have to include something a bit folky,' says Richard. 'Folk was a big thing through the sixties, and by 1967 it was beginning to fuse with rock music – consider Bob Dylan's famous electric guitar moment. This is a jolly Irish tune – a traditional one, made famous by the Dubliners – about a poor young man who is transported unjustly to the colonies after being betrayed by a lovely young barmaid. It could happen to anyone.'

Bill has a sense of what sort of thing is coming. 'Christ,' he thinks, almost out loud but not quite, 'next thing it will be ribbons on fucking kittens.' But the choir sing "Black Velvet Band" with such relish that he gives way, just a little.

There is a twenty-minute interval while people go through to the bar and refill their glasses. Bill would like to leave, but he is sure Viv has seen him, and it wouldn't do to reinforce her idea of him as someone who runs out of situations, rudely. She would tell Joanie. What is he going to say to her? What is she going to do to him? He hopes he can avoid her.

'Well Oggy,' says Richard. 'You got here in the end then.'

'I might miss out on the second half,' says Bill. He knows he is being ungracious.

'Why?'

'Just this music – it's not really my scene. I didn't think it would be yours. All these pretty tunes.'

'I have to keep people happy,' says Richard. 'But you can go through to the bar if you like and wait for us there. We have a bit of a gathering afterwards – don't get too drunk before we get there though.'

'I can't drink much,' says Bill. 'I've got to drive the van back to the site.'

'Well stay and listen then. In fact, if you don't, you'll miss a real treat. I won't tell you what, but our last piece – well I think it will be worth it.'

'Does it bring it all back then?' says Rachel, laughing.

'Not really,' says Joan. 'I remember some of them of course, but as far as I remember, they didn't touch me at the time.'

Nothing touched me. My mother died. I took my 'A' levels and my mother died and I was never able to tell her how I did. And I went down to Essex – and it felt as though I was sent, like a punishment – and I was so miserable and they were all snooty about northerners and said awful things as if we were all smoky chimneys and coal in the bath, and I had no friends and that's why I took up with Trish and her bunch of god-botherers.

The concert resumes and they launch into "Happy Together" without any introduction.

'This one,' says Richard, 'may be unfamiliar to some of you. It comes from the second album by the Incredible String Band, released in 1967. Not very popular stuff, it has to be admitted, and our version is a little less weird than the original. It's called "Painting Box".'

The applause for this one seems a little tentative, thinks Viv. People like things they know, as Sandra said. She worries about the next one too, that it might be too odd, even though she likes it a lot.

'It can't be denied,' says Richard, 'that there was an element of drug referencing in many of the songs of that time.' Richard is getting into his stride now. He loves showing off at the front of the choir, thinks Viv, but it takes him a while to lose his self-consciousness. 'Our next song may or may not be directly about hallucinogenic substances, but certainly, if you look on Youtube, you can see a remarkably silly video of a group of young men who are certainly not completely sober. They were Pink Floyd, and the song is "See Emily Play".' Yes it is odd, for a choir, but Viv loves the way the men support the higher parts, as if they are really guitars and drums, she loves the difficulty of the alto part, which took such a long time to get right, and was so worth the effort.

'And while on the subject of young men in a park,' says Richard, 'here's one that I could not leave out, because I grew up near this very park, in Ilford, Essex. The original recording was by the Small Faces, as you will know, but our way of doing it borrows also from the version by M People. Ladies and gentlemen – "Itchycoo Park".'

Bill feels a little better. He can remember that this was Rosemary's favourite, or at least, she and her friends used to sing it together, usually while waiting at bus stops. He hasn't retrieved that memory for forty years or more, but there it is, undimmed.

'"Waterloo Sunset",' says Richard, 'needs no introduction. Some say it is the best song ever written. I have chosen it for myself, because in the so-called Summer of Love I was living in London, supposedly studying music, but more realistically having a good time. At least I thought I was having a good time. Mostly I was getting my heart broken and this is the wistful sort of song that takes me back there.'

Joan feels comfortably sad at hearing this. The original would be more than she could bear, but just the words and the tune, without the baggage of the real version, is, well, bearable. Pleasantly nostalgic. Much of the evening, in fact, has been pleasant. Keith Fairlie, still sitting next to her, has been silent, but it's been an easy silence, surrounded by singing.

'Our final piece,' says Richard, 'deserves a little more introduction.' The choir gives a sort of collective wriggle of anticipation.

'Now,' he says. 'There, in San Francisco, in 1967, were two young men called James Rado and Gerome Ragni. They were writing a little play you might have heard of, if you were around in the sixties. It was the musical *Hair*. It opened on Broadway in April 1968, and in England in September that same year. It contained, as most of you will know, nudity, references to drugs and a strong anti-war message. At the time, it was a sensational piece of theatre.

'So, here is something from *Hair*, as you have never heard it before. It's what we want to leave you with, so we won't be giving any encores this evening. Some of us will be in the bar next door after this and will be delighted to see you there. Here is our last little piece of the Summer of Love.'

And the women of the choir begin, a capella, in two parts, – 'what a piece of work is man.' As they finish, 'the paragon of animals,' the men come in, overlapping. 'I have of late, but wherefore I know not, lost all my mirth.'

Not that I had much mirth in the first place, thinks Joan to herself.

At the end of the men's part, there is an attempt to applaud from the audience, but it is hushed, because the women start again, the sopranos this time higher and more insistent. 'What a piece of work is man.'

But by the end of the phrase the men are back too. 'Wherefore I know not lost all my mirth.'

'The beauty of the world,' sing the altos.

'Seems to me a sterile promontory,' sing the men.

'Bloody women,' thinks Bill, 'getting all the best lines.' And they start again, 'This brave oe'erhanging firmament, this majestical roof,' holding the last note while the men grumble underneath them, 'foul and pestilent congregation of vapours.'

Then a pause, while the audience wonder again if they should be clapping, and then the men gather themselves, and seem to grow taller, and begin again, with a key change that has caused them a great deal of anguish before they got it right. "Let the Sunshine In".

And the whole choir sings joyfully and, amazingly, tears are shed, on the stage and in the audience. And when they stop there is more applause than they have ever had and some at the back even stand up to clap. Viv feels as if she could float away with elation. Richard turns and bows and waves his hand to acknowledge the choir, and the choir applaud him, and it seems that everybody loves everybody.

The concert has gone well. The bar is crowded with choir members and their friends and relations. Keith Fairlie has gone, with a swift and embarrassed goodbye to Joan, as if there was something he needed to avoid. Joan feels better about him now that they seem to be on a more natural footing, as they used to be. She is sorry she ever involved him in her problems – but what else could she have done? The concert has done something to warm her up, she feels a little more human. She has even allowed herself to be persuaded by Rachel to have just one drink.

Viv feels giddy. The annual concert is her favourite night of the year, better than Christmas, exhausting and exhilarating, and unlike Christmas, never disappointing. She feels as if she is at her own party, where she knows everyone, and likes everyone, and everyone likes her and is grateful to her for inviting them. She has in her hand the largest glass of red wine the pub can sell and she weaves through the bar, sipping, smiling, saying hello and picking up snippets, little shreds of conversations, without knowing or caring what they mean. If she died now – if I died now, she thinks, it wouldn't be so bad.

Her next door neighbours – she must get used to calling them by their names, now that she knows them – seem to know a few of the choir.

'It was lovely,' Elaine is saying to Yvonne and Derek. 'You must have been practising for months.' At the same time she is looking round, as if searching.

'I think he went,' says Frank.

Richard is missing too because he has taken his aged mother home, promising to come back soon. A corner of the bar already has a small collection of drinks for him. As always, the evening belongs to him. His was the vision, his was the work of arranging and writing and printing the music, and then dragging the choir through it, even against their protests. He told them it would be all right and it was. Each time, they find it hard to trust him, until, finally, they have to. It takes it out of him though, you can see that.

Viv stops to talk to her neighbour Frank – she feels she knows him much more tenuously than she knows Elaine, but he is always quite a jolly little man, and now he says all the right things.

'And thank you for inviting us,' he says. 'In fact, I think I might like to join, if the man would have me.'

Viv sees Richard making his return entrance. She actually sees him pause at the door, rearrange his face, take a breath and enter the room, as if it was a stage. He has taken off his tie and jacket and pulled his shirt outside of his trousers; you can see the creases where it was tucked in so short a time ago.

Viv feels a pang of tenderness towards him. She foresees a time when he no longer has his mother and will need someone else to iron his shirts and generally keep him up to scratch. She thinks she might apply for the job herself. If I'm around, she thinks. And I'd make him shave off that beard.

Viv sees Pamela heading towards her in a determined way, but it turns out it is Frank she wants to accost. She takes the arm of Frank and grasps it affectionately, so that he turns away from Elaine, who is still comparing grandchildren with Yvonne. Viv perceives that Frank looks pleased to see Pamela, which is not something, she thinks, that can often happen. She moves closer to hear what they are saying.

'What did you think of it?' demands Pamela.

'I thought it was great,' he says. What else did she think he was going to say?

'Did you hear the sopranos miss a beat coming in? In "Happy Together"? I can't believe you didn't notice. And I think the tenors could have been louder in some of their harmonies. Don't you think?'

He smiles, apparently fondly. 'You're a perfectionist,' he says. 'Not everyone has your high standards.'

'Well they should have,' she snaps. He does not seem surprised.

'You know what,' he says. 'This looks like a great choir to belong to, but I wonder if you shouldn't be in something a bit more professional. Why don't you go for the Teachers' Operatic?'

'Don't you know who runs it?' she says. Almost spits.

'There must be other choirs though,' he says. 'Go and have a look in the reference library. Wait, I'll ask Elaine, – Elaine, haven't they got lists of choirs in the reference library?'

His wife (wife? Viv doesn't know) turns. 'Lists? By the thousand.'

Pamela takes a step backwards. 'Oh,' she says. 'I didn't know – is this –? I mean –'

'This is Elaine,' he says. 'You haven't met before?'

'No,' says Pamela.

'I know you from somewhere,' says Elaine.

'What were all that about?' says Viv, when she has Pamela to herself.

'That's not his wife,' says Pamela. 'I know people who have seen his wife, and that is definitely not her.'

'Well, he lives with her,' says Viv. 'I can vouch for that, they live next door to me. What's your problem?'

But Pamela wouldn't say.

Rachel is on her way to the bar. 'I've persuaded her that I need another drink,' she says. 'Do you want one?'

'Why not,' says Viv. 'Thank you.'

'She enjoyed it you know,' says Rachel. 'She did her best not to, but she did. She was tapping her foot and smiling. And now she's found people she knows to talk to she's like a different woman.'

'He were there you know,' says Viv.

'Who? Him?'

'That Bill, or whatever his name is. I'm sure it were him. He came in just as we were starting. Late as usual. Sat at the back.'

'Is he here now?'

'Haven't seen him. Haven't been looking actually. If I meet him or if I don't, it's all the same to me.' She accepts the large red wine that Rachel passes her, realises she now has one in each hand and pours some into the new glass, then drains what is left. Shakes her head to clear it.

'Do you like her hair?' says Rachel. 'That was a battle I can tell you. But now it's done I think she feels better.'

The crush in the bar seems to be growing denser. The noise of chatter is getting louder.

'She'll want to go in a minute,' says Rachel. 'But she does seem to be better, in general. I don't feel as scared about her as I was at Christmas.'

'I miss her,' says Viv. 'When you come down to it, we go back a long way. I have other friends, but I don't have much in the way of family, and that's what I miss now that I don't see her. I don't want much from her, just to know that she thinks of me as family still.'

'I'm sure she does,' says Rachel.

'I'm sure she doesn't. Do you know, I haven't even got her spare key any more, not since her lock were changed. Like she doesn't trust me. Like she thinks I were in cahoots with that Bill, like I were on his side, not hers.'

'She'll come round,' says Rachel, but Viv cannot think of any previous instances where Joan has done any coming round.

'I'll come and say hello to her,' says Viv. 'Not that it will do any good.'

As the two of them push through the crowd on their way to Joan, they come face to face with Bill.

'Ha,' cries Viv.

'Is this who I think it is?' says Rachel. Both of them are a little giddy from the wine.

'Thank you,' says Viv, politely, 'for sending my earrings back. It was very thoughtful of you.'

Bill does not answer.

'I don't know,' says Viv, changing gear, 'how you have the cheek to turn up here. Have you seen Joan? *Joanie*. Have you come to apologise for breaking her door down?'

'Is she here?' he says, looking around – unsuccessfully as his immediate view is of heads and shoulders and hands holding glasses.

'Or maybe you have been in touch with her,' says Viv. 'Maybe she got in touch with you to tell you she forgives you for all the inconvenience you caused her.' She sees from his face that he has not had any contact with Joan. She continues. 'I bet you couldn't even recognise her, could you?'

'Is she here?' he says again.

'But you recognise me, don't you. You remember how much inconvenience you caused me, don't you.'

'Did I?'

'You know bloody well you did.'

'I came back to look for you,' he says.

'I'm supposed to believe that am I?'

'You'd gone. What was I supposed to do?'

'What was I supposed to do? I could have been murdered for all you knew.'

'You weren't though. I phoned you if you recall, next day. You were fine, you said so.'

'Quite late the next day, if I recall correctly. Not first thing. Got through a few other jobs first, did you.'

Rachel speaks for the first time. 'Is it true you broke into my mother's flat?'

He looks at her, not recognising her.

'Was it you?' she says. 'Because I think that was a despicable thing to do. I think Viv here should have reported you to the police, that's what I would have done. I don't know why she didn't.'

Viv doesn't know either, except that she had felt that she had implicated herself in the affair by her own actions.

'I'm sorry about that,' he says.

'I should think you ought to be sorry. I can't believe you dare to show your face here after the way you behaved. I think you should come now – now – and tell my mother that you are sorry.'

'I will,' he says. 'I came here, I came back here, to see her – and Viv – and I wanted to make it all straight between us. But not tonight, not with all these people around – I want to see her on her own, not with you.'

'I don't care what you want,' says Rachel briskly. 'I'm going to get her.' She gestures in a vague direction. 'Viv, you stay here and hold on to him.'

239

Viv finds that she can think of nothing to say – nothing that won't either give him an excuse to take offence and go away, or make him believe that he has been unaccountably forgiven. As well, she is becoming aware of a strong need to visit the ladies, when they are interrupted by Richard, holding two full pints of beer.

'Rick,' says Bill.

'Did you stay for the second half? What did you think?'

Bill nods. 'You did all right there mate.'

'Still not your style though?'

'Doesn't matter,' says Bill graciously. 'The result was impressive.'

'Take one of these off me,' says Richard, holding out one of the glasses. 'I've got more lined up on the bar than even I can get thorough before closing time.'

'I should be going,' says Bill.

'Oh no you don't,' says Viv. 'You're waiting here for Joan, don't forget. Stay here, I'll go and see where they've got to. Don't let him go Richard. And look after my glass.'

She is right, there is queue in the toilets, and when she eventually emerges she is thinking that for better or worse Joan and Bill will have met by now, or if not, that he must have escaped. Not my fault, she thinks. Then she sees Joan sitting not far away, with Sandra, and at the same moment Rachel is by her side, just arriving.

'Where did you get to?' says Viv.

'Loo,' says Rachel. 'Massive queue and then I met someone from school. Have you lost him?'

'Probably.'

'Mum.' Joan looks up at Rachel, appears not to see Viv. 'I think I'd like to go,' she says to Rachel.

'Are you sure? You don't want to talk to Viv?'

'Not now.'

'But some time? I bet she misses you.'

'I shouldn't think she does. Come on, lets go.'

Joan is too late. Viv is in front of her. 'Well? What did you think?'

'I enjoyed it,' says Joan. 'Didn't we, Rachel?' But Rachel is not listening; she has turned to talk to someone Joan can't see.

'And did I see you sitting next to Mr Fairlie?'

'We met him by chance as we came in.'

'And?'

'Nothing. He had to go.'

'And I,' says Viv, 'can tell you why. He didn't want to run into his wife. Ex-wife. Do you see that woman over there, with that short man? Look, her in green dress. Well, I've found out, she's Fairlie's wife. And it's true, she has left him, and she's living with that bloke. Frank, they call him.'

'How do you know?'

'They live next door to me,' says Viv. 'They bought Marjorie's house. Remember Marjorie?'

'Not really,' says Joan. She looks with mild curiosity at the erstwhile Mrs Fairlie and realises that Viv could be right and her presence is probably what sent Keith scurrying off. Then she turns away.

Viv sees the interest leave Joan's face and fears that she will be wanting to go home. 'Don't go,' she says. 'Not yet. Come and sit down for a minute. I haven't hardly talked to you since Christmas.'

They sit together and Viv finds that she has nothing to say. 'Rachel's looking well,' she says. 'Is she still with that young man? Ryan?'

'I haven't asked,' says Joan, as if she too can think of nothing to say.

Viv comes to a sudden decision, surprising herself. 'I have to have a colonoscopy,' she says. She thinks Joan will probably pretend she hasn't heard, so she is further surprised when Joan turns to look at her properly for the first time and says, sincerely, 'That sounds horrible. Poor you. When is it?'

'Next week.'

'I hope it's a false positive,' says Joan. 'Isn't that what they call it? Let me know how it goes.'

Richard walks by, carrying two full pint glasses. He does not appear to see Viv, or else he hopes that she will not see him.

'That's the dog man,' says Joan quietly, as if to herself.

'What?'

'Dogs, two dogs, in the park. Weimaraners I think they're called.'

'That's right, Richard, man in park, same person.'

They see Richard pause and look around, and call, 'Oggy.' Joan looks, she can't help it. She sees that Richard is waving to someone nearby, calling him to come to the bar. She looks – she really can't help it – to see who he is calling. A slight figure, not someone she knows. White of hair and creased of face he is, and then by some magic, his face resolves into who he really is, and she recognises Aughton. At the same second he recognises her.

'So we meet at last,' he says.

'Aughton?'

'Don't you recognise me?'

'You've changed.'

'We all have. Maybe you not so much.'

'Older. We're all older. I didn't expect you to look so – conventional.'

'You thought I'd still be wearing flares and a Led Zeppelin t-shirt?'

'I remember you how I last saw you. Cut off jeans and a yellow vest. Silly isn't it, how things stick.'

'And you, I always think of you in that red caftan. And your red hair.'

'I dyed it for years,' she says. 'Redheads lose their colour early you know.'

'Why did you stop?'

'I just did. Last year. I was a bit ill, I think.'

'I was a bit insane,' he says. 'I'm sorry. I mean, if you think I was stalking you. I wasn't thinking straight.'

'I don't know what you mean. But then I don't know much about anything.'

'I thought that Viv would have told you all about it.'

'No. I wouldn't let her tell me.'

'Then I'll have to confess it all to you.'

'You don't have to. In fact, please don't. And anyway, I made a mess of things as well. And you had more excuse than I did. People do strange things when their partner has just died.'

'Lydia would have told me off. I mean, properly told me off. She often thought I was foolish.'

'I thought so too. You are sometimes foolish, don't you think.'

'Maybe I am. But Lydia needed a bit of foolishness in her life. So do you.'

He wonders – he wonders this for the first time – when he broke into Joanie's house, when he drove all the way to Scotland to look for her, on that bloody Viv's say-so, where was she? Where did she go?

'I'm sorry,' he says.

'For?'

'I broke into your house,' he says. 'The police came. I must have caused you some trouble.'

'They gave me a crime number,' she says. 'The insurance paid out for a new door. There wasn't anything else.'

'Where were you?'

'Me?'

'You weren't at home. You weren't at your daughter's.'

'I was away,' she says.

'Where?'

'I was in Brightlingsea,' she says. She looks into his eyes. Her dark eyes, his dark eyes, they meet. 'I got your postcard, but too late. I came to see you.'

Briefly, he wishes he had never asked. 'And I wasn't there?'

'It didn't matter,' she says.

'I suppose not.'

'It's changed. It was all so different from the way I remember it.'

'I suppose so,' he says again. 'Where did you stay? Did you stay? Or just look around and go away again?'

'Five nights,' she says. 'Guest house called Seawinds. Do you know it?'

Yes he knows it. 'You never told me you were coming.'

'I phoned you. But you were never there. It didn't matter.'

Five days. He suspects there is something she is not telling him.

Rachel comes and stands next to them, saying nothing.

'Are you ready to go?' Joan says to her.

'If you are.'

Joan picks up her bag, puts it over her shoulder. She holds out her hand to Bill, to Aughton, A.J, Oggy, whoever he is. Holds out her hand to be shaken. He does not take her hand.

'Nice to see you,' she says, lowering her hand.

'I'm glad we met at last,' he says carefully. 'I hope I see you again. Before too long.'

She does not reply but she does allow herself to smile at him. He does not smile back. I know where you live, he thinks.

Viv is finishing her large glass of wine when Joan and Rachel pass by on their way to the door.

'So,' says Viv, 'that's the long-haired hippy lover of yesteryear. Will we be seeing much more of him?'

'I doubt it,' says Joan calmly, but Viv is not sure she means it. She has one of her premonitions. Joan will get together with Bill. She will move down to the Essex coast and take up where poor dead Lydia has left off. Joan will invite Rachel down and Rachel will take her, Viv, too. Or maybe Bill will invite Richard and he will ask Viv to come along. It's true that Richard is not as good-looking as Bill but he would be way more malleable. But who could she pair off with Keith Fairlie? Pamela, she decides and laughs out loud into her wine glass.

'Are you all right?' says Rachel.

'I'll be fine,' says Viv. 'Pamela is giving me a lift home. Shall I see you tomorrow? Come for lunch, bring your mother.'

'I'll see what I can do,' says Rachel.

Richard has tried to work his way through the backlog of beers that have been lined up on the bar for him, but even with help from Bill, he has run out of time.

They walk out together into the night, as far as where Bill has parked the van.

'So is it true?' says Richard. 'That you came all this way to see that woman? Is that the one I saw you talking to?'

'Joan,' says Bill. 'She says she sees you in the park, with your dogs.'

'Does she?'

'I think you've got that condition,' says Bill. 'You know, when you can't recognise faces. Like dyslexia but with faces.'

'I think I have,' agrees Richard. 'It's been said before. But let me hear a voice and I can always remember it. But this Joan person? Any luck?'

'Too soon to say,' says Bill.' Anyway, we're different people now. Not twenty any more.'

'I suppose you miss your wife?'

'I suppose I do.'

'Happy, were you?'

'I suppose we were. It seems like it now anyway. Were you?'

'Couldn't have been could we? She left.'

'So did you miss her?'

'A bit,' says Richard. 'But there were compensations. You get more done.'

They are silent, standing under the street light.

'You off home tomorrow?'

'I think so. No plans to stay, not this time.'

'You'll keep in touch?'

'With you? Course I will.'

'And with her?'

'Maybe. It may be too soon. Why are you asking – do you want to try your luck?'

'I don't think so,' says Richard. 'I don't think she'd look at me anyway. Just sometimes – I think it might be nice to have a bit of female company. You know?'

'What you want,' says Bill, 'is to try – you know – approach – that Viv.'

'She that little chubby one?'

'That's right. Friend of Joan's. Probably a lot more fun though, if the circumstances are right.'

'Meaning?'

'I'll tell you one day,' says Bill. 'But honestly, she was giving you a look – I saw her – tonight. She'd be up for – whatever. You could do worse. She'd know how to keep you in order. Good sense of humour though. Doesn't bear a grudge. Just the sort of woman you need.'

Richard laughs. 'What would my mother say?'

'How old is your mother?'

He thinks. 'Ninety-something.'

'Then it doesn't matter what she says. She won't be around for ever.'

'Hm,' says Richard.

It is a dry clear night. Joan walks home with Rachel. 'So,' she says, 'are you glad you went?'

'I should be asking you that,' says Rachel.

Joan does not answer directly. Then, 'How is your young man? Ryan, is it?'

'Gone,' says Rachel cheerfully. 'We split up. Don't worry, it was never going to be a goer.'

'So you're all right?'

'Absolutely fine,' says Rachel. 'Actually there's another man now. Older this time.'

'Not married is he?'

'Not any more,' says Rachel. 'Still early days. We'll see.'

'I want you to be happy,' says Joan.

'I know Mum. It would be nice if you could be happy too. If you could just let it happen.'

Is that all I have to do, thinks Joan, just let it happen. Is Rachel telling her something about Aughton? What does she know? Would she see him again if he asked her? Would she approach him even? There are many questions Joan would like to ask Viv, and probably Rachel too; many questions that she has been sitting on for months now. I could say something now, she thinks. But says nothing.

'Come with me to Viv's tomorrow,' says Rachel.

'I suppose I could,' says Joan.

'Of course you could. Nothing easier. She'll be ever so pleased if you do.'

Joan remembers what Viv told her. Sounds nasty, colonoscopy. Sounds scary. Should she offer to go with her to the hospital for some support? It's what Viv would do if their positions were reversed, she knows that. Well, Viv can always ask her, and if she asks, then –. But Joan knows that Viv will not ask, not now. Not unless she herself makes it possible.

They reach home, she takes the dog out to pee. She stands waiting, humming softly as Minnie has a last sniff round the nearest gatepost. Gradually the tune she is humming gathers words. "Let the Sunshine In".

Bill is aware that he cannot drive the van back to the campsite. He unlocks it and lies down on the bunk. Some time later he sits up, takes off his shoes and gets inside the sleeping bag. Briefly, he thinks miserably about how law-abiding he is these days. He is old, his days of driving while intoxicated are long gone.

He turns over, knows that he will wake in the morning with a stiff back and a headache, sneers again inwardly at the meaningless drivel that Rick made him come all this way for. But there was Joanie as well, and she was not hostile. What does he feel for her now, after all these years? He can't tell. He hauls up the memory of Joanie with her long hair, with her white bikini, with her wide smile and tries to believe that the woman he spoke to earlier this evening was her. He tries to imagine what he would feel if she told him to get lost and never bother her again. He can't tell.

He said he hoped to see her again, but he doesn't know if it's true. She didn't say no but she was probably just being polite. His actions of last autumn are obscure to him now. What was he doing, lurching from one daft impulse to another, what was he hoping for?

What is he hoping for now? A romance? No, it was not romantic, but she held out her hand to him. Could they even manage a friendship? There were no violins but she said the word nice. A friendship might be nice.

He resolves that he will take it slowly; he will consult the memory of Lydia in terms of proprieties; he will make allowances for the possible feelings of Emily and Laura; he will do nothing rash.

When he wakes in the morning feeling exactly as he knew he would, there is a song revolving through his head, that will not go away. He knows that it will be with him all the way home, taunting him. "Let the Sunshine In".

Viv wakes in the morning later than usual. She stretches. She had expected to feel a little flat and exhausted after the concert but no, she still has the feeling from last night, of achievement, of something completed, of standing on a peak. Then, Colonoscopy, she thinks, and then, False positive, that's what I have to hope for. Wasn't there a time when positive was a good thing and false was a bad thing? I could lose my hair, she thinks, and wonders if anyone would recognise her without her bundle of black, albeit dyed, springy hair, going its own way. A wig, she thinks but would it be worth the money if she's only going to die? Her thoughts threaten to spiral away down that hole and she catches hold of them. Oh sod it, nothing to be done, just roll with it Viv. Think about last night.

Last night Joan was all right with her, that Bill managed to pretend at least to be humbly apologetic, Richard even appeared to recognise her.

Today she has to prepare some lunch for Rachel, an arrangement that might even include Joan, if she can be cajoled. Though why should we bother, thinks Viv. We should just leave her to her own devices if that's what she wants.

She gets out of bed and opens the curtains. Let the sunshine in, she thinks involuntarily. Let it in.

ABOUT THE AUTHOR

Susan Day has been making up stories since before she could do joined up writing, but it took a while before she became brave enough to let other people read them. *Who Your Friends Are* was her first book, and she hasn't stopped writing since.

Susan was brought up in Enfield and lived in Colchester, Leicester and Paisley before settling in Sheffield. She has a husband, three children and a garden.

Also by Susan Day

WHO YOUR FRIENDS ARE

Plain Pat and Lovely Rita – childhood best friends who shared lives and confidences through the 1950s and 60s.

As the two friends follow different paths through the 70s, they grow apart, but Pat stays loyal to her friendship with Rita and her sisters.

Now, years later, Pat finds herself with time on her hands, and begins to look back on her relationship with Rita – at the same time as she has a crisis in her own life and problems in her grown up family.

A wonderful book about rites of passage – from the 1950s to the present day. Sometimes raw; often poignant; with deft dialogue and a feel for the realities of teenage friendship and subsequent family life and its unexpected twists and turns.

Robin Kent, author of *Agony Aunt Advises*

A deceptively simple story that makes you think about relationships, self-deceit and how we fail to spot the obvious.

Barbara Bannister, author of *The Tissue Veil*

THE ROADS THEY TRAVELLED

Four girls set out one wartime morning, on a day that will bind them together for years to come. Work and marriage, children and divorce, change and death.

Many years later they are still in touch, and still trying to resolve the tragedy that has been a constant in their lives. What did happen to Marcie?

Read carefully and you may recognise some of the characters from *Who Your Friends Are*.

Ordinary is made extraordinary by the intricacies shared in this beautifully woven tale of lives shaped by the forces of history... The reader is drawn into a skilfully painted picture of lives, changed forever by war.

Bryony Doran, author of *The China Bird*

Offers fresh new perspectives on lives lived – its pages are filled with moments and stories that are a pleasure to take into the imagination.

Docs and Daughters Book Group, Bristol

HOLLIN CLOUGH

CONCEALMENT: (*Verbs*) To conceal, hide, put out of sight, screen, cloak, veil, shroud, muffle, mask, disguise, camouflage.

There are families that would fall apart if the truth came out.

Jen admires her father and Frank believes that his daughters are happy, but no one in any family knows the whole story.

This family has fractured before, and been patched up by secrets and evasions.

Now things are about to change.

The more I read, the more I enjoyed it. A real page-turner – well-written and believable.

Laura Kerr, Botanical Book Group, Sheffield

A book that makes you think. Susan Day expertly tackles the relationships within families and their dynamics; her characters are very convincingly drawn and deftly written. Thoughtful and entertaining.

Steven Kay, author of *The Evergreen in Red and White*

Other Leaping Boy titles

THE CHILD WHO FELL FROM THE SKY
Stephan Chadwick

Untold secrets of a post-war childhood.

A true story of a child born in war-torn London soon after the Second World War whose early memories are of the care and security given to him by his grandmother and a guardian angel who watches over him. At six he finds out a devastating secret that changes his life. He withdraws into his own world, searching for understanding and meaning. Isolated from his family and children of his own age he turns to his angel for love and guidance but even she cannot save him from what is to come.

'Sometimes a book can just sneak up on you and contradict your expectations and this is such a book. There is nothing flashy about it, but nor is it didactic, and it has a raw, poetic quality that to my mind puts much more scholarly writers to shame.'

Amazon review

'This is an extraordinary, raw, and powerful book.'

James Willis, author of *Friends in Low Places*

HOW TO TALK TO TEENAGERS

If you have teenagers in your life – at home, at work, or in your neighbourhood – this book may stop you tearing your hair out! It will give you insights into how teenagers tick, and strategies to get their co-operation.

- ➤ Explains how teenagers see the world
- ➤ Packed with examples from day-to-day life
- ➤ Focuses on what to say to get them on board
- ➤ Includes 'maintaining boundaries' and 'avoiding conflict'
- ➤ Gives tips on how to stop the nagging and shouting
- ➤ Encourages adults to see the positive in teenagers
- ➤ Concise chapter summaries for easy reference

'Lucinda has captured the art of dealing with teenagers in a fantastic, easy to use guide.'

John Keyes, Social Inclusion Manager
Arsenal Football Club

'A superb guide – the key issues and techniques of interacting with young people are covered in a practical, easy to understand way. A great introduction to working with young people. I'd recommend it to anyone.'

Mark Todd, Chief Executive
Ocean Youth Trust South

Books for children

The TOM AND JAKE Series
Helen MccGwire

Six charmingly written and illustrated little books about Tom and Jake, two small boys who live with their family and animals in an old farm-house in Devon. The stories are based on the experiences of the author's five children during the 1960s, whilst living in the countryside.

Tom and Jake

More About Tom and Jake

Tom and Jake & The Bantams

Tom in the Woods

Tom and Jake & Emily

Tom and Jake & The Storm

'Enchanting ... it takes us back to the 1960s and the adventures of the two young heroes, living in the countryside with the world to discover. Ideal for grandparents and young listeners, and a springboard for reminiscences, too. The story and prose are realistic and precise, the illustrations nostalgic and have detail for young eyes to explore and absorb. Thoroughly recommended.'

Richard Newbold, Amazon
Top 1000 Reviewer

THE VERY SKINNY WHIPPETY DOG
Kate Tomlinson
Illustrated by Sue Luxton

A beautiful picture book about a skinny whippet who finds joy playing hide and seek in the woods and fields of Devon, and contentment in the comfort of a loving home.

The delightful illustrations make this a perfect book for dog lovers, or to read to small children.

Other work by artist Sue Luxton can be viewed at www.sueluxton.com

Any of our books can be purchased online at:

www.leapingboy.com

9 781999 840143